From Slave Cabins
to the White House

From Slave Cabins to the White House

Homemade Citizenship
in
African American Culture

KORITHA MITCHELL

UNIVERSITY OF ILLINOIS PRESS
Urbana, Chicago, and Springfield

First Illinois paperback, 2021
© 2020 by Koritha Mitchell
All rights reserved
Manufactured in the United States of America
2 3 4 5 6 C P 6 5 4 3 2
∞ This book is printed on acid-free paper.

Library of Congress Cataloging-in-Publication Data
Names: Mitchell, Koritha, author.
Title: From slave cabins to the White House: homemade
    citizenship in African American culture / Koritha Mitchell.
Other titles: Homemade citizenship in African American culture
Description: Urbana: University of Illinois Press, [2020] | Series:
    The new black studies series | Includes bibliographical
    references and index. |
Identifiers: LCCN 2020005316 (print) | LCCN 2020005317 (ebook) |
    ISBN 9780252043321 (cloth) | ISBN 9780252052200 (ebook)
Subjects: LCSH: American literature—African American authors—
    History and criticism. | American literature—Women authors—
    History and criticism. | Women and literature—United
    States—History. | African American women in literature. |
    African Americans in literature. | African American women—
    Intellectual life. | African American women—Social life and
    customs. | African Americans—Race identity.
Classification: LCC PS153.N5 M575 2020 (print) | LCC PS153.N5
    (ebook) | ddc 810.9/896073—dc23
LC record available at https://lccn.loc.gov/2020005316
LC ebook record available at https://lccn.loc.gov/2020005317

Paperback ISBN 978-0-252-08631-1

For the ancestors.
May we truly see the evidence you left.

Contents

Acknowledgments

I have lived with this project for several years, and many people have helped me sharpen my thinking along the way. This book benefited from every single encounter, despite my inability to name each one.

First, I thank two people who wouldn't let me stay discouraged when I encountered obstacles: Dawn Durante and Tanya McKinnon. Dawn and I hit it off in 2011, when *Living with Lynching* emerged, and she has continued to help me see the value of my contributions. You've been an important voice in my head, and I'm grateful. Even after a storm in her own life, Tanya helped me weather the storms that threatened this project. Thank you for modeling grace.

The profession is full of scholars who inspire me. It is a special gift when some of those people provide guidance and intervene on one's behalf. For me, those people include Robert Reid-Pharr, Barbara McCaskill, Harvey Young, Mark Anthony Neal, John Ernest, Martha S. Jones, Carol Anderson, Margo Crawford, and John L. Jackson Jr. Thank you for making the time.

I gladly acknowledge my debt for an early intervention from Gabrielle Foreman. I began presenting on Michelle Obama in 2011, but I somehow never saw that material as part of this study. Gabrielle convinced me that was a mistake. I remain grateful you did.

Some of this project's earliest interlocutors came my way because colleagues invited me to speak at their institutions. In this regard, I am especially grateful to Lindsay Reckson, who brought me to Haverford College to interact with an engaged audience from around the Philadelphia area. Graduate students at the University of Chicago invited me for a seminar. They were encouraged by Adrienne Brown, who made my visit memorable. Similar opportunities facilitated by Magdelyn Hammond Helwig at Western Illinois University invigorated me. Magdelyn assembled various groups whose questions helped my thinking for months. (Shout out to Maurine Magliocco, Timothy Helwig, and Shazia Rahman.) Also important for my thinking during this project's gestation was a remarkable visit to Texas Christian University, organized by Theresa Gaul.

I had generative conversations about this material with audiences at Dartmouth College, Bowdoin College, and during two visits to Brown University—one sponsored by the Pembroke Center for Teaching and Research on Women and one sponsored jointly by the Center for the Study of Race and Ethnicity in America and the Department of American Studies. I am especially grateful for intellectual engagement from Kevin Quashie, Tricia Rose, Matt Gutterl, Naoko Shibusawa, Adrienne Keene, Elena Shih, Ralph Rodriguez, Monica Muñoz Martinez, Leticia Alvarado, and Dixa Ramírez. The timing of those conversations made a real difference. Also linked to this fruitful time were my interactions with Leela Gandhi and Diego Millan. And I'm still in awe of the intellectual rigor and generosity offered by Tess Chakkalakal and Judith Casselberry during my visit to Bowdoin.

At crucial moments that made more of a difference than I can say, scholars I deeply admire made time to read portions of the book manuscript. For their thorough and constructively critical feedback, I am forever grateful to Sharon Holland, Brittney Cooper, and Evie Shockley. Likewise, I have grown from valuable conversations with, and exceptional support from, Robin Bernstein, Kyla Tompkins, Salamishah Tillet, and Brian Herrera.

Many thanks to Christopher Morris for research assistance and to readers I sought for particular chapters, including Adélékè Adéẹ̀kọ́, Brian McHale, Katherine Marino, and Cathy Hannabach. I am also grateful to the various anonymous manuscript reviewers. Every reaction helped me make the work stronger.

Also, though circumstances prevented this project from being the main one I worked on while in residence at the Notre Dame Institute for

Advanced Study, the Institute supported it with a fellowship, affirming in both intellectual and material ways my belief in its importance. The people who made my year at Notre Dame special include Jarvis McInnis, Perin Gürel, Alex E. Chávez, Paul Ramírez, Haruko "Hal" Momma, Tia Madkins, Rufus Burnett, Korey Garibaldi, Z'étoile Imma, Dianne Pinderhughes, and Greg Laski.

As anyone who knows me can attest, I would not be in the profession if it were not for the Ford Foundation Fellows community. You helped me through another monograph. Thank you. Over the years, the intellectual community that has entered my life via the Black Performance Theory working group has attempted to make me a more limber thinker. I'm still trying. Much gratitude to the many artists and scholars who have helped me develop through *Callaloo* conference gatherings. My work has been forever changed because of those encounters. In recent years, I've been inspired and energized by connections with the sisters of ABWH (Association of Black Women Historians), Zora's House, and #CiteBlackWomen. Rock on!

And, of course, I could not have endured all the ups and downs of this project without friends and family. Craig Jones, I remain in awe of your support and grateful for your wicked sense of humor. Carie Brown, you helped me through some of my darkest days, empowering me to do this work. What a joy to have you in my life, benefit from your impact on my life, and witness the many ways you do the same for others. Leila Ben-Nasr, our get-togethers have seen me through this entire process and much more. Laverne Mitchell, you remain my most consistent and committed interlocutor. You are behind every word I've ever written, and it is a privilege and an honor to say so.

From Slave Cabins
to the White House

Introduction

House Slaves, Housekeepers, Homemakers

African American culture is best understood as a dynamic, multivalent, ongoing conversation about how to define and pursue black success in a hostile environment—the United States of America. Even as their accomplishments have been discouraged, denied, or destroyed, African Americans have continued to strive, no matter how often they must adjust their conception of what constitutes achievement. Because black success so often inspires white violence, pursuing accomplishment requires African Americans to discuss not only the strategies for attaining it but also its very contours and parameters; they debate how one will even know if one has achieved. Because it requires caring enough to want to influence another's worldview, debate is an embodied practice of belonging, and such practices constitute the community conversation. By participating in that conversation, African Americans create a citizenship that is homemade. Denied basic ingredients, like safety, by the land of their birth, they cultivate a sense of belonging from scratch.

With U.S. citizenship built on the denial of black citizenship,[1] African Americans' success at asserting that they belong consistently inspires hostility. And yet, this reality remains shrouded because Americans ignore the effort expended to erase the accomplishments of nonwhite populations. Appreciating how profoundly achievement shapes black cultural practices therefore requires some housekeeping. As feminist theorist Hortense Spillers explains, because black people are represented in ways that are "loaded with mythical prepossession," "there is no easy way for the agents buried beneath to come clean" (203). The necessary housework begins with acknowledging what actually structures experience in the United States. That structuring mechanism is what I call *know-your-place aggression*, the flexible, dynamic array of forces that answer the achievements of marginalized groups such that their success brings aggression as often as praise.[2] Americans celebrate white men's accomplishments, but any progress by those who are not straight, white, and male is answered with a backlash of violence—both literal and symbolic, both physical and discursive—that essentially says, *know your place!*

Within African America, examples abound.[3] During slavery, holding on to one's dignity (or simple belief in one's humanity) made those in bondage targets for extra abuse. During the Civil War, when black soldiers were finally allowed to fight, they successfully contradicted assertions that they were too servile and cowardly for combat. As a reward, African American men gained the right to vote. In response, white Americans abandoned Reconstruction policies and undertook a decades-long campaign in which officials disfranchised African Americans with Black Codes, and both officials and civilians terrorized them with lynching. Black soldiers again fought in World War I and earned respect from Europeans as they secured a victory of which the United States was proud, but when they returned to the land of their birth, Anglo Americans lynched them in their military uniforms during the Red Summer of 1919. The pattern repeated after World War II so that, during the 1940s and 1950s, the United States offered black veterans more insult and injury than GI Bill benefits. In the 1960s and 1970s, African Americans secured victories in the form of not only voting rights but also legislation supporting their access to decent housing. In response, white Americans claimed black households were pathological, overrun by emasculating matriarchs and welfare queens. No matter how closely black families resembled the nation's ideal, they could not escape depictions of themselves as dysfunctional.

Clearly, meeting American standards has not meant black success will be respected or rewarded with civic inclusion, but African Americans keep embracing everything associated with the ideal citizen, including an impressive work ethic, entrepreneurship, and military service, as well as traditional homemaking.[4] Though systematically denied access to resources that would support their doing so, African Americans often achieve the nation's most revered domestic configuration: the heteronormative nuclear family.

Why do African Americans continue to invest in achieving conservative goals, especially heteronormative domesticity, when they know their accomplishments will more likely inspire attack than respectability and safety? What does this pattern of investing against the odds reveal about African American culture? *From Slave Cabins to the White House* argues that it reveals *homemade citizenship*.

Homemade citizenship is a deep sense of success and belonging that does not depend on civic inclusion or mainstream recognition. African Americans understand the nation's commitment to attacking black accomplishment while claiming it never existed. So, when African Americans seem to be investing against the odds, they are not responding to the forces that oppose them so much as they are continuing community traditions of affirming themselves while acknowledging that the resulting success will attract hostility. Understanding that violence—whether physical or discursive—emerges to keep them in their "proper" place, African Americans have no problem acknowledging violence without being distracted by it.[5] To identify homemade citizenship, scholars, teachers, and general readers must look through the lens of achievement, rather than protest. Doing so quickly reveals that African Americans have always focused more on creating possibility for themselves and each other than on responding to oppression. Upon understanding that reality, protest can be appreciated in proportion to how it actually functions in African American history and culture. It also becomes clear that it is a mistake to view black expressive culture that acknowledges white violence in terms of resistance. Like black people more generally, the community's cultural producers orient themselves toward racial self-affirmation—but that does not keep them from acknowledging white brutality. Noticing relentless white hostility does not distract them from their creative goals, and their primary goal is rarely protest.

Black people pursue and achieve success, white aggression counters their progress, and then violence becomes part of any accurate representation of African American communities. Like the lives depicted, the representations do not exist to counteract racist attacks. If African Americans are to achieve, they must create a sense of belonging despite the violence that answers them, and there is overwhelming evidence that they have done this in the lived world and in (and through) expressive culture. In their demeanor, words, and actions, which constitute the community conversation, those who are marginalized refuse to ignore violence—even as they persevere in spite of it.

Because the community conversation includes cultural production, homemade citizenship exists in the lived world, but it is also a heretofore unrecognized trope in African American art and literature, and the heteronormative nuclear family is its metonym. Traditional black families signal the cultivation of homemade citizenship, which is all about defining and pursuing accomplishment while recognizing the hostility it attracts. Every form of black success inspires aggression, but the heteronormative nuclear family emerges as the metonym for homemade citizenship to demonstrate that traditionally defined black domestic success draws the country's most vicious assaults and to emphasize that African Americans have always known that. After all, black people routinely prove more invested in nurturing themselves and each other than in pursuing particular domestic configurations, but whenever their intimacies even resemble the heteronormative nuclear family, African Americans become irresistible targets, in need of being put in their "proper" place.

From Slave Cabins to the White House uses the insights of performance theory to engage the dynamism of U.S. history by recognizing the power of embodied practices.[6] This is a study not of identity but of the activities through which besieged communities cultivate success and belonging. Rather than focusing on subjects and their presumably stable identities, this project follows words, actions, gestures, and demeanors to discover how texts (both written and performed) engage in practices that produce homemade citizenship. That is, as a cultural project that African Americans engage in, the tendency to *pursue success while acknowledging hostility* is an endeavor of articulation and performance that does not assume stable identity so much as discussion and debate, as well as both harmony and discord in action. And because house slaves, housekeepers, and homemakers contribute profoundly to the debates about success through which African American communities cohere, taking seriously black people's preoccupation with achievement yields new appreciation for women in these roles. I examine black female cultural production from the Civil War to the present, including Michelle Obama's public persona, which I treat as a performance text. By focusing on woman-authored slave narratives, novels, dramas, and Mrs. Obama's first lady persona, I spotlight creative contributions to the community conversation that defines, affirms, and fuels black success in a nation hostile to it.

This book declares know-your-place aggression to be "the weather" in which African Americans sustain themselves and each other in the march toward accomplishment. Christina Sharpe argues that "the weather is the total climate; and that climate is antiblack" (104). I complicate this powerful concept by foregrounding the reactionary nature of white supremacy and the violence that necessarily accompanies it. Scholars speak in terms of "antiblackness" but then proceed as if it were primary—as if antiblackness comes first and then black people must respond to and grapple with it, rather than the other way around.[7] In actuality, as Nell Painter's *The History of White People* demonstrates, white supremacy is reactionary, even though white people manufactured whiteness by conjuring up blackness. Claudia Rankine, recasting Frantz Fanon, puts it this way: "It is the white man who creates the black man. But it is the black man who creates" (128–29). Recognizing know-your-place aggression helps us stay clear about the actual cause-and-effect relationship that structures dominant culture. *Black success is the reason antiblackness became "the weather."* White supremacy and antiblackness became (and continue to be) so relentless because they spring into action in hopes of discouraging, diminishing, and destroying black people's every achievement and every assertion of belonging.

Looking Anew at Success, Citizenship, and Domesticity

Writing my first book, *Living with Lynching*, taught me that African Americans have long documented the link between their accomplishments and the white-authored violence they face; their doing so has always been a crucial part of the community conversation on success. African Americans who lived at the height of mob violence wrote plays demonstrating that mobs most often targeted black men, not because they were criminals but because they were accomplished heads of household in heteronormative nuclear families. Black men with traditionally defined achievements were the ones who had forgotten their "rightful" position in American society, so their deaths served as a warning to survivors: *know your place!* Black-authored lynching dramas spotlight stable African American families and show how whites attack their success while insisting it never existed—insisting, in fact, that black communities are full of criminals, specifically black rapists who target white women. Casting African Americans (regardless of their behavior) as rapacious, sexually irresponsible, or uninterested in domestic stability amounts to discursive violence, and violence, whether physical or discursive, has one major purpose: to mark who belongs and who does not. Violence is a way of reminding everyone of the target's "proper" place, a way of insisting that certain people should not feel secure in claiming space and resources. In other words, violence is a performance of the denial of citizenship, an active rejection of the idea that one belongs. Attacks—whether physical or discursive—fortify the boundaries around citizenship, and they become most necessary when purportedly inferior people are proving their mettle.

African Americans have always pursued success while knowing their accomplishments make them targets, but historians and cultural critics often fail to appreciate this dynamic. Scholarship typically proceeds as if acknowledging violence and affirming oneself are mutually exclusive. When examining African American history, researchers often present a series of episodes in which white violence provokes black protest. Examples include lynching and antilynching campaigns or segregation and antisegregation activism. For those who study literature and art, the pattern is similar: identify injustice and the artistic works denouncing it. When examining art that does not seem to respond to white violence, scholars treat it as evidence that African Americans affirm themselves by creating spaces of refuge and escape. In other words, this form of cultural criticism is often based on two faulty assumptions: (1) black artists usually react to white violence, and (2) when black artists affirm themselves and their communities, their self-affirmation is unrelated to violence.[8] Approaching black people's activism and art as if African Americans either protest injustice or avoid it is a mistake, because affirming oneself and contending with oppression so often go together.

In fact, the pattern of African American culture is best described this way: Africans and African-descended people in the United States strive for and achieve success, so when African American artists tell the truth about their communities, they depict success. The achievement recorded is sometimes so modest that it hardly resembles "success" and seems better described as "survival." And yet, when your people were never meant to survive (especially with any self-regard intact), survival is a victory, and victories (whether big or small) inspire know-your-place aggression. Racist violence then becomes part of any accurate portrait of these communities. To read the record of black expressive culture with any precision, scholars, teachers, and general readers must grapple with what black intellectuals, activists, and artists who lived surrounded by intense violence asserted: that their success inspired attacks. In her 1892 pamphlet about lynching, *Southern Horrors*, Ida B. Wells made it plain: "The mob spirit has grown with the increasing intelligence of the Afro-American" (62). W. E. B. Du Bois was equally clear when he declared in 1915, "There was one thing that the white South feared more than Negro dishonesty, ignorance, and incompetency, and that was Negro honesty, knowledge, and efficiency" (qtd. in Litwack xiii–xiv). Thinking in terms of protest versus self-affirmation obscures African Americans' understanding that black success beckons the mob. Aware of the inevitable backlash, African Americans have marched toward accomplishment nonetheless.

Given the precision with which Wells and Du Bois described African Americans' predicament one hundred years ago, it is time for a theory of cultural criticism that maintains clarity about the cause-and-effect relationship between the achievement of marginalized communities and the violence of dominant culture. A more precise approach exposes the aggression embedded in mainstream America's most common words and deeds. For instance, dominant discourses and practices[9] assert that strong, heteronormative families are the bedrock of society; at the same time, they ensure that, in the nation's imagination, the ideal family is white. American culture consistently excludes black and brown people from its family portraits. Far from a coincidence or benign tradition, this pattern amounts to discursive violence. For as long as the nation has claimed to cherish "family life," it has also insisted nonwhite people fail to share those values. Dominant discourses and practices represent black and brown households primarily in terms of single mothers, absentee fathers, anchor babies, and delinquent children. That inclination robs nonwhite citizens of the most powerful shorthand for declaring themselves to be stable, moral, and trustworthy.[10] This is no accident. It reinforces the idea that their "proper" place is on the margins, if not on the other side of borders. Keeping nonwhite heteronormative nuclear families outside the nation's family portraits does great violence.

Likewise, in a society that claims to value strong families, women purportedly earn respect and protection by creating domestic havens, but throughout the nation's history, when black and brown women become model mothers and wives, it is more likely to inspire aggression than secure safety and respectability. When media outlets constantly cast black and brown mothers as welfare recipients or drop-and-leave culprits,[11] and that characterization seems legitimate no matter what the women are actually doing, that is violence. When one's behavior is irrelevant because of the persistence of stereotypes, that is violence. Meanwhile, even with evidence to the contrary, American "common sense" (Omi and Winant 11) insists that the model family is white and middle class. When Americans speak of treasured wives, mothers, and families, they typically mean white wives, mothers, and families; therefore, their categorical opposites—cadres of baby mamas and bad hombres[12]—must be black and brown. Women from these populations might have been indispensable house slaves, and they might become decent housekeepers . . . but they will never be seen as homemakers.

Acknowledging the racial connotations attached to representations of house slaves, housekeepers, and homemakers is crucial because although many Americans claim a commitment to "the citizen" in its presumably inclusive abstraction, demographics determine how people are viewed and treated. Because this corporeal approach to citizenship shapes the nation's present no less so than its past,[13] we must view American rhetoric as always both linguistic and embodied—we must be attentive to both words and deeds, both the archive and the repertoire.[14] When American discourse casts black and brown citizens primarily as single mothers and absentee fathers, it justifies the social and political exclusion of people of color. To suggest particular groups have weak families is to label them *noncitizens*. By animating stereotypes, American laws, political rhetoric, and popular culture create figures—multivalent entities. The meanings evoked by such figures, and the emotions accompanying them, prove to be almost irresistibly persuasive. As performance theorist Diana Taylor explains, questions of "true/false" fall away: "instead, the affective is the effective" (*Performance* 92).

It is therefore wise to follow cultural critic Sharon Holland in viewing racism "as the emotional lifeblood of race; it is the 'feeling' that articulates and keeps the flawed logic of race in its place" (6). Merely mentioning a familiar figure such as the welfare queen or anchor baby instantly pathologizes black and brown families, powerfully asserting (without needing to do so explicitly) that people of color do not contribute to society and therefore should not expect the rights, privileges, and basic benefits of citizenship, including the assumption that the police and courts exist for their protection. This is why, when a police officer kills an unarmed teenager of color, the American public is so often told the teen came from a "broken home."[15] It is a way to explain why using public resources for their benefit would have been a waste; they were headed toward tragedy anyway.[16]

That Americans use mere claims about less-than-ideal households to blame victims for their own deaths is another example of know-your-place aggression. While crucial scholarship has revealed the limits of heteronormative domesticity,[17] this study focuses on homemaking in order to honor African Americans' keen awareness of their domestic vulnerability and their commitment to being homemakers nonetheless. Black families who are successful according to the nation's standards are not rare, but negative portrayals of black households circulate relentlessly. Mainstream discourses and practices negate evidence of African Americans' ability to achieve what the nation's laws and policies are designed to prevent them from accomplishing.[18]

Dominant culture attacks African American achievement of every kind, but nothing seems to inspire more hostility than black domestic success; thus, family-centered racial violence is a long-standing American tradition. In slavery, white people categorically declared it impossible for a black woman to be raped, because her body did not belong to her. A "master" could use an enslaved woman as a breeder, forcing her to have sex with him or with other captives.[19] These dehumanizing practices emerged because there was so much evidence that black captives were human. If their humanity had any chance of being denied, it had to be brutalized out of them. Brutality was never completely effective, though, as confirmed by the many testimonies about black women who loved black men of their choice, thereby infuriating their so-called "masters."[20] Practices like breeding should therefore be understood as violent *responses* to black people's success at holding on to humanity and agency. This violence attempted to make the bondwoman's feelings for her partner irrelevant and her emotional connection to her children immaterial. After all, these bonds could be attacked because they had been nurtured and therefore existed.

After Emancipation, one way African Americans asserted their freedom was to reassemble their families and make their marriages legal.[21] For many, these reunions represented success, so racist violence arose to counter it. Indeed, as black people invested in the inviolability and legal protections of marriage, white Americans again disregarded those bonds. Whites ignored these intimate attachments by, for instance, asserting that black men were rapists obsessed with white women. This discourse contradicted the image of black men happily paired with black women; it was discursive violence in response to black people's success at loving each other against the odds. For similar reasons, queer intimacies and domesticities attracted violence. The "crime" in those cases was the victory of refusing to believe that sexual conformity was a prerequisite for humanity and belonging.[22] In all instances, discursive violence was accompanied by physical aggression. As historian Hannah Rosen documents in detail, even while declaring that black coupling was nonexistent and that white households were in danger, mobs "ku-kluxed" black homes, often raping the wives of successful black men (Rosen, *Terror*, 187–90).

Violence emerged in this precise (domestic) form because African Americans had created monogamous marriages and self-sustaining households. Mainstream discourses and practices counter the success of purportedly inferior people who nonetheless embody exactly what the nation respects: the traditional domesticity that should prove them worthy of citizenship. Creating a traditional family does not make one worthier of belonging, but American discourse claims it does. In that context, excluding African Americans who create heteronormative nuclear families sends a powerful message to them and to everyone else. Personifying heteronormativity does *not* interrupt the other-ing the United States does to those considered black. What better way to show everyone that African Americans will never be citizens?

In other words, the real purpose of negatively portraying families of color (thereby erasing actual families) is to fortify the message that merit and whiteness always go together and that citizens are white.[23] Again, black people nurturing each other through queer intimacies, or in alternative domestic configurations, also attract violence. However, black expressive culture faithfully records the intense opposition to African Americans enjoying anything resembling what white people put on a pedestal and claim only they are capable of achieving.

Because the nation insists on linking citizenship to traditional domesticity, homemaking has long defined who is and is not a citizen, so the traditional domestic success of those who are not straight, white, and male is routinely attacked. Sometimes, the violence is discursive, such as Fox News calling Michelle Obama a "baby mama."[24] In a society built on the denigration of black women, the truth of who Michelle Obama is easily becomes a nonissue. Sometimes, the violence is physical. And, quite often, it is family-centered. Whether physical or discursive, aggression is always a response to some degree of success. It was Michelle Obama's achievements, including becoming a wife and mother at a level usually reserved for white women, that inspired some Americans to revel in taking her (and those who admire her) down a peg by labeling her a baby mama. Besides being a Princeton- and Harvard-educated lawyer, she was pursuing first lady status, complete with well-behaved children and an affectionate husband. To call her a baby mama is to associate her with a caricature of an uneducated woman of a lower socioeconomic class and with a domestic image that does not involve being publicly claimed by a man of stature. Recasting a black wife and mother as a baby mama puts her in her "proper" place; she can't possibly be a homemaker. This example demonstrates that, like citizenship, traditional domesticity seems to be an inclusive abstraction—recognizable by behavior, not demographic—but in the United States, inclusive theories rarely shape praxis. As a result, aggression flows toward certain domesticities more than safety and respectability, no matter how well they measure up to stated standards.

Hostility toward Michelle Obama's domestic success took many forms. While Mrs. Obama embodied the role of "Mom-in-Chief" with dignity and grace, her husband was disrespected, denigrated, and sometimes "lynched." A state representative shouted, "You lie," while President Obama addressed Congress in 2009, and a governor shoved her finger in the Commander-in-Chief's face.

Figure 1. When President Obama visited Arizona in January 2012, Governor Jan Brewer was disrespectful, to say the least. Not all Americans were disturbed by this sight, but I daresay all Americans recognized the disrespect. (Photo Credit: Haraz N. Ghanbari via AP Images)

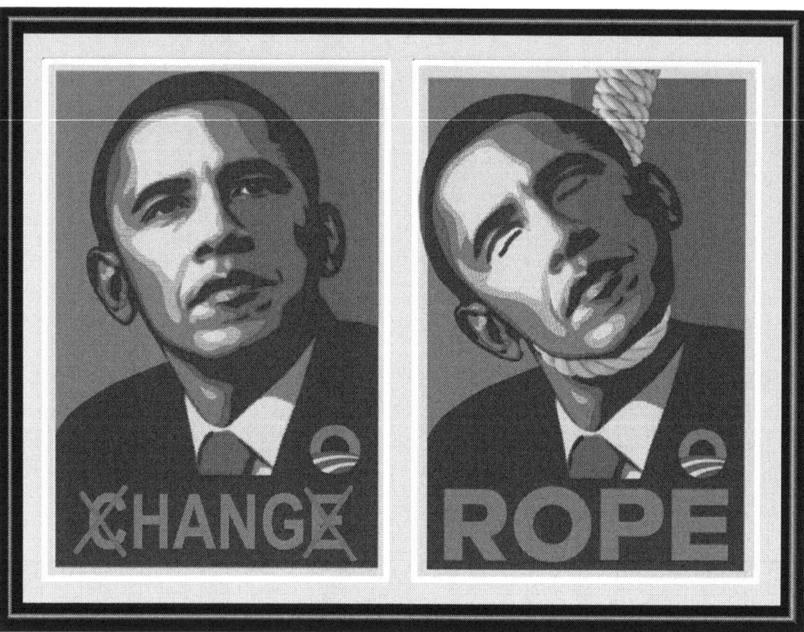

Figure 2. In the lead-up to the 2008 presidential election, the Obama campaign message often revolved around "Hope." Watching Obama succeed in generating enthusiasm around this message inspired the emergence of a revision: "Rope." Several versions continue to circulate.

More tellingly, as investigative journalist Ronald Kessler reports, "Once Obama became president, the Secret Service experienced a 400 percent increase in the number of threats . . ., in comparison to President [George W.] Bush" (225). Also, depictions of a lynched Barack Obama have received "likes" on Facebook and Twitter[25] and continue to circulate on the internet. When making his first bid for president, Obama galvanized potential voters with the idea of "Hope and Change," and the campaign released an iconic red, white, and blue *HOPE* image that was quickly revised to *ROPE*. The modification endures as an example of the sort of discursive violence that I call *know-your-place aggression* because Obama's success at generating excitement about hope was answered with the circulation of pictures of his neck in a rope. Several versions of the modified illustration remain readily available online, including high-quality renditions suitable for printing.

Some fantasy lynching images capture life-size dummies made to resemble Obama.

Figure 3. Life-sized dummies made to look like President Obama have been hanged and photographed for circulation. This example is from June 2012 in front of the Dove World Outreach Center in Gainesville, Florida. (Photo Credit: Matt Stamey for *The Gainesville Sun*)

Still, the most striking example emerged after Clint Eastwood's empty chair routine at the 2012 Republican National Convention. Eastwood had pretended to be speaking to President Obama as he chastised an empty chair, and the next day, an empty chair hung from a noose in the front yard of a middle-class neighborhood near Austin, Texas.[26] Could the message be any clearer? *You may be president of the United States of America, but you're still a—. Americans will not only ask to see your papers [birth certificate and transcripts]; some will relish the idea of seeing you in a noose.*

Together, the Obamas embody the heteronormative nuclear family that Americans claim to respect, yet American words and deeds seek to remind them of their "proper" place. If prominent figures like the Obamas face know-your-place aggression, ordinary members of the community certainly do. Like the characters in lynching plays, African Americans live their lives, tell their truths, and affirm themselves, and when they seem to be enjoying too much success and acting like they believe they belong, they receive a reminder of their "proper" place.

As expressed through U.S. law, public policy, and popular culture, the heteronormative nuclear family remains the standard, and this book highlights how routinely aggression follows African Americans even when they embody exactly what the nation values. Rather than contradict the unjust bias, I underscore the injustice of having one's achievement of an ideal become the reason for attack. In this way, I follow the lead of black expressive culture, which often uses heteronormative nuclear families to debate not only strategies for attaining success but also how to define it in the first place, given that every version of success attracts hostility.

To read through the lens of achievement and notice how often the heteronormative nuclear family signals the cultivation of homemade citizenship is also to notice how regularly artists articulate values not limited to that norm. Because they march toward accomplishment, African Americans look for ways to nurture themselves and each other. As they do so, their sustaining connections attract violence, especially when those connections resemble what the powerful want to reserve for themselves. In tracing black women's investment in moving from house slaves and housekeepers to homemakers, I demonstrate that even while serving as house slaves and housekeepers, black women operate as homemakers. Their definitions of "homemaker" do not always look like the mainstream image. Indeed, they routinely recalibrate their conception of homemaking success. Sometimes, they redefine achievement in the wake of white violence, but focusing on success allows readers to appreciate black homemakers' victories and to notice that not every move is a reaction to white people.

Recognizing the heteronormative nuclear family as the metonym for homemade citizenship highlights how African Americans debate definitions of success rather than simply internalize mainstream conceptions. Even if their homemaking practices look like those the nation respects, how motivated by white acceptance can African Americans be when they understand that to achieve according to mainstream standards is to all but invite injury? The same can be said for measuring accomplishment in capitalist terms. It is tempting to view black consumerism as a simple triumph of mainstream ideologies. That is, if conduct manuals for African Americans proliferated after Emancipation, promoting store-bought rather than homemade goods, then black Victorians' shopping and interest in home décor must have signaled the internalization of dominant discourse. Or, if the federal government ran "Own Your Own Home" campaigns beginning in the 1930s, then presumably only black people who believed the hype wanted to live in the suburbs. However, slave narratives record bondspeople earning and spending money, giving each other gifts, and grappling with the tension between material worth and other types of value. Acquiring anything white people cherished made African Americans vulnerable both before and after Emancipation, so simple acceptance of dominant ideas could not have fueled black people's actions. Similarly, in the 1930s, 1940s, and 1950s, when they knew moving into suburban houses placed targets on their backs, does it make sense to assume that African Americans simply trusted the nation's promises and uncritically invested in the American Dream?

Preoccupied with their success-oriented journeys, black people define, redefine, and pursue achievement, and whites often work to interrupt black progress. Rankine's *Citizen* captures this dynamic by articulating a matter-of-fact lack of interest in reacting to white aggression. As Rankine's persona meditates on racist comments from a "friend" and "colleague," she concludes: "It is not only that confrontation is headache-producing; it is also that *you have a destination* that doesn't include acting like this moment isn't inhabitable, hasn't happened before" (10, emphasis added). African Americans have always marched toward accomplishment, while being attacked for doing so, and they have sustained themselves and each other in this march by engaging in an ongoing community conversation about success.

Community Conversation as Methodology

When I say African Americans support each other in their journeys toward achievement with a *community conversation* on success, I'm referring to the broad, dynamic discussions among African Americans about the countless issues affecting community members' life chances and well-being. These discussions are wide-ranging and multivalent, encompassing real-life exchanges as well as the poems, plays, songs, and narratives that community artists produce. And, like broader American (or even Western) conversations, the community conversation is never limited to language.[27] Meaning is created and conveyed through not only words but also gestures, objects, and movement—indeed, all embodied practices and all the ways a body can convey meaning. In other words, the community conversation is advanced by a person's facial expressions or their cooking or dancing as well as by the artistic work that emerges from black enclaves. The community conversation is too dynamic and all-encompassing for this study to examine it comprehensively. By focusing on slave narratives, novels, and dramas authored by women and on the performance text of Michelle Obama's public persona as first lady, *From Slave Cabins to the White House* spotlights creative contributions to the conversation.

Even as I focus on cultural production, I do not disregard the lived world, however, because black artistic contributions engage real-world experiences. In highlighting community conversation, I acknowledge how, from enslavement onward, Africans in the United States and their descendants have articulated an improvised nationalism and the precarity of their status as a political constituency. As Saidiya Hartman argues, because enslaved people were not citizens, scholars are encouraged to view their lives and actions as being outside of politics. And yet, "the black captive" constituted "the ground of the master's inalienable rights, being, and liberty" (*Scenes* 69). My theorizing around community conversation acknowledges black people's simultaneous exclusion from and centrality to American citizenship, and it builds on Benedict Anderson's definition of nation as "an imagined political community—and imagined as both inherently limited and sovereign" (6). Expressive culture contributes to this imagined community, linking African Americans in an effort to define and pursue success when they are opposed at every turn.

Thus, I conceive of the community conversation as the discussions and debates among African Americans that cultivate *homemade citizenship*—belonging that can never be defined by U.S. politics and mainstream standards. Homemade citizenship exceeds American citizenship; its value does not rely on civic inclusion. In fact, homemade citizenship exists only inasmuch as community members assume civic inclusion to be an impossibility, precisely because they recognize the nation's investment in know-your-place aggression. Theorist Fred Moten has conceived of this idea as "stolen life" ("The Case" 179), allowing him to see that "blackness is prior to ontology" ("Blackness" 739), and it is akin to what the enslaved called "community among ourselves." And, as Hartman makes clear, this sense of belonging was not defined by "the centrality of racial identity . . . nor merely by the condition of enslavement but by the connections forged in the context of disrupted affiliations [and] sociality amid the constant threat of separation" (*Scenes* 59). In other words, examining the community conversation to understand how it cultivates homemade citizenship helps readers appreciate the constant, proactive creation of black sociality and communion in hostile environments. A community conversation approach also acknowledges what Anderson calls the "national imagination," which assumes a "sociological landscape of a fixity that fuses the world inside the [text] with the world outside" (30).

Given the link between the world represented in art and the world art enters, recognizing know-your-place aggression is crucial. Moten asks, "How can we fathom a social life that tends toward death, that enacts a kind of being-toward-death, and which, because of such tendency and enactment, maintains a terribly beautiful vitality?" ("The Case" 188). When one understands that black people march toward success, and white violence steps in to counter them, then one appreciates that African Americans tend not toward death but toward accomplishment. And they have always done so while understanding that their countrymen insist upon answering black achievement with insult, injury, and death rather than respect. When one recognizes this pattern, it becomes clear that whiteness is far more reactionary than assured in its superiority and dominance. Whiteness springs into action to deny to black people all that it claims for itself: humanity, dignity, citizenship.

For African Americans, pursuing success means all but inviting injury. Therefore, when one appreciates the reactionary nature of know-your-place aggression, the notion that African American culture is geared toward defending black humanity seems misguided. While many believe brutality emerges when people have trouble seeing another's humanity, black experience proves otherwise. In fact, African American history corroborates the critique of humanist assumptions that guides philosopher Kate Manne's description of how misogyny works. Even when "people participate in mass atrocities under the influence of dehumanizing propaganda," Manne argues, "their actions often betray the fact that their victims must seem human, all too human" (135). Manne continues, "Many of the nastiest things that people do to each other . . . proceed in full view of, and are in fact plausibly triggered by, these others' manifestations of their shared or common humanity" (149). "If anything, the more similar these others are to ourselves, the more one may have to watch out for them" (154). In short, "one need not think poorly of one's rival in order to regard him as a rival, or even a nemesis. Indeed, quite the contrary—if one did not have some appreciation of his merits . . ., then competing with him would" be less compelling

(155). Black humanity is a given, and white violence only certifies white people's cognizance of that fact. And, as I argue, the same is true for black belonging in the United States.

African American expressive culture takes black humanity and citizenship for granted. It simply remains for scholars and readers to adopt interpretive frameworks that enable them to appreciate the resulting dynamics. Namely, during slavery and long afterward, African Americans have not responded to white-authored violence so much as white aggression has sought to interrupt black people's journeys toward their goals, especially a sense of home and belonging. Recognizing this tradition will help scholars and general readers appreciate how consistently African Americans have refused to ignore violence . . . even as they persevere in spite of it.

Black culture is literally constituted through its investment in thriving—as well as defining the characteristics of surviving and thriving and every variation in between. When I examine African American culture, I find it grappling with questions such as: What does success look like for an enslaved person? How does she assess achievement and whether life is worth living? Just as important, might taking her own life represent accomplishment? With so many bearing witness to infanticide and suicide in the antebellum era,[28] the community conversation has consistently considered success in terms of keeping white people from profiting from black life and labor. After Emancipation, when so many rights were (and are) withheld because one is not considered white, how does a person who has known no other country understand their citizenship? When a person's experience falls short of what white counterparts enjoy, do they accept the nation's message that they are not a citizen—or do they devise a more complex definition of citizenship?

The community conversation asks and answers these questions and enables me to identify homemade citizenship as a more complex conception of belonging than would be possible if African Americans merely sought U.S. citizenship. In other words, I do not assume that black people simply internalize mainstream ideologies. However, to the extent that they strive for that which resembles mainstream accomplishment, African Americans' success-oriented journeys may seem based on an investment in a nationalist project of settler colonialism, capitalism, and imperialism. As Tiffany Lethabo King argues when examining encounters between Indigenous peoples and Black communities, "'innocence' does not exist within the lifeways of this hemisphere or the modern world. The endeavor of surviving under conditions of conquest is never clean" (xi). Thus, I do not argue that African Americans are never colonizers and never implicated in capitalist and imperialist projects. I do not assert that African Americans always reject these ideologies. I simply recognize a dynamic reality: even if African Americans who staked their claims in the United States (rather than emigrating) embraced a violent regime, they also deliberately highlighted the country's violent exclusion of them. That is, they underscored how routinely they were attacked even while embodying everything the nation reveres.

Tracing homemade citizenship involves grappling with realities that Judith Butler helps readers understand. Namely, African Americans do not achieve "a 'pure' opposition, a 'transcendence' of contemporary relations of power" (241). Instead, they engage in the "difficult labor of forging a future from resources inevitably impure" (ibid.). The resources available in the United States are tainted, to say the least, and this is one way to understand homemade citizenship in relationship to mainstream American culture. African-descended people in the United States have made a tradition of affirming themselves and each other while knowing the resulting success will invite aggression as often as praise. Because hostility has shaped black experience, African Americans could not survive and create a culture without grappling with violence as their inheritance. As James Baldwin understood, "the Negro has been formed by this nation, for better or for worse, and does not belong to any other. . . . The paradox—and a fearful paradox it is—is that the American Negro can have no future anywhere, on any continent, as long as he is unwilling to accept his past. To accept one's past—one's history—is not the same thing as drowning in it; it is learning how to use it" (*Fire* 333). What does it mean to use African American history? Baldwin devoted much of his life to answering that question. Influenced by his insights, I offer my own, and I insist upon an approach that acknowledges how focused on success African-descended people have always been.

In the process of recognizing that white culture is far more reactionary than black culture but also that African Americans cannot escape their Americanness, this project corroborates E. Patrick Johnson's findings regarding black sexualities and community building. Just as straight African Americans revise the whites-only portrait of healthy domesticity, "black gay men challenge the notion of the domestic site as only a heterosexual paradigm" (77). At the same time, black belonging is threatened from within the community. The "labor of allegiance" is disrupted by "black cultural conservationists who seek to demarcate blackness as unproblematically heterosexual" (Johnson 103). Nevertheless, connections remain. As Johnson asserts, "black heterosexuals and homosexuals exist in the vortex that is the process of identification" (ibid.). This study engages texts that primarily feature heterosexual intimacies, but as these works highlight the vulnerability of sexually conservative African Americans, they deepen appreciation for the aggression that hounds all assertions of black belonging.

That is, both straight and queer black people must make themselves at home in the midst of hostility. Figures who are read as straight seem to conform to mainstream standards of heteronormativity, and figures who are read as LGBTQ+ seem to flout them. Because queer intimacies seem to divest from capitalist regimes of productivity, LGBTQ+ African Americans are understood to create alternative domestic spaces "where they 'make themselves from scratch' [. . . and] 'make do' with the leftovers from a world that has disowned and abused them" (83). However, tracing black people's success-oriented journeys makes it clear that African Americans do not simply respond to dominant discourses and practices—whether those words and deeds reign in mainstream society or in black enclaves. African Americans of every gender and sexuality participate in the embodied debates that constitute black culture, and that culture is more proactive than reactive, supported as it is by the community conversation that keeps African Americans striving despite the opposition they face at every turn.

Examining the community conversation therefore allows me to demonstrate the importance of another question about an earlier time period: How effective can cultural criticism be if it assumes that identifying and claiming gradations of success would have been irrelevant to men, women, and children in bondage? How illuminating can criticism be if it assumes that, because they cannot avoid grappling with the "afterlives of slavery" (Hartman), African Americans have been forced to "tend toward death" (Moten) or to accept failure? Even while extracting a complex understanding of enslaved people's lives (from archives designed to prevent her from doing so), Hartman argues that "the *history* of black counter-historical projects is one of failure, precisely because these accounts have never been able to install themselves as history, but rather are insurgent, disruptive narratives that are marginalized and derailed before they ever gain a footing" ("Venus" 13, original emphasis). The problem here begins with conceiving of "black counter-historical projects" at all. Whiteness aggressively denies to blackness everything it claims for itself, so whiteness is the ultimate counter-historical project. Scholars must resist the temptation to grant victories to white supremacy that its desperately reactionary nature contradicts. As Hartman articulates in another context, to study African American culture is to study that which was created by people who "didn't need others beneath their feet to establish their value" (*Wayward*, 270).

Homemade Citizenship: It Was Always There

To assert that scholars have overlooked how routinely affirming oneself and grappling with violence go together is to encourage greater appreciation of practices that African Americans have always undertaken. I am thinking along with critical geographer Katherine McKittrick, who shows how black women's place-making and meaning-making have always existed but have been obscured by dominant discourses and practices. Rigorous cultural criticism must therefore disclose or reveal what is already there, and expressive culture provides an important access point (xxiii–xxvii).

Because they so deliberately sustain black people in the hostile environment of the United States, those who are both artists and analysts prove to be especially powerful guides. Novelist and critic Toni Morrison used her writing and speaking to engage in and document the practices of racial self-affirmation my study examines. In her contribution to the essay collection, *The House That Race Built*, she explains, "These questions . . . have troubled all of my work. . . . [H]ow to convert a racist house into a race-specific yet nonracist home? How to enunciate race while depriving it of its lethal cling? They are questions of concept, of language, of trajectory, of habitation, of occupation" (5). My project thinks along with Morrison to understand how defining and pursuing accomplishment has required African Americans to grapple with these same questions. Claiming success that the nation is committed to withholding demands race-specific yet nonracist strategies; it requires understanding the death-dealing meanings that cling to blackness without internalizing those meanings.

To cultivate homemade citizenship is to embody and enact a belief that has reverberated for generations: one may not be able to escape the racism and sexism the United States heaps onto particular groups, but that does not mean one cannot create more inhabitable spaces in the midst of hostility. Especially as house slaves and housekeepers, black women have had lots of practice doing precisely that. I examine evidence left by those who achieved while bombarded with racist and sexist violence. While some African Americans have advocated leaving the country for better opportunities around the globe,[29] the artists discussed here illuminate the strategies of those determined to stake their claims in the United States while facing its aggression. To adapt the insight offered by another artist and cultural critic, James Baldwin: for African Americans to come into their own, they had to make themselves up as they went along, and "this had to be done in the not-at-all-metaphorical teeth of the world's determination to destroy [them]" (*Nobody* 279).

Complementing Morrison and Baldwin, poet and scholar Evie Shockley gestures toward the kinds of practices I prioritize when examining African American culture—practices of racial self-affirmation in the midst of grappling with hostility. Her assessment of academia is applicable to black people's experiences in the United States more generally: "I am neither homeless nor at home in the academy; rather, I am making-myself-at-home. 'Making-myself-at-home' is both a state of being and a process in which I am ongoingly engaged. . . . I am doing what I can . . . to make the place where I find myself feel like a home (for myself and for my students) by acting like (not pretending, but behaving as if) the academy is ours. We've been invited in. The situation is often hospitable. But you don't have to be invited into your own home."

Because black presence in the United States has been shaped by kidnapping and 250 years of slavery, this is not quite home, so black people are always making themselves at home. What they can grasp is not quite citizenship, so they are always making citizenship from scratch. By contributing to a multivalent community conversation that empowers them to face the worst odds and achieve nonetheless, African Americans make themselves at home.

In identifying practices of *making-oneself-at-home*, this book helps readers appreciate that, for black communities, citizenship is not in question so much as it must be defined and pursued in ways that call upon an authority beyond the nation-state. Its value does not derive from civic inclusion. Many African Americans understand that black people often better embody American ideals than do the straight white men who are the country's archetypal citizens. However, because national citizenship by definition includes state recognition, it is for nonwhite people what feminist scholar Salamishah Tillet describes as a "peculiar citizenship" at best. So, cultivating homemade citizenship, creating a sense of belonging from scratch (without basic ingredients like safety) is a way of making mainstream recognition less important because the nation's withholding of recognition is simply another example of know-your-place aggression anyway. As literary historian Derrick Spires has found when examining African American culture from the 1780s to the mid–nineteenth century, black people did not simply track the loss of rights; they "actively worked to generate new ways of understanding citizenship and being citizens outside rights discourse" (17). This project therefore aligns with that of Spires: "Rather than ask how black citizens could achieve citizenship or had achieved citizenship as a destination defined by the state or white recognition, [this study] asks how black citizens defined citizenship themselves, *claiming their everyday activities as doing the work of citizenship*, often outside of or despite dominant political frameworks" (13, emphasis added).

Quite powerfully, members of black communities have made themselves at home without ceasing, even though black agency is often "limited and transient" (Hartman, *Scenes*, 61). As Hartman explains, African American community relations cannot be appreciated without understanding the losses engendered by slavery and its afterlives: "These relations can neither be reduced to domination nor explained outside of it" (ibid.). However, recognizing know-your-place aggression highlights that it is not just African American agency that is limited and transient; so too is domination. Domination does not simply endure; it keeps reacting to every sign of black success and every assertion of black belonging. This project therefore places pressure on conceptions of power. In "The Subject and Power," Michel Foucault argues: "Power is exercised only over free subjects, and only insofar as they are free . . . . Where the determining factors saturate the whole, there is no relationship of power; slavery is not a power relationship when man is in chains" (790). Afro-pessimism often aligns with Foucault on this point,[30] but African American expressive culture offers countless examples of how slavery failed to obliterate free will. As Ibram X. Kendi puts it, "Black people were people. Although their enslavers tried, they had never been reduced to things. Their humanity had never been eliminated" (183). Enslaved people engaged in a range of practices that demonstrate that they never relinquished what Foucault calls "the intransigence of freedom." Foucault insists that controlling actions requires total domination. In all other cases, "instead of manipulating and inducing actions in a calculated manner, one must be content with reacting to them after the event" (794). That is how I propose we understand practices like breeding and the separation of families. White-authored violence reacts to black-authored success. Foucault continues, "It would not be possible for power relations to exist without points of insubordination which, by definition, are means of escape. Accordingly, every intensification, every extension of power relations *to make the insubordinate submit* can only result in the limits of power" (ibid., emphasis added). White brutality produces horrible conditions, but it does so as a response to reminders of its impotence.

As a result, viewing black life and art as reactions to white violence will always yield misreadings. It is far better to examine black culture through the lens of achievement. Doing so reveals "the predicaments posed by a general state of obstructed agency with respect to other human actors or to the social" (Ngai 3). African Americans experience "obstructed agency" in that their ability to overcome obstacles, and meet or exceed standards, brings violence as often as praise. When cultural critics and general readers attend to achievement as faithfully as African Americans do, they will appreciate the perseverance of black communities. They will truly understand how routinely black success inspires aggression *from the nation it helped build*.

Becoming Better Readers

Because current interpretive frameworks obscure more than they illuminate, I argue for a reading practice attuned to what has actually formed African American culture: a fierce orientation toward accomplishment. The archives on which researchers depend disproportionately prioritize white voices and perspectives. For black people, "the archive is [frequently] a death sentence, a tomb, a display of the violated body, an inventory of property" (Hartman, "Venus," 2). Those are not the only resources, however, because many African Americans created their own records. Forebears left evidence about not only what was most important to them but also how they sustained themselves and each other in the pursuit of what was most important. And yet, alternative archival material does little good if scholarly paradigms dull perception.

Common reading practices limit what historians and cultural critics see when encountering the archives that predecessors struggled to leave. Just as documents produced and preserved by oppressors require particular strategies for accessing accurate information about African-descended people,[31] the same proves true for black-authored texts. Generations of critics have prioritized identifying what Henry Louis Gates Jr. famously called signifyin(g). They have been on the lookout for double meanings and coded language because white culture is assumed to be so totalizing as to require vigilance regarding African Americans' inevitable reactions to it. Perhaps preoccupied with sly indirection, critics have overlooked that which has been directly represented: black people's laser focus on success.

Expressive culture is an access point to a broader, multivalent community conversation, and focusing on women's cultural production offers particular rewards. Because the accomplishments of marginalized groups inspire hostility, black women's texts illuminate strategies of perseverance at the intersection of both racist and sexist violence, at the intersection of aggression designed to keep both African Americans and women in their "proper" place. As Kimberlé Crenshaw teaches, when one studies those hounded by more than one form of oppression, the findings shed light on the experiences of those who live at intersections with less traffic. So, I believe black women's works will be more revealing than men's for understanding how African Americans as a group cultivate home-made citizenship. As Crenshaw's forerunner Anna Julia Cooper argued in 1892, "no man can represent the race. Whatever the attainments of the individual may be, unless his home has moved on *pari passu* [side by side], he can never be regarded as identical with or representative of the whole" (*Voice* 30). Cooper's insistence upon using the home to measure representativeness underscores the value of a particular time frame—from slavery to the Obama administration—for tracking black achievement and the backlash it inspires. Because the United States is especially brutal toward black domesticities and intimacies, beginning this study's exploration in the mid–nineteenth century proves illuminating. The Civil War represents a moment of extraordinary potential for changing what black homes could become as well as a moment of painful continuity in terms of the assault on black families and households.

I focus on texts authored by black women that now enjoy canonical status. Because sexism determined how literature entered the curriculum and how it circulated outside classrooms, woman-authored texts weren't incorporated into African American literary history until the 1970s and 1980s, when a critical mass of black feminists undertook recuperative labor. Examining canonical works by black women exposes cultural criticism's most durable assumptions because demonstrating the significance of neglected contributions required making them legible according to the most accepted protocols. One reliable framework involved viewing black expressive culture in terms of either self-affirmation or resistance. By focusing on some of the most frequently anthologized, taught, and/or discussed creative contributions made by African American women, I reveal what an affirmation-versus-protest approach has obscured. I also prioritize narrative because scholars have privileged it when working to understand black culture; replicating that focus allows this study to enter a long-standing discussion. However, slave narratives and novels are part of a dynamic conversation comprised of not only the written word but also tone, gesture, and movement. Thus, rather than place narrative on a literary pedestal that may or may not be relevant to the "real" world, I consider it as one of many contributions to community debates about achievement. As important, I place drama and media performances on par with narrative to acknowledge the diversity of creative expression that constitutes the community's ongoing effort to define and pursue black success and thereby cultivate homemade citizenship.

The nation has long attacked black familial bonds while insisting they never existed, so African Americans have always been aware of their domestic vulnerability. At the same time, community members have often defined accomplishment in ways that center heteronormative homemaking. For example, in the 1890s and early 1900s, black club women taught less-educated mothers how to create domestic havens and gave lessons on how to comport oneself as a restrained and refined lady. As black women activists represented themselves as avatars of moral and sexual propriety, they produced and supported art that bolstered those efforts by defining achievement in terms of traditional domesticity. In examining such work, leading scholars have generally understood it in terms of the politics of respectability,[32] which has led many of them to view the artistic legacy through the lens of protest.

Becoming better readers requires attention to how these works contribute to a community conversation concerned more with defining black achievement and asserting black belonging than with defending black people's humanity, morality, or even citizenship. I approach the archive and repertoire of African American culture looking not for protest but for an investment in defining black success in a society bent on denying it. New insights await scholars and readers who tune in to black accomplishment, because cultural criticism has typically stopped short of challenging the assumption that African American artists primarily react to mainstream misrepresentation.

For example, indispensable studies such as Hazel Carby's *Reconstructing Womanhood* (1987), Claudia Tate's *Domestic Allegories of Political Desire* (1992), and Ann duCille's *Coupling Convention* (1993) examine black domestic novels as evidence that black women resisted their exclusion from the mainstream conception of "true womanhood."[33] Yet, their findings do not address the reactionary nature of dominant culture. The nation's investment in excluding black women from the cult of true womanhood intensified precisely because black women were increasingly seen to meet the standards of genteel femininity, and black men were providing marital protection. Indeed, these sorts of achievements inspired real-life violence as white men "ku-kluxed" households by raping the wives of successful black men. As always, discursive violence and physical violence reinforce each other, and black cultural production acknowledges both. However, because they worked to demonstrate that black women authors "transformed," "reconstructed," and "subverted" dominant ideologies, black feminist studies overlooked the fact that whites became desperate to weaponize ideologies precisely because African Americans were meeting or exceeding stated standards. That is, black achievement inspired aggression, including the discursive violence of stereotyping black women as whores.

Historians and cultural critics have shown how black artists and activists persistently placed a spotlight on their community's domestic successes while mainstream discourse cast African Americans as sexual deviants uninterested in traditional home life. These findings should be considered in light of what W. E. B. Du Bois, Ida B. Wells, and others living and writing in the midst of mob brutality made clear: African Americans were anything but oblivious to the link between domestic terrorism and black achievement. The discursive violence of insisting that black women are not women must be read as a *response* to African American success, and accomplishments in the domestic realm have always been met with particular force because the nation insists upon tying citizenship to traditional home life, which only whites are supposed to enjoy. *From Slave Cabins to the White House* therefore models a black feminist reading practice that maintains clarity about the direction of the cause-and-effect relationship between black accomplishment and white supremacist terrorism—a clarity inspired by the lessons of my previous book, *Living with Lynching.*

It is powerful to recall foundational black feminist studies of the 1980s and 1990s in our current moment, as we are encouraged to develop reading practices that align with the need not only to assert that #BlackLivesMatter but also to insist that Americans #SayHerName. Faced with evidence of the vulnerability of black women and girls—but also with the fact that their struggles easily fall out of focus—more media commentators and researchers are paying attention to black female citizens. Still, recent interventions emphasize biography and history over black women's creative and artist contributions. This has left a gap in our understanding that this study fills.[34]

Reading Responses to a Black First Lady

Understanding that American citizenship has been produced through know-your-place aggression, *From Slave Cabins to the White House* refuses to allow unjust exclusions to remain unmarked. This study, like the community conversation, focuses on key truths: in the United States, racist attacks and black achievement are intimately linked because the success of marginalized groups inspires aggression as often as praise. Answering with violence the accomplishments of those who are not white, male, straight, and propertied has been the American way from the time there was anything like the United States.[35] And the violence has always included insisting that certain folk can be house slaves and housekeepers but never homemakers.

Responses to Michelle Obama expose the nation's rigidity about who is understood as a homemaker. As discussed, Mrs. Obama is a married woman who prioritizes her relationship with both her husband and her children, but when she became a public figure, critics couldn't resist trying to diminish her with the label "baby mama."[36] Several years later, at the 2012 Democratic National Convention, she claimed the title "Mom-in-Chief,"[37] and some declared this to be an affront to the women's movement.[38] For others, it was not enough to ignore or diminish Mrs. Obama's marriage and motherhood. Especially when she prioritized her own children, her success as a wife and mother prompted aggression. Not only did the Obamas receive an extraordinary number of threats,[39] but the couple's doting on their children, not just on white children, sparked criticism. An effective National Rifle Association (NRA) advertisement insisted the president and his wife shielded their children while trying to strip Americans of the ability to protect theirs.[40] The NRA essentially promoted the belief that, despite being the first family, the Obamas were not truly America's family.

African American cultural production has been committed to representing black women's movement from serving in someone else's home to being *woman of the house*, and Michelle Obama's public persona is part of this tradition. However, the journey has always been less about becoming a homemaker than about receiving respect, rather than hostility, for one's homemaker status. This book discusses that pattern in relationship to both enslaved women *who were nonetheless homemakers* and contemporary black women. As feminist theorist bell hooks has suggested, it is significant that *The Help* emerged as a sensation when the country finally had a black first lady.[41] This very popular book and movie reinforces the idea that black womanhood best fits the servant role—that black women are housekeepers, not homemakers. The franchise's overwhelming popularity, spawning everything from cookbooks to packaged tea, should be understood as a reaction to the unconscious distress caused by seeing a black woman as woman of the house. This is nothing new, of course; as historian Kimberly Wallace-Sanders demonstrates, the marketability of Aunt Jemima "hinged on a Black woman pretending to be a slave in 1893, so that its success revolved around the fantasy of returning a Black woman to slave labor" ("Dishing Up" 218). A similar cultural purpose was served by black women pretending to be 1960s maids in 2009 (novel) and 2011 (film). Indeed, the value Americans place on supposedly innocuous (but racist) nostalgia was confirmed when the film industry bestowed Academy Awards and nominations on *The Help*'s black actresses. This coveted recognition asserted that the performers had contributed to American culture by affirming mainstream beliefs about where black womanhood belongs.[42] And it matters that they had the opportunity to do so (in a blockbuster hit) when Michelle Obama was so conspicuously out of her "proper" place.

When the nation's most prominent wife and mother so routinely has her marriage and motherhood ignored, diminished, or attacked, what does that say about the United States, which insists that women prove to be national treasures by becoming wives and mothers? This book emerges, in part, to address that question—a question whose relevance refuses to fade. According to mainstream rhetoric, a woman makes undeniable contributions to the country when she marries a man and has children in an admirable household. Nevertheless, married black women and their stable, intact families never seem to be viewed in this light, even when the black woman in question inhabits the nation's most revered home.

Reading This Book

From Slave Cabins to the White House examines black cultural production as an access point to the community conversation among African Americans, from its engagement with slavery and the Civil War to its appreciation for the unprecedented freedom marginalized communities enjoy in the Age of Michelle Obama. In the process, I trace homemade citizenship, finding that the need for making-oneself-at-home never fades, despite historical shifts since slavery. The book's six chapters engage different decades, but I am less concerned with comprehensive coverage than with what selected canonical texts reveal about the politics of representation in the United States. I attempt to answer why mainstream conversations never tire of animating certain figures, even as others struggle to gain traction—for instance, why black and brown women can always be cast as house slaves and housekeepers but not as homemakers.

Chapter 1, "A Home of One's Own," demonstrates how intensely African Americans defined and redefined success even while enslaved. With an emphasis on Harriet Jacobs's *Incidents in the Life of a Slave Girl* (1861) and Elizabeth Keckley's *Behind the Scenes; Or, Thirty Years a Slave and Four Years in the White House* (1868), this chapter charts black women's determination to move from slave cabins to the nation's most iconic house. Strikingly, in all environments, the authors highlight practices of making-oneself-at-home, the activities that sustain black women and their loved ones no matter how hostile their surroundings. Even when the environment is assumed to be less hostile—given the prestige of the White House, for example—women must assert their rightful place as they encounter opposition every step of the way.

Chapter 2, "No, Really: A Home of One's Own," examines representative works of the black domestic novel tradition, Frances E. W. Harper's

Iola Leroy (1892) and Pauline Hopkins's *Contending Forces* (1900). This genre inspired the foundational black feminist criticism of the 1980s and 1990s, which expanded understandings of African American literary traditions by decentering male-authored texts and taking women writers seriously. That indispensable work placed black women's literature in the context of the cult of true womanhood, which insisted that real women were white and therefore black women were some other order of being. However, in this chapter, I deepen understandings by refusing to see black domestic fiction primarily as a response to dehumanizing discourses and practices. If one does not assume that these narratives mainly protest exclusion from "true womanhood," what insights await? This chapter highlights the trope of homemade citizenship that has always been there but that scholars have overlooked in their assumptions that every artistic work is either protesting or ignoring the reasons for protest. Both *Iola Leroy* and *Contending Forces* revolve around racial uplift, and because they define it as collective practices of making-oneself-at-home, they highlight the importance of the community conversation to help black women claim their right to every aspect of success, including romantic love.

Chapter 3, "New Negroes, New Homes," uses Nella Larsen's *Quicksand* (1928) and Zora Neale Hurston's *Their Eyes Were Watching God* (1937) to understand the impact "race motherhood" had on community definitions of success. Race motherhood, the idea that black women best contribute to racial uplift by supporting men, gained traction in the 1920s and 1930s. Though questioning race motherhood made black women vulnerable to harsh criticism and possible ostracism, black women authors suggest that this ideology emerged to coerce women into advancing a black male-centered agenda. Larsen's and Hurston's protagonists are preoccupied with achieving what they define as success and a sense of belonging. Along the way, they expose the harm caused by race motherhood, an ideology that many in the community embraced despite its tendency to disregard black women's right to pleasure, not simply survival and service.

Chapter 4, "Home as Human Right and Black Power," examines two significant dramas, Lorraine Hansberry's *A Raisin in the Sun* (1959) and Alice Childress's *Wine in the Wilderness* (1969). Together, these plays gesture toward the consistency with which African Americans' definitions of success involved conceiving of one's household as either a fundamental human right or a sign of black independence and power. Importantly, both plays spotlight intimate settings that presumably facilitate racial self-affirmation but in which single black women find little refuge. By highlighting the hostility these women encounter in their own communities, Hansberry and Childress suggested that rigorous debate remains crucial if African Americans are to enjoy the sense of belonging and achievement, as well as the independence and positive self-regard, they so richly deserve.

Chapter 5, "Still the Master's House?" examines two novels that revisit slavery, Octavia Butler's *Kindred* (1979) and Toni Morrison's *Beloved* (1987). These powerful texts exemplify black women's attempts in the 1970s and 1980s to create spaces of empowerment for modern women and places of honor for women ancestors at a time when Alex Haley's *Roots* and Kunta Kinte had overtaken the community conversation. These works expose the damage done when African Americans assume their female forebears functioned primarily as race traitors and matriarchs.

Chapter 6, "The Ultimate Home: Michelle Obama in the White House," analyzes the first lady's public persona as a performance text, highlighting her facility with not only claiming success for herself but also inspiring its pursuit in others. As a self-proclaimed Mom-in-Chief, Mrs. Obama embodied a variation of the strong black woman, and her strategies for inspiring others resembled those of black club women of the 1890s and early 1900s. As mentioned, club women not only taught other women best practices for feeding their children and cleaning and decorating their homes; they also gave advice about, and considered themselves models for, how best to style one's hair and dress appropriately—all for the good of the race. Likewise, Mrs. Obama made deliberate choices about her hair, clothes, and overall bodily presentation, and she decorated the White House in ways that continued Jacqueline Kennedy's legacy but that also acknowledged the hostility hounding her first family because it was not white.

The Coda tells a basic truth that nevertheless cannot be left unsaid: the investment in know-your-place aggression led many Americans to embrace the idea of taking the country "From Mom-in-Chief to Predator-in-Chief." Americans' most common words and deeds aim to keep people who are not straight, white, and male in their "proper" place. What better way to tell women, especially women of color, that they aren't at home than with the election of Donald Trump, despite his admitting to sexual predation? Americans spoke loudly and acted out of their belief that the

American Dream might be for white men who damage communities and institutions, but it is certainly not for accomplished black women.

* * *

African American women have consistently pursued and achieved success in every possible arena, and their victories have made them targets—and this is especially true of their domestic accomplishments. Black women have always been exemplary wives and mothers in admirable households, and mainstream discourse has relentlessly discouraged, diminished, and worked to destroy their achievements. This tendency took center stage when a black woman became woman of the nation's house. As this study demonstrates, however, the tradition of know-your-place aggression did not begin with the Obamas. It has been a response to the most ordinary, even downtrodden, examples of black familial success. Literally, *From Slave Cabins to the White House.*

A Home of One's Own

By the mid–nineteenth century, the political and cultural landscape of the United States had been shaped for at least 200 years by lifelong servitude for those believed to have "African blood." In concert with Enlightenment thinking, white Americans assured themselves that God had created some groups for the purpose of serving others (Kendi). Systematically subordinating people who were not inferior required aggressive assertions about the difference between those in power and those vulnerable to them. Family and reproduction were effective areas for constructing difference that supposedly proved natural inferiority,[1] so Anglo Americans insisted their (sometimes) darker counterparts felt little that resembled their own intimate attachments. These assertions must be seen as reactive violence. It was because the humanity of enslaved people was so apparent that denials of it had to be continual and brutal. As Cedrick Robinson puts it, "the cargoes of laborers also contained African cultures, critical mixes . . . of language and thought, of cosmology and metaphysics, of habits, beliefs, and morality. These were the actual terms of their humanity" (124). Yet, even when most were in chains, black people in the United States did not act simply on their awareness of their humanity; they pursued greater and greater success. African-descended people succeeded, and their triumphs included the creation of homes despite being denied basic resources for domestic stability. As demonstrated in the

Introduction, black accomplishment is always attacked, but achievement in the realm of traditional domesticity is particularly so.

The aggression that answered black success included the American Colonization Society, founded in 1817; the Fugitive Slave Act of 1850; and the Dred Scott decision of 1857. The American Colonization Society constituted know-your-place aggression in that it emerged from the idea that, if black people were not going to be enslaved, they should reside somewhere other than the United States. The organization gained traction as abolitionists found common cause with proslavery activists. Though they seemed ideologically opposed, these groups agreed it was unreasonable to expect white Americans to tolerate the presence of, to say nothing of rights for, free black people. Of course, some blacks embraced emigration. Convinced they would never enjoy decent treatment in the United States, they were willing to seek more just possibilities elsewhere. Black advocates of colonization and emigration took a stance that makes sense.[2] Who wouldn't want a life in which one's achievements aren't answered with violence? Still, the good sense of their stance only underscores the degree to which debate has always characterized the community conversation about success.

Because many African-descended people in the United States did not seek life elsewhere but acted on the belief that they belonged in the country they helped build, the aggression of the American Colonization Society was joined in 1850 by the violence of the Fugitive Slave Act. This legislation countered what Robin Kelley calls "freedom dreams" with discursive violence that encouraged both discursive and physical violence. Facing tremendous odds and brutal punishment if captured, enslaved men and women nevertheless often fled. Their doing so constituted a victory in that the enslaved had retained enough self-determination to resist staying in their "proper" place.[3] The national government responded to that victory with hostility. Ratified in 1850, the Fugitive Slave Act required all citizens to assist in returning to bondage anyone suspected of having run away from slavery, and it obliterated a fugitive's right to a jury trial. Cases would be handled by special commissioners who would be paid $5 if an alleged fugitive were released and $10 if handed over to the claimant. The law literally offered incentives for being hostile to an entire population's human desire for freedom. The message was clear: there would be federal cooperation with enslavers and federal opposition to anyone acknowledging freedom might be a human right, even for those not considered white.

This legislation's 1850 ratification expressed the government's resistance to conceiving of nonwhite people as humans with a right to the fruit of their labor. For those caught in slavery's web, it also communicated that familial bonds would continue to be attacked with the blessing of the country's leaders.[4] After the Fugitive Slave Act went into effect, free black people who otherwise had no interest in leaving the United States became convinced emigration was their people's best hope, reluctantly aligning with white activists who had founded the American Colonization Society and its colony in Liberia. Others fled to Canada and encouraged their brethren to follow. For instance, Mary Shadd relocated there and founded the *Provincial Freeman* newspaper, giving black readers in the United States information that made Canada less intimidating and more inviting, thereby acknowledging imagined community and contributing to its multivalent community conversation. Also, "from 1830 until well after the Civil War, once captive and already free Blacks came together in state, regional, and national conventions to strategize about how they might achieve educational, labor, and legal justice" (ColoredConventions. org). Through the convention movement, African Americans defined and redefined accomplishment, and participants viewed the Fugitive Slave Act as an assault, as a reaction to community members' success at refusing to internalize the notion that they were inferior to white counterparts and should have no aspirations.

The violence of the Fugitive Slave Act was not enough to satisfy the nation's appetite for know-your-place aggression; in 1857, the Supreme Court declared black people had "no rights which the white man was bound to respect" in *Dred Scott v. Sandford*. This decision is best understood as a reaction to black success.[5] Harriet and Dred Scott had commanded recognition of their humanity and their rights when allowed to marry each other in a public ceremony in a free territory. They had lived as free people for years but filed suit in 1846, hoping the court would recognize that their having relocated to the slave state of Missouri had not changed their status. They likely took these extraordinary legal steps because Scott's former owner had died, creating the possibility that his heirs would sell him, thereby separating him from his wife Harriet (Hunter, *Bound in Wedlock*, 82). Such a move would constitute a brutal assault on the life they had successfully built by returning them to their "proper" place. Years before, Scott had been listed in a territorial census as "the head of his household, which affirmed that [he and Harriet] conducted themselves as a married couple and as free people" (ibid. 81).

The court's decision to strip the couple of the status former enslavers had acknowledged was designed to insist nonwhite people have privileges, not rights. This judgment must be seen as a violent reaction to an entire population, the homes they build, and the triumphs they secure against the odds.[6]

Even as the United States reinforced the belief that those who are not straight, white, and male can only belong *to* the nation and its acknowledged citizens, black women remained focused on how to keep claiming success.[7] One observes this investment in two Civil War–era texts that showcase practices of making-oneself-at-home while never ignoring white-authored attacks on black people's aspirations and achievements. Harriet Jacobs's *Incidents in the Life of a Slave Girl* (1861) and Elizabeth Keckley's *Behind the Scenes; Or, Thirty Years a Slave and Four Years in the White House* (1868) highlight black women's efforts to move from being house slaves to having homes of their own.[8] Yet, readers attentive to success will notice that even when deprived of households of their own, African Americans cultivate a sense of home and belonging nonetheless. Slavery does not diminish their investment in pursuing achievement, even the type most likely to be attacked: domestic stability. As Saidiya Hartman might put it, black women constantly face the "absence of a proper domain" (*Scenes* 109), so they make it from scratch and in the midst of violence. This chapter therefore follows Deborah McDowell's lead by considering how black women's cultural production "dramatizes not what was *done* to slave women, but what they *did* with what was done to them" (146, original emphasis).

Slave Cabins as Spaces of Triumph

Harriet Jacobs's *Incidents in the Life of a Slave Girl* is a novelized autobiography in which the author presents herself as Linda Brent, the heroine of a sentimental coming-of-age story, but Jacobs concludes by insisting her protagonist's journey had been more a quest for freedom than for marriage. Educated white women readers made sentimental novels a sensation, and these stories revolved around the development of a virtuous heroine who learns to "feel right," to prioritize morality and to sympathize with the less fortunate, and her doing so yields the reward of having a husband and children to nurture. Understanding these expectations, but also challenging them, Jacobs's narrator explains, "Reader, my story ends with freedom; not in the usual way, with marriage. I and my children are now free! [However,] The dream of my life is not yet realized. I do not sit with my children in a home of my own, I still long for a hearthstone of my own, however humble. I wish it for my children's sake far more than for [mine]" (167). Jacobs's definition of success prioritizes freedom over marriage, but freedom is not truly satisfying without a home of one's own. It is therefore revealing to examine the text for its drive toward achievement and for how often Linda defines accomplishment in relation to homemaking. Though the concluding passage downplays her domestic desire by emphasizing her children, the narrative focus on domesticity exposes how relentlessly Linda defines, redefines, and pursues success while taking note of white violence.

Because Jacobs depicts practices of making-oneself-at-home even while addressing a white audience whose abolitionist support she seeks for those still in bondage, *Incidents* reflects and advances the community conversation that fuels homemade citizenship. Black readers and interlocutors are never neglected. The text contributes to self-affirmation no less than it protests conditions, and its protest is not at all separate from self-affirmation.

Jacobs frames Linda's life story by highlighting know-your-place aggression; she emphasizes that white Americans are aware that the enslaved succeed in maintaining dignity, so they deliberately try to brutalize that dignity out of them. When Linda's father dies when she is around 6 or 7 years old, rather than allow her to be with her family, she is "ordered to go for flowers, that my mistress's house might be decorated for an evening party. I spent the day gathering flowers and weaving them into festoons, while the dead body of my father was lying within a mile of me" (13). The narrative pinpoints why enslavers make such demands: "He was merely a piece of property. Moreover, they thought he had spoiled his children, by teaching them to feel that they were human beings" (ibid.). As narrator, Linda tracks black self-affirmation no less than she identifies reactionary white aggression. For instance, when her uncle Benjamin runs away and is captured, his holding on to his sense of self constitutes a victory whites seek to brutalize out of him. His enslaver places him in jail, vowing to leave him there until he is "subdued." If he is not subdued, his oppressor swears to sell him even if the price is low. During the six months that Benjamin is imprisoned, the indignities he endures include being chained and covered with vermin (24). When he is finally to be sold, the trader is hesitant because he has "heard something of his character, and it did not strike him as suitable for a slave" (ibid.). Benjamin's body has been mutilated and his psyche assaulted, but *Incidents* records his victory. In this, the text corroborates what a real-life mother said of her son, that "it would be 'hard work for him to bring his mind to be a slave'" (D. Berry 65). Every entity supporting subjugation aims to destroy all signs of black humanity and self-regard, and Jacobs's text is ever alive to that reality.

As it showcases Linda's determination to claim success by creating a home for herself and her family, *Incidents* never loses sight of the nation's investment in stomping those aspirations out of them. By focusing on households, the text gestures toward enslaved women's awareness that domesticity, as an ideology, casts the "properly" domestic woman as "the modern reconstruction not just of the female self but of selfhood in general" (Romero 25). This orientation is part of Jacobs's skillful appeal to white women familiar with sentimentality. However, if one reads not simply for how the text protests conditions to recruit for its cause but also for how it affirms its author and her family and community, then additional insights await. By age 14, Linda has begun accepting the correlation between houses and selfhood by watching her grandmother, but Jacobs also highlights the debate about definitions of success that this correlation prompts. Even as youngsters, Linda and her uncle Benjamin—who is so close in age "that he seemed more like my brother than my uncle" (10)—envy Aunt Martha. Jacobs has Linda explain: "By perseverance and unwearied industry, she was now mistress of a snug little home, surrounded with the necessaries of life. She would have been happy could her children have shared them with her" (18). While noting the pain her grandmother feels at being separated from loved ones, Linda insists Aunt Martha's cabin is preferable to her own situation, living in the Flint household. With this, even though Aunt Martha is free, Linda corroborates what historian Erica Dunbar has found, that most bondswomen would have preferred the living quarters occupied by field hands because, even if conditions were rough, such cabins "offered what house slaves longed for: privacy" (57). Because she and Benjamin make no secret of their misery, Aunt Martha encourages them to view their lot as "the will of God: that he had seen fit to place [them] under such circumstances; and though it was hard, [they] ought to pray for contentment" (18). However, Linda is unequivocal; she and her uncle Benjamin "*reasoned* that it was much more the will of God that we should be situated as she was. We longed for a home like hers" (ibid., emphasis added).

Here, Jacobs highlights debate as an embodied practice of belonging that sustains African Americans. Linda and her young uncle do not agree with Aunt Martha, and their discussion expresses and bolsters the attachment they feel to each other. As important, especially because Linda and Benjamin cannot immediately change their circumstances, Jacobs's representation of their articulated dissatisfaction becomes an example of making-oneself-at-home both in the text and in the lived world. For Linda and Benjamin as well as for Jacobs, holding fast to their own standard for being content constitutes self-affirmation even while unable to escape know-your-place aggression. Linda and Benjamin cannot claim a home of their own, but they do not accept the logic that capitulation is the appropriate response.

Though Linda cannot live with her grandmother, she benefits from her having succeeded in securing a home of her own. Aunt Martha provides Linda with treats as well as with necessities to make her life more comfortable than the Flints do. For, "little attention was paid to the slaves' meals in Dr. Flint's house. If they could catch a bit of food while it was going, well and good" (13). Thus, Jacobs shows that Aunt Martha achieves an efficient domesticity, offering her loved ones relief and helping them cope. The narrator recalls, "I was frequently threatened with punishment if I stopped there; and my grandmother, to avoid detaining me, often stood at the gate with something for my breakfast or dinner. I was indebted to *her* for all my comforts, spiritual or temporal. It was *her* labor that supplied my scanty wardrobe" (ibid.). As modest as these achievements are, they are met with know-your-place aggression. Being able to provide comfort and support surely gives a sense of purpose to Aunt Martha's lifetime of struggle, and there is no doubt she considers her current situation an accomplishment, but her granddaughter is threatened because enslavers insist upon diminishing black achievements.

While honoring what Aunt Martha does to alleviate the cruelties of the Flint household, Jacobs will not allow Linda to silence a painful truth: "Even the charms of the old oven failed to reconcile us to our hard lot" (19). At one point, Linda's brother William says he wishes he had died with their father because the world is bad, and everyone seems unhappy. Linda corrects him by insisting not everyone is miserable; people with "pleasant homes, and kind friends, *and who were not afraid to love them*" are happy (ibid., emphasis added). Jacobs thereby notes that, by age 14, Linda understands that slavery makes those in its clutches afraid to love—not only afraid to love their friends and family but also their homes.

With love deemed dangerous, how will Linda define success? At least temporarily, her answer involves good behavior. Linda tells her brother, "We must be good; perhaps that would bring us contentment" (ibid.). Using domesticity to make sense of daily realities, Linda weds good behavior to contentment and perhaps eventual justice. After all, she believes her grandmother's "perseverance and unwearied industry" had yielded a home of her own, a space representing not only relief and succor but also success. Yet, this conclusion requires Linda to ignore the fact that white people need not behave decently to enjoy benefits, including homes of their own.

The injustice of a focus on good behavior becomes undeniable when Linda narrates one of her grandmother's greatest homemaking victories, but Jacobs refrains from having Linda comment on it directly. Aunt Martha's son Benjamin does not want her to buy his freedom, so he claims it himself by running away, but because her son Phillip does not, she eventually purchases him. Linda reports, "She paid eight hundred dollars, and came home with the precious document that secured his freedom. The happy mother and son sat together by the old hearthstone that night, telling how proud they were of each other, and how they would prove to the world that they could take care of themselves, as they had long taken care of others" (26–27). The chapter closes on a particularly ironic note: "We all concluded by saying, 'He that is *willing* to be a slave, let him be a slave'" (27, original italics). Thus, Aunt Martha pays white Americans $800 for a man whose uncompensated labor had already benefited them. In exchange, she and her son get to "prove" they can take care of themselves, can create the sort of home life that deserves respect and protection. Here, the text interacts with African Americans' lived experiences. Though it was as rare as successful escape, many enslaved people worked tirelessly to buy loved ones. As usual, American institutions thrived on denying black humanity while also relying on it. If black familial bonds meant nothing, white people would not have been able to profit from such sales. The violence inhered in white people's insistence upon simultaneously recognizing and disregarding black humanity.[9] Of course, Aunt Martha and Phillip had been taking care of themselves all along; they simply had not been "free" to take care of themselves. Yet, they had always had the freedom to do what they were now doing with that bill of sale: provide for themselves while enriching white people. What did they gain, then? As narrator, Linda does not comment directly on the incongruence of their defining this as a moment of triumph, but she ends with what the family had gathered around to *say*, thereby suggesting they had simply gained the ability to *express* that they were not willingly enslaved. One might ask, "who was willingly enslaved?"

By assuming they are somehow different from their peers, the mother and son help Jacobs highlight the degree to which debate characterizes the community conversation, which defines success. As the text gestures toward debate, it acknowledges debate's crucial role both inside and outside the text in helping African Americans create a sense of belonging. And belonging to each other often requires struggling toward not belonging to white "masters," including the government. For some, this means operating within completely unjust, dehumanizing rules that funnel material resources away from black families. For others, this means refusing to "pay any man or woman for her freedom, because she thinks she has a right to it" (164). Ultimately, *Incidents* honors Aunt Martha without accepting the values she seems to hold dear. As Gabrielle Foreman argues, the narrative's "polyvalent pull highlights its parodic bitterness and the ultimate rejection of the grandmother's piety" (36); in fact, "*Incidents* calls into question the tenets of motherhood—domestic contentment and submission to God's will—by illustrating the limited maternal power true womanhood ostensibly brings to Black women under slavery" (36).

Even in this most victorious moment, Aunt Martha primarily makes enslavers richer while she and her family must continue to struggle for subsistence, as if they had not been working all their lives. The toil that Aunt Martha's modest accumulation of money represents, especially when considered alongside the unpaid labor Phillip has done all his life, makes for a bitter illustration of "limited maternal power," indeed. As Jacobs represents these scenes, defining success proves to be an activity enslaved people take seriously.

Jacobs's text notes how contradictory and piecemeal victories can be, but overlooking black people's preoccupation with achievement would only advance the goals of the know-your-place aggression they face. Because it registers the painful irony of this black familial success but refrains from commenting on it directly, *Incidents* refuses to discount the nonmaterial value and meaning of Aunt Martha's mothering. By purchasing her son, Aunt Martha claims sovereignty for some of her family; she tries to lessen whites' ability to control their lives. As Dorothy Roberts reminds us, while enslaved women's domestic labor and sacrifices should not be romanticized, their "devotion to their own households defied the expectation of total service to whites" (55). That is, "whites had the brute power . . . to steer the course of their slaves' reproductive lives; but they could not dictate the full value of procreation and mothering for Black women" (ibid.). In *Incidents*, expectations of total service come to the fore via Linda's aunt, Nancy, whom Mrs. Flint had forced to sleep outside her bedroom door, destroying her health. When Nancy dies, Mrs. Flint "became very sentimental. I suppose she thought it would be a beautiful illustration of the attachment existing between slaveholder and slave, if the body of her old worn-out servant was buried at her feet" (Jacobs 123). Just as purchasing her son Phillip shows Aunt Martha's mothering mattered in ways that could not be measured financially, *Incidents* recognizes Phillip's affection when he asks "permission to bury his sister [Nancy] at his own expense" (ibid.). Linda notes, "slaveholders are always ready to grant *such* favors to slaves and their relatives" (ibid., original italics). So, the benefit to white people is clear, but the narrative records these embodied practices of belonging with respect.

As Jacobs's novelized slave narrative reflects and contributes to a community conversation that debates definitions of success, it also grapples with the hierarchy of homebuilding practices. All black households are vulnerable, but those based on blood are sometimes tolerated while those based on choice are always attacked. To subordinate enslaved people, whites devalue all black familial bonds, but even if they sometimes abide the attachment enslaved people feel to their children, "masters" revel in preventing the enslaved from cherishing a mate of their own choosing. Linda had witnessed this dynamic through Mrs. Flint's treatment of another woman, but Dr. Flint soon forces her to contend with it herself. Jacobs's narrator reports, "I once heard [Mrs. Flint] abuse a young slave girl, who told her that a colored man wanted to make her his wife. 'I will have you peeled and pickled, my lady,' said she, 'if I ever hear you mention that subject again. Do you suppose that I will have you tending *my* children with the children of that nigger?'" (35). Linda's direct experience begins when she is 15 years old and has fallen in love with a free young man who wants to buy her freedom. Though Mrs. Flint is suspicious of her husband's interest in Linda, the slave girl expects no help because Mrs. Flint is like other white women. Namely, she "seemed to think that slaves had no right to any family ties of their own; that they were created merely to wait upon the family of the mistress" (35).

Linda's experience leaves an indelible impression. Dr. Flint refrains from hitting Linda until the day she admits loving a man of her choice. "How dare you tell me so!" he yells (37). Dr. Flint is offended she not only wants to marry but wants to marry a free man of color. He says, "Well, I'll soon convince you whether I am your master, or the nigger fellow you honor so highly. If you *must* have a husband, you may take up with one of my slaves" (36). The confrontation ends with several threats from Dr. Flint: "Never let me hear that fellow's name mentioned again. If I ever know of your speaking to him, I will cowhide you both; and if I catch him lurking about my premises, I will shoot him as soon as I would a dog. Do you hear what I say? I'll teach you a lesson about marriage and free niggers!" (Jacobs 37–38).

What Linda learns about "marriage and free niggers" proves irreversible, and the pain of this lesson reverberates throughout Jacobs's text. Linda agonizes, "There was no hope that the doctor would consent to sell me on any terms" (39). She realizes black homebuilding based on romantic coupling inspires especially intense hostility. To preserve enough agency—while enslaved—to have a desire, and to express it, constitutes success, and that victory inspires know-your-place aggression. In documenting awareness of this pattern, Jacobs shows enslaved people thought about achievement and developed and refined their definitions of it. Hereafter, Linda's homemaking goals become painfully different.

Adjusting her definition of success, Linda bids her first love farewell. Jacobs writes, "hard as it was to bring my feelings to it, I earnestly entreated him not to come back. I advised him to go to the Free States. . . . He left me, still hoping the day would come when I could be bought. With me the lamp of hope had gone out. The dream of my girlhood was over" (39). Jacobs/Linda parts with her beau because she does not want to link his fate with "my own unhappy destiny" (ibid.). When Linda encourages her beloved to forget her, she expresses affection that white supremacy worked to prevent and attacked when it couldn't prevent it. Linda does not stop making herself at home, though; she must simply do so under circumstances she does not choose. As Saidiya Hartman reminds us, any evidence of community among the enslaved should make readers appreciate "the difficulty and the accomplishment of collectivity in the context of domination and terror" (*Scenes* 60). When read for its focus on accomplishment despite the violence it brings, Jacobs's text corroborates

Hartman's claim. While being deprived of basic ingredients, Linda succeeds at making home and a sense of belonging nonetheless. She reports: "I still had my good grandmother, and my affectionate brother. When he put his arms round my neck, and looked into my eyes, as if to read there the troubles I dared not tell, I felt that I still had something to love" (Jacobs 39). Even as she notes the victory of maintaining and nurturing these bonds, she acknowledges that such modest success—though it is made from scratch and with the remnants of crushed dreams—would only inspire aggression: "If [Dr. Flint] had known how we loved each other, I think he would have exulted in separating us" (39–40). As Linda cultivates that which American society would prevent her from enjoying, it is clear enslaved people care about defining and redefining success.

Realizing Dr. Flint would never sell her and allow her to have a mate of her choice, Jacobs has Linda articulate recognition of what legal scholar Dorothy Roberts would later identify as the significance of such experiences. Namely, enslavers sought to control black women's reproduction, and the nation enabled them to do so, because it was "the most effective means of subjugating enslaved women, of denying them the power to govern their own bodies and to determine the course of their own destiny" (55). As historian Daina Berry puts it, "the institution of slavery in the United States extended its reach into women's bodies" (13). Forced to grapple with injustice, Linda begins relinquishing her original ideas about how homes and selfhood correspond—or at least how they could correspond in her life. If allowed to marry a free man of color who purchased her freedom, she could presumably abandon her house-slave status and create a home of her own. Even if still working in the Flint household, she would be more of a housekeeper whose domestic situation would not be completely determined by white people. After this devastating separation, however, she believes she would never be a "virtuous, free, and happy wife" (Jacobs 53). There was "no chance for me to be respectable" (68). Linda will not be allowed to embody the most accepted definitions of respectability, virtue, and freedom.

Upon recognizing the hierarchy of homemaking, whereby households based on romantic coupling are the most prized, Linda can accept the "properly" subordinate place Dr. Flint and the United States have for her, or she can acknowledge the closed doors and devise definitions that keep another version of success within reach. She chooses the latter; she becomes involved with a white man who does not own her, bearing his children and thereby frustrating Dr. Flint's plans for her life.

The hierarchy of homemaking is a violent mechanism designed to keep African Americans in their "proper" place, and *Incidents* underscores the violence when Linda's mourning of "the dream of my girlhood" contains a pivot point in which she clings to a new domestic vision. In short, she settles for a domesticity like that of Aunt Martha, one that does not include a partner of her own choosing.

Because Linda does not initially choose this path, it requires her to revise her definition of accomplishment, so *Incidents* encourages readers to distinguish between homemaking based on parenting and homemaking based on coupling. As Gabrielle Foreman notes, very often, "being sold surpassed almost all punishment" because it took its victim away from loved ones. Thus, "the pledge not to sell one's slaves was the next best thing to a promise of freedom" (28) because it meant remaining with family and friends. Historian Heather Williams confirms the importance of this insight in *Help Me to Find My People*, which tracks how tirelessly African Americans searched for family members who were torn from their lives by sales. However, when one accounts for differences in familial bonds, as Williams does by examining the separation of parents and children apart from the separation of husbands and wives, one must contend with the nuances of Linda's coming of age as it relates to her homemaking ideals. Foreman concludes that Flint's threat, "I will never sell you," becomes a victory for the "slave girl." According to Foreman, Linda "tactically outmaneuvers her own owner and victimizer; she nullifies the loss she most fears and preserves perhaps not her virtue—but her family" (29). This may be true if the family most worth preserving is that which she has by blood, not by choice, but there is evidence she wanted some chosen family.

As it reflects and contributes to the community conversation that debates success, Jacobs's narrative offers an opportunity to scrutinize not only definitions of accomplishment but also what women feel entitled to assert as the basis of their definitions. *Incidents* ends declaring Linda wants freedom more for her children than for herself. Wanting freedom for herself is somehow too unacceptable to be uttered; she must qualify her desires, even her domestic ones. Yet, if one considers the situation slavery has forced upon her in response to her success at maintaining enough self-regard to desire a man of her choice, one gains a deeper appreciation for its brutality. Much of slavery's violence resided in the fact that, in controlling black women's reproductive lives, "it forced its victims to perpetuate the very institution that subjugated them" (Roberts

24). When the narrative concludes with Linda emphasizing her children's presumed desires more than her own, it gestures toward a defeat suffered in slavery. Any success Linda creates after sending her beau away must be fashioned not only from meager resources but also out of the remnants of crushed dreams. She does not completely choose the father of her children, nor does she choose to have children at all. Her predicament therefore highlights the poignancy of Anna Julia Cooper's 1893 pronouncement about the deepest desires of enslaved women. Cooper explains, "The painful, patient, and silent toil of mothers to gain a fee simple title to the bodies of their daughters, the despairing fight, as of an entrapped tigress, to keep hallowed their own persons, would furnish material for epics" (*World's Congress* 712). Jacobs's narrative—and the transformation Linda's homemaking desires undergo—highlight the importance of the order in which Cooper lists black women's struggles. Working to claim a title on her daughter's body remains the foremost preoccupation because it is the realm of most possibility. Her daughter's existence is so often the result of not being able to dictate what happens to her own body, so shielding her daughter from a similar plight feels even more urgent and more hopeful.

Linda's experience has followed this pattern, and it seems to apply to Aunt Martha (the text's paragon of true womanhood) as well, so *Incidents* anticipates Cooper's 1893 description of the painful epics in which enslaved women are forced to become heroines. In this light, the story *Incidents* relates about an unnamed enslaved woman proves significant. When her mistress prepares to marry and offers to free her family, the woman declines. Linda says she had not been surprised because "I had often seen them in their comfortable home, and thought that the whole town did not contain a happier family" (46). The family declines freedom because the mistress "had always been their best friend, and they could not be so happy any where as with her" (ibid.). Jacobs's text thereby demonstrates that there is no single definition of achievement. Even among the enslaved, "success" and "manumission" are not necessarily synonyms. Linda, as narrator, tells the family's story this way: the "pious mistress"

> was an orphan, and inherited as slaves a woman and her six children. Their father was a free man. They had a comfortable home of their own, parents and children living together. The mother and eldest daughter served their mistress during the day, and at night returned to their dwelling, which was on the premises. The young lady was very pious,

and there was some reality in her religion. She taught her slaves to lead
pure lives, and wished them to enjoy the fruit of their own industry. *Her*
religion was not a garb put on for Sunday, and laid aside till Sunday
returned again. The eldest daughter of the slave mother was promised
in marriage to a free man; and the day before the wedding this good
mistress emancipated her, in order that her marriage might have the
sanction of *law*. (ibid.)

In essence, when a cabin is a home of one's own, its being a slave cabin
is less important.

However, when the white woman's new husband arrives, he asserts
his patriarchal "rights." Linda describes the fate of the enslaved woman's
remaining daughters:

One little girl, too young to be of service to her master, was left with the
wretched mother. The other three were carried to their master's plantation. The eldest soon became a mother; and when the slaveholder's
wife looked at the babe, she wept bitterly. She knew that her own husband had violated the purity she had so carefully inculcated. She had
a second child by her master, and then he sold her and his offspring to
his brother. She bore two children to the brother and was sold again.
The next sister went crazy. The life she was compelled to lead drove
her mad. The third one became the mother of five daughters. (ibid.)

The unnamed woman had had no objection to inhabiting a slave cabin
because it had been inviolate, but conditions changed.

Jacobs highlights the fact that enslaved people define achievement,
so her text does not simply protest in hopes of recruiting abolitionists;
it affirms black people with a spotlight on their various strategies for
claiming success because they routinely focus more on that than on
white people. It is white supremacy that reacts to them out of its need
to counter black people's every achievement and every assertion of belonging. Of course, the anonymous woman's situation is unusual because
her domestic success had been respected. The moment know-your-place
aggression emerges, her experience becomes typical.

Most bondswomen could not protect their own bodies as this woman
had, so Linda seems to include this story to reconcile herself to prioritizing her children's well-being over her own. It is too late for her—as
it was for Aunt Martha. Linda therefore extracts a sense of purpose
from her ability to redefine success in ways that prioritize the domestic

configuration oppressors find less threatening because it is based on blood, not based on choice. She is forced to value a home built on blood relations because it occupies a lower position in society's hierarchy of homebuilding. Nevertheless, she finds a way to make the power structure's constraints accommodate some sense of victory. Clearly, having experienced an inviolate home life with a free husband means less when one's daughters end up sexually violated. What are the chances Linda would have enjoyed a home based on her own romantic love choice only to see her children exploited later? Using the unnamed woman's story to put that slim possibility into the community conversation, Jacobs justifies Linda's decision to relinquish her original definition of domestic success.[10] Even while enslaved, Linda is always pursuing accomplishment. Those considered white use their power against her, but she is always pursuing accomplishment, and she represents a much larger pattern. African Americans must often change their definitions of achievement, but nothing diminishes their preoccupation with it.

Given that the anonymous woman declined freedom because she had not known slavery's cruelty while the mistress was single, Jacobs's narrative suggests slavery is not simply a political reality; it is a domestic one. As Claudia Tate explains, "Jacobs depicted freedom not simply as escape from the political condition of slavery but as the gaining of access to the social institutions of motherhood, family, and home" (32). Clearly, the anonymous woman had considered herself free and successful even while enslaved because she operated as a mother and wife in a home of her own. Her seeming misapprehension of what defines freedom underscores the fact that, in any society, contingency reigns. There is no inherently good or safe domestic configuration; there is only what society will protect and respect or at least leave unmolested. The woman's contentment had resulted from having a home of her own to which she and her daughters returned each night, corroborating historian Dylan Penningroth's findings about the degree to which oppression can thrive even among material resources and recognition of individual merit (78). Like familial ties, the recognition of merit encouraged enslaved people to remain where they were, as the unnamed woman does and as Aunt Martha's son Phillip does. Penningroth argues: "Masters who permitted their slaves to earn and keep property were not necessarily 'kind' or 'indulgent' toward slaves . . . although ex-slaves sometimes described them that way" (57). In this case, Linda recalls the mistress "was very pious, and there was some reality in her religion. She taught her slaves to lead pure lives, and wished them to enjoy the fruit of their own industry" (46). Yet, one would do well to note the subtle qualification—*some* reality in her religion—because these practices benefited enslavers. After all, "earnings went to buy clothes and food that masters would otherwise have provided" (Penningroth 65). This must have been especially true in this case because the unnamed woman's husband was a free man. Like Jacobs's grandmother, he likely provided for his wife and children, leaving even more of the mistress' resources for her own benefit. Having "some reality in her religion" may not be high praise, then, and it certainly did not constitute an unequivocal boon for those on her plantation.

Furthermore, as with Aunt Martha, when it matters most, the freedom of the enslaved woman's husband does not allow him to purchase his children, keep his family together, and keep their household intact. A nation invested in slavery ensures that deep emotional ties among enslaved people never interfere with an enslaver's "right" to do whatever he wants with his property. Black people would simply never be allowed to control what would happen to their loved ones (H. Williams 51–53, 65, 82). Ultimately, the most effective forms of know-your-place aggression target domesticity, preserving for those in power the unjust authority to allow or destroy black homebuilding. Because their every victory is met with violence, enslaved people actively engage success, doing the painful work of adjusting their definitions.

The labor required for making-oneself-at-home while being denied at every turn can be seen in African American culture from slavery to the age of Michelle Obama. *Incidents* exposes this labor by foregrounding awareness that living according to the standards Americans claim to respect will not bring safety and respectability to one's doorstep—if one is allowed to have a doorstep at all. Jacobs's narrative makes clear that individuals are safe, protected, respected, or at least unmolested based on demographics or the protection of someone in a powerful demographic. One's character and behavior provide no guarantees. If they did, far fewer white Americans would be safe at home, and many more black people could love each other without fear and heartbreak.

Homebuilding in the Midst of Violence

Elizabeth Keckley's *Behind the Scenes* showcases practices of making-oneself-at-home in hostile environments and highlights its author's ability to continue these practices in the ultimate home, the White House, when she becomes seamstress and confidante to president Abraham Lincoln's family. As an autobiography published shortly after Emancipation, it contains reminiscences of slavery but also details postbellum life. As William Andrews has shown, authors of postbellum slave narratives often present themselves as agents of national unification, and this text offers opportunities for such interpretations, but the narrative is primarily animated by Keckley's pursuit of achievement. Not every personal and business endeavor goes smoothly, so the text also tracks shifting definitions of success.

The narrative begins with a spotlight on making oneself at home while facing white violence by showcasing Keckley's parents. Despite declarations that the enslaved have weak familial bonds, Keckley frames her narrative with her parents' enduring love. Claimed by different men in the same town, they are separated when her mother's enslaver moves. They see each other only twice a year, at Easter and Christmas. Then, the mother's enslaver decides to reward her hard work by convincing her father's enslaver to allow him to live on the plantation with his wife and daughter. They are confined to a slave cabin, but they make a home of it with their love. They may not have enjoyed domestic peace as long as the unnamed woman in *Incidents*, but they similarly grasped the achievement within reach. Unfortunately, "the golden days did not last long" (22). Keckley recalls, "while yet my father and mother were speaking hopefully, joyfully of the future, Mr. Burwell came to the cabin, with a letter in his hand" (23). In "two hours," Keckley's father must join his enslaver again, and they would immediately depart for the Western states. With this, "he, my father, was gone, gone forever" (ibid.).

During the forced separation, the couple continues practices of making-oneself-at-home. Keckley includes letters her father dictated, pouring out his heart to her mother. Through the years, the mundane violence that makes slavery function keeps them from being under one roof or even in the same state. Nevertheless, they maintain bonds of affection—creating a sense of home despite being robbed of the resources to have a household, even a slave cabin.

Keckley's parents preserve what they can of their love bond, and white aggression answers their modest victory. As Keckley puts it, "deep as was the distress of my mother in parting with my father, her sorrow did not screen her from insult" (24). The woman of the house tells Keckley's mother, "Stop your nonsense; there is no necessity for you putting on airs. Your husband is not the only slave that has been sold from his family, and you are not the only one that has had to part. There are plenty more men about here, and if you want a husband so badly, stop your crying and go and find another" (24–25). Thus, the know-your-place aggression that answers black romantic love is highlighted in Keckley's text no less than in Jacobs's; as these works reflect and contribute to the community conversation, they also record white aggression's consistency. Given the mistress's discursive violence, Keckley's declaration that her parents "kept up a regular correspondence for years" demonstrates they created domestic success against the odds. Furthermore, she affirms the value of these efforts both in the text and in life when she identifies her father's letters as "the most precious mementoes of my existence" (25).

As Keckley remembers her parents, their journey offers examples of how African Americans' definitions of accomplishment shift but their focus on achievement never does. They do not respond to white-authored violence so much as white aggression interrupts their progress toward success and a sense of home. They acknowledge the interruptions and keep pressing ahead. Keckley's parents' journey begins with finding each other, having their daughter, and being together as a family. When separated by a move, homemaking success becomes cherishing Easter and Christmas, the two times per year they are allowed to see each other. Next, they rejoice in the victory of having their bond acknowledged with an arrangement that enables cohabitation, despite their enslavers living in different towns. This modest triumph attracts opposition. Because the nation insists upon keeping African Americans in their "proper" place, their cabin is violated by the matter-of-fact discursive violence of a letter from the man who claims Keckley's father as property.

Keckley's narrative highlights the intimacies maintained against the odds as well as the know-your-place aggression that hounds them. Immediately after recounting the separation of her own family unit, Keckley recalls the first time she witnesses a slave sale. Upon realizing her small son is not returning, an enslaved woman becomes inconsolable. Keckley reports, "she was whipped for grieving her lost boy" because her oppressor "never liked to see one of his slaves wear a sorrowful face, and those who offended in this particular way were always punished" (29). Requiring that the facial expressions and demeanors of enslaved people convey contentment constitutes violence. This demand punishes African Americans for being human.[11] To violently suppress grief is to enforce the lie undergirding the institution, that black people do not cherish familial bonds. Keckley notes both the intimate connections and the violence they attract.

With the slave cabin turned into a space of vulnerability and sorrow, what Keckley enjoys about being assigned at age 4 to care for her owner's new baby is that the "duty transferred me from the rude cabin to the household of my master" (20). It does not take long for the disadvantages to become clear, however. She is beaten at age 4 after rocking the baby out of its bed, and by age 14, she has heard constantly that "I would never be worth my salt," despite all the work she does (21). In this hostile environment, Keckley resolves to help her overburdened mother as much as possible. In other words, Keckley's definition of success revolved around benefiting her mother, not winning white people's favor. She inhabits the hostile environment of an oppressor's house, but within it, she actively engages in practices of making-oneself-at-home by attending to her mother and their bond.

Nurturing the connection with her mother affirms Keckley's belief in her self-worth and right to belong, and her success at holding onto these resources is met with aggression when she is loaned out to her enslaver's oldest son, a minister. This loan separates the 14-year-old from her mother. By the time Keckley is 18, the Rev. Burwell becomes a pastor, and the local schoolmaster, Mr. Bingham, becomes a family friend. Empowered by Mrs. Burwell, Mr. Bingham strives to "subdue what he called my 'stubborn pride'" (36). He tears down her dress and whips her (34). She demands to know from her enslaver why Bingham has been allowed to abuse her, and he answers by attacking her with a chair (35). The next week, Bingham greets her with "a new rope and a new cowhide" (36). She struggles with him, and he beats her severely with a stick. She reports, "Again, I went home sore and bleeding, but with pride as strong and defiant as ever" (36–37). The next week, "Mr. Bingham again tried to conquer me, but in vain" (37). He strikes "many savage blows" and she stands "bleeding before him" but when he is "nearly exhausted with his efforts, he burst into tears, and declared that it would be a sin to beat me any more" (ibid.). When Bingham informs Rev. and Mrs. Burwell that he will no longer beat Keckley, the woman of the house commands her husband to do it himself. Keckley again fights back, and the man does not stop beating her until his wife begs him to, so Keckley is bedridden for five days (37–38). Keckley emphasizes that this is a man "who preached the love of Heaven, who glorified the precepts and examples of Christ, who expounded the Holy Scriptures Sabbath after Sabbath from the pulpit" (37). Clearly, as much as Christianity shapes Keckley's self-conception as she writes her life story, she does not use dominant definitions of Christian attainment, and her narrative demonstrates why that is the case as it lays bare her determination to remain faithful to her sense of self and her sense of achievement. While relentlessly pursuing success, she proves to be a better Christian than the men who brutally interrupt her journey.

The white violence designed to negate any modest victory an enslaved 18-year-old Keckley could muster takes more than one form. In addition to the aforementioned "savage efforts to subdue my pride," another white man "had base designs upon me. . . . Suffice it to say, that he persecuted me for four years, and I—I—became a mother" (39). She follows this brief mention of rape with a passage highlighting the fact that her mother cherishes letters from her daughter as much as Keckley cherishes her parents' love letters. Keckley reproduces a letter she sent to her mother that her mother kept. Keckley's letter declares her love for her mother and requests that she "give my love to all the family, both white and black" (41). Keckley also marks the regularity with which material expressions of affection are exchanged among those stripped of their freedom: "I was very much obliged to you for the presents you sent me last summer" and "tell Aunt Bella that I was much obliged to her for her present; I have been so particular with it that I have only worn it once" (ibid.). Keckley even notes that "there have been six weddings since October" and that she has been asked to be first attendant as well as a bridesmaid (ibid.). African Americans clearly made homes in hostile environments (purportedly) dominated by white power.

These details revealing the depth of her family and community connections constitute evidence of making-oneself-at-home in the midst of every effort to convince black people that they cannot pursue success and will never be at home. While assured that they do not belong except to the extent that they belong *to* the nation and *to* white citizens, Keckley and her entire community cultivate homemade citizenship. They acknowledge dehumanizing assaults but never heed them. Keckley's narrative resonates with *Incidents* by demonstrating how routinely the enslaved take care of their own material needs and by gesturing toward that which is not material. Keckley's focus on these letters seems similar to Jacobs's emphasis on Uncle Phillip's paying for his sister Nancy's burial. Whites always benefit financially, but the value of the affection expressed cannot be measured in dollars.

Still, what is most striking about this letter to her mother is Keckley's representation of it in the narrative. Keckley mentions the violations that yield her son, and then suddenly introduces correspondence as a mechanism for maintaining (chosen) emotional bonds. Indeed, the letter focuses on black love, not white violence, "although I could fill ten pages with my griefs and misfortunes" (42). So, in the midst of beatings, rapes, and so much more, Keckley nurtures connections to her mother and to community members who include her in their weddings. Further, as her narrative both reflects and contributes to the community conversation on success, it preserves evidence that she had always nurtured these intimate attachments and done so in the midst of white aggression. After all, she closes her letter primarily because "Miss Elizabeth says it is time I had finished" (ibid.).

Besides recounting her time in bondage, Keckley's narrative shares her journey from slave cabins to the White House; in the process, Keckley discusses marriage and highlights definitions of success. Mr. Keckley, whom she had known in Virginia, comes to St. Louis and proposes. She initially refuses the proposal because she does not want more children who will inherit her slave status. She had already asked to buy herself and her son and been refused. Only after her enslaver has relented and named a price does she consider marrying Keckley (49). They wed and remain together for eight years. Unlike Linda Brent in *Incidents*, Keckley chooses her mate, but their life together does not meet her standard. Mr. Keckley, she reports, "proved dissipated, and a burden instead of a helpmate" (50). Mutual aid is key to Keckley's definition of domestic success, and her marriage falls short. However, she places this information alongside the fact that she had so fully supported the Garland family that she could not save enough money to purchase herself and her son. She had "kept bread in the mouths of seventeen persons for two years and five months" (45), but the nation's laws and customs ensure she would not enjoy the fruit of her labor. Though her marriage does not offer what she expects, it is far from the reason she does not have a home of her own.

The post-slavery portion of *Behind the Scenes* most concerns itself with Keckley's movement from slave cabins to the White House, so it underscores not simply Keckley's access to the nation's house but her value within it. On the night the president is shot, she had not helped Mrs. Lincoln dress for the theater, but when tragedy strikes, she is the person whose presence is most desired (189). Furthermore, "I was [Mrs. Lincoln's] only companion, except her children, in the days of her great sorrow" (193). Keckley always prioritizes achievement, but she revises her definition, moving away from her heteronormative nuclear family with Mr. Keckley and toward a domestic configuration that better supports her ambitions: "Ever since arriving in Washington I had a great desire to work for the ladies of the White House, and to accomplish this end I was ready to make almost any sacrifice consistent with propriety" (76).

Keckley's presence in and value within the White House creates an alternative domestic success akin to that of Aunt Martha in *Incidents*; it enables a level of agency and authority for a black woman that is nearly unheard of in the United States of the nineteenth century. She reports, "When I entered the room [where the president lay in state], the members of the Cabinet and many distinguished officers of the army were grouped around the body of their fallen chief. They made room for me" (190). Could there be a better way to declare Keckley's success? From there, the text details the integral part Keckley plays in comforting Mrs. Lincoln through her grief. Most important to Keckley's emphasis on having made it out of slave cabins and into the White House, she gestures toward the many white women who could not claim what she could. She reports, "Mrs. Lincoln was extremely nervous, and she refused to have anybody about her but myself. Many ladies called, but she received none of them" (195–96).

Keckley makes herself at home in the White House, and the nature of her achievement in doing so becomes clearest with her handling of her own son's death. Keckley's narrative withholds the details of her family's situation while making a display of powerful white people's vulnerable moments. She reverses the direction of spectacle from how her story begins—with an account of her own family's separation and the sale of a young boy—and places the spotlight on a white family in distress. This reversal is not about white people so much as it highlights her achievement of having moved from slave cabins to the White House.

When the Lincolns lose their son Willie, Keckley offers details that highlight the family's pain and grief. Lincoln's vulnerability is showcased: "great sobs choked his utterance. He buried his head in his hands, and his tall frame was convulsed with emotion" (103). As she stands at the foot of the bed, Keckley's eyes are "full of tears, looking at the man in silent, awe-struck wonder" as "his grief unnerved him, and made him a weak, passive child" (ibid.). Mrs. Lincoln's pain is also highlighted as Keckley represents dialogue between the couple. Keckley says the president points to an insane asylum and warns his wife, "try and control your grief, or it will drive you mad, and we may have to send you there" (104–5). What is striking about the detail of the scene is that Keckley follows it with a single paragraph about the death of her own son. She reports, "previous to this I had lost my son," who had joined the Union army after having attended Wilberforce (105). Immediately after this paragraph, she lays the Lincolns' mourning even more to bear by reproducing a newspaper tribute to Willie that Mrs. Lincoln had saved in a scrapbook. By making such brief, passing mention of her son's death in a story about her own life, Keckley keeps her struggle private. As critic Janet Neary demonstrates, "Ripping the slave narrative apart at the seams and refashioning it," Keckley "refuses the conflation of her subjectivity with pain" (76, 62). She seems to, as Darlene Clark Hine might say, engage in dissembling, seeming to reveal so much while actually shielding from public view her innermost thoughts and feelings (912). When claiming the White House as home, Keckley claims some privacy for herself and her family—what she could not secure while in a slave cabin or the white-owned space she occupied when she was raped.

This reversal of spectacle also pertains to the alternative home she has created within the black community. Even as she tells her life story, she protects the safe havens she has created. This accomplishment manifests in terms of both the physical home with Mr. and Mrs. Walker Lewis, the black couple with whom she lives, and the space of privacy and dignity her text preserves even as it claims to reveal so much in order to defend her reputation. She only mentions living with this couple immediately before detailing the night of the assassination—a narration of her exceptional success. By acknowledging the couple, Keckley honors the fact that community definitions of success involve the heteronormative nuclear family even though Keckley no longer defines her own achievement that way. In other words, she gives space to others' definitions while claiming another option for herself. Perhaps more important, Keckley gestures toward deep connections to the black community without putting them on display. This proves significant because Keckley says her main motivation for writing is that harsh judgments of the former first lady extend to her, given that she has been "intimately associated with [Mary Lincoln] in the most eventful periods of her life" (xiv). She insists that "the veil of mystery must be drawn aside" (ibid.), but her concern for her reputation does not lead to a desperate display. As literary historian Elizabeth Young reminds us, black women often chose "rhetorical disembodiment" when entering national discourse because they were "overembodied in racist white culture" (111). Furthermore, as the opening scenes of family separation underscore, too much exposure is exactly what occupying slave cabins entails, and Keckley has left slave cabins behind.

When one reads *Behind the Scenes* for how it reflects and contributes to the community conversation on achievement, practices of making-oneself-at-home become particularly striking in relation to the Confederacy and slaveholders. Keckley speaks affectionately about her former enslavers; after all, she can "afford to be charitable" (xiii). Still, when she recounts her visit with them, she emphasizes not only how far removed she is from having occupied slave cabins but also that she feels so at home in a slaveholder's house that her success is undeniable. After traveling and encountering strangers who help her reach her destination, "I was carried to the house in triumph. In the parlour I was divested of my things and placed in an easy-chair before a bright fire. The servants looked on in amazement" (250). Further, she notes how eagerly her former owners prepare and serve her breakfast rather than allow their current cook to do it (252).

These scenes take on even more significance as Keckley emphasizes the setting: Rude's Hill, which "was once occupied by General Stonewall Jackson for his head-quarters" (ibid.). Indeed, "marks of war could be seen everywhere on the plantation" (253). Nevertheless, "the location was delightful" (252) and Keckley "was shown every attention" in the very place where the people "worshipped [Stonewall Jackson] as an idol" (253). Keckley presents herself as triumphantly occupying the space of the Confederacy. She makes herself at home where those who wanted her deemed subhuman once dominated. In fact, "the room in which I sat in the daytime was the room that General Jackson always slept in" (ibid.). Further, she portrays herself as quite comfortable while being served by the white women of the house. She embodies a decidedly post-slavery status; she is the personification of achievement.[12] And, of course, the fact that she shares these self-portraits by writing and publishing a narrative that becomes part of the community conversation on success also underscores her participation in embodied practices of belonging in the lived world. Her text encourages African Americans to continue pursuing accomplishment, showing little regard for the know-your-place messages they cannot escape.

Keckley's visit with her former owners on Stonewall Jackson's old stomping ground adds significance to another scene of triumph. Earlier in the text, Keckley shares that she visits Chicago immediately after the Civil War. A charity fair benefiting "the families of those soldiers who were killed or wounded during the war" had been held at a building containing "a wax figure of Jefferson Davis, wearing over his other garments the dress in which it was reported that he was captured" (74). Keckley reports that, "in examining the dress," she "made the pleasing discovery that it was one of the chintz wrappers that I made for Mrs. Davis, a short time before she departed from Washington for the South" (74–75). Furthermore, "when it was announced that I recognized the dress as one that I had made for the wife of the late Confederate President there was great cheering and excitement, and I at once became an object of the deepest curiosity" (75). According to Young, "Keckley uses the imagery of feminization to humiliate Davis. No longer wearing the gown of Confederate leadership . . . Davis is now wrapped in the feminized chintz of disgrace, dummied into wax and preserved in prose. In her account, she implicitly humiliates him not once but three times: by making the very dress that is his reputed downfall; by staging her confirmation of the dress for an appreciative audience; and by including the story in her memoir. Despite her professed admiration for Davis, the image of the cross-dressed ex-president functions implicitly to rip apart the legacy of the Confederacy" (133).

Given that Keckley's countless beatings and rapes are an important part of "the legacy of the Confederacy," one wonders why a critic would expect Keckley to honor it. Leaving that aside, though, readers attuned to black achievement despite the attacks of white supremacy will appreciate that this scene is less about humiliating Davis than about demonstrating that, even in a northern city in which the Confederate president is honored with a wax figure, Keckley commands recognition. She is successful in multiple ways throughout her life's journey, and she is preserving evidence of that fact. To have people at the museum (and readers) appreciate the truth she records is less about denigrating Davis than about celebrating her own accomplishments.

Even with her reclamations of Confederate space, Keckley's visit with two white women she had served before going to the White House highlights the degree to which definitions of black success involve choice. She calls Mrs. Meem her "foster child," emphasizing that she had chosen to operate in that role toward her. In contrast, her son had come into the world without her consent. "For four years a white man . . . had base designs upon me. . . . Suffice it to say, that he persecuted me for four years, and I—I—became a mother" (39). It is in this context that readers should interpret Keckley's report that "my mother took care of my son, and Miss

Nannie Garland [now Meem] . . . became my especial charge" (239). She had slept in Keckley's bed and "I could not have loved her more tenderly had she been the sister of my unfortunate boy" (ibid.). Thus, even if there is some victory in making-oneself-at-home in former Confederate headquarters and being served by former enslavers, there is no escaping the lack of choice Keckley has had in the configuration of her family. Slavery took away her father and forced a child into her womb because society "deemed it no crime to undermine the virtue of girls in my then situation" (39).[13] Like Linda in *Incidents*, Keckley redefines domestic success in order to keep marching toward achievement, even after her options have been limited by others. Ultimately, African Americans make home, and they do so while contending with white violence every step of the way.

*   *   *

Incidents in the Life of a Slave Girl and *Behind the Scenes* demonstrate that "black women write and express their existence through and beyond slavery" (McKittrick 39). As they reflect and contribute to the community conversation, they reveal how people of African descent affirm themselves and each other with embodied practices of belonging, even as whites respond with physical violence and devastating legislation, like the Fugitive Slave Act and the Dred Scott Decision. While African Americans undertake affirming practices, their white counterparts and the government answer with assertions that black people can claim space only to the extent that their presence, words, and deeds benefit others. *Incidents* and *Behind the Scenes* showcase the dynamic practices black communities employed to stay on a journey directed, not by domination, but by ambition.

One way to appreciate the priority placed on their own aspirations is to note the degree to which both *Incidents* and *Behind the Scenes* embrace goals that seem simply to align with mainstream ideologies but whose meaning deepens when one considers black women's awareness that to achieve according to dominant standards is to all but invite injury. For instance, Linda remains invested in individual behavior and personal character, despite noticing that these do not determine outcomes nearly as much as demographics do. Clearly, faithfulness to individual merit is not submission to white violence or conformity to dominant standards so much as it articulates reverence for Aunt Martha. Linda's loyalty never wavers, despite how harshly Aunt Martha judges her when she has children with a white man in town. As Tate offers, "the grandmother's excessively insensitive and punitive response is also an index of Jacobs's desire to make feminine sexual propriety unconditionally available to black women. That is, the more extreme the grandmother's censure, the more Jacobs sought to sanction absolute sexual autonomy and continence for black women, conditions that could only exist if black women were free political subjects" (30).

In this way, *Incidents* exemplifies what Carrie Hyde might call the "subjunctive orientation" of the community conversation that cultivates homemade citizenship. That is, "the possible (what might or could be)" collides with "the prescriptive (what should or ought to be)" (Hyde 16).[14] As Gabrielle Foreman argues, Jacobs presents her grandmother as a black woman whose home is a sealed-off space in which inhabitants adhere to "the purity and domesticity that are, according to *Incidents*, almost impossible to realize under slavery" (38). Jacobs also has Linda claim inviolate agency for herself in a heated exchange with Dr. Flint: "You have tried to kill me, and I wish you had; *but you have no right to do as you like with me*" (35, emphasis added). Here, Linda asserts what Foreman calls "discursive property rights" by claiming that which the United States denies her but which she envisions as reality in the world she wants to see—a world she makes from scratch with her text. Despite the odds against them, black women use cultural production to honor and assert, in Tate's words, "domestic allegories of political desire." Refusing to give up on possibilities, they extract victories even when they cannot escape defeat.

Behind the Scenes similarly asserts belonging via embodied practices. In the post-Emancipation portion of Keckley's narrative, she travels through the South, an activity understood to be dangerous for unaccompanied women and certainly for unaccompanied black women. However, in Keckley's account, she suffers no indignities, and several strangers help her. Given the shameful stories of travel told by Keckley's contemporaries, such as Frances E. W. Harper and Sojourner Truth,[15] one might view Keckley's travelogue as an example of discursive property rights akin to Linda Brent's declaration that Dr. Flint could not use her as he pleased. Keckley portrays herself as fully embodying the role of modern citizen, with all the mobility and dignified access to transportation that citizenship is understood to entail. She thereby refuses to be limited by the nation-state and her fellow Americans.

In all of these instances, the texts gesture toward the community conversation's investment in affirming black people's aspirations. It is not revenge or even resistance that most motivates them. Desire is an index of their humanity, and their humanity is a given, but holding onto desire is also a victory. Black humanity is never in question, even if African Americans die and even if they die in what others consider defeat.[16] And yet, there is also victory in preserving one's agency through a lifetime of grappling with white violence. White people knew this. That's why they insisted black people could not express basic human emotions, such as the desire to choose one's mate or sorrow at being separated from loved ones. In other words, white people forced the enslaved to perform the difference that the discursive violence of claiming they were another order of being was said to simply describe. It is time for scholars to recognize how thoroughly black people understood the forces arrayed against them as they nevertheless claimed victories. It is time to notice the many ways African Americans defined and redefined gradations of achievement.

No, Really

A Home of One's Own

If the modest achievements of the enslaved inspired the American Colonization Society, the Fugitive Slave Act, and the Dred Scott decision, the victory of Emancipation was bound to motivate backlash. The abolition of slavery inspired both legislative violence and bolder physical aggression. Besides instituting Black Codes—laws to limit African American employment opportunity, land ownership, and voting—the former Confederacy made its presence felt through what is best described as night riding, invading black communities at night. The Ku Klux Klan was responsible for much of the violence, but others adopted its methods. Night riders brutalized and/or killed African Americans who had achieved anything at all, and they created a culture of terror that articulated "an ingrained feeling that the blacks at large belong to the whites at large" (Union Colonel Samuel Thomas, qtd. in Feimster 42). In other words, the decades following Emancipation were marked by the commitment among the newly free to pursue their definitions of success and by white efforts to put them in their "proper" place of servitude and subordination. This pattern only intensified after the brief attempt at Reconstruction; the post-Reconstruction era was marked by repression, eventually being dubbed "the Nadir," the lowest point of race relations. The intended message was unmistakable: African Americans did not belong *in* the nation, but *to* it and its "real" citizens.

African Americans had defined and redefined success for themselves in the midst of slavery; they continued to do so in the context of freedom and found that white opposition was not diminishing. Goals were oriented toward what the formerly enslaved Julie Tillory described as the ability "to 'joy my freedom." She wanted "to protect her dignity, to preserve the integrity of her family, and to secure fair terms for her labor" (Hunter, *To 'Joy*, 2). African Americans operated with "the guiding assumption that wage labor should not emulate slavery" (ibid. 27). As important, because sexual exploitation had characterized the peculiar institution, "newly freed black women were unwilling to return to the antebellum sexual and racial status quo that allowed white men to rape and brutalize them with impunity" (Feimster 41). As African Americans pursued goals that seemed newly achievable, other Americans' most common words and deeds reiterated the belief that citizenship was simply never meant for nonwhite people. Because know-your-place aggression always arises to diminish or destroy the achievements of certain groups, it makes sense that the Ku Klux Klan first gained traction in Tennessee, the first state to extend suffrage to black men (Rosen 187). White vigilantes articulated to victims during attacks why they were being punished, and "violations" included voting; previous service in the Union Army; and "insubordination" to white people, which could include refusing to work for them. In other words, "the actions for which freedpeople were allegedly punished represented the exercise of choice that accompanied freedom and citizenship" (ibid. 189).

White supremacist violence was most often carried out in black people's homes. "Night riders' intrusion into African American homes asserted that . . . rather than autonomous realms of black patriarchal power, freedpeople's homes were to continue to be penetrable at any and all moments by the power of white men. Neither were private black domains to constitute independence and the rights of citizenship. When white men attacked freedpeople's private identities as husbands and wives, they were also attacking their worthiness for public rights as citizens" (ibid. 192).

Such brutality emerged because African Americans were succeeding at embodying all that the nation claims to respect. The precise form of attacks is therefore revealing. As historian Hannah Rosen demonstrates, "[Night riders'] actions forced freedpeople to manifest an apparent difference from whites through coerced performances of unchaste daughters and wives, incapable patriarchs, and a lack of moralizing and protective domestic domains" (ibid. 207). What could make these forced performances necessary except the fact that black people were proving to be chaste daughters and wives as well as capable patriarchs?

In the post-Reconstruction decades, Americans claimed that individuals prove ready for full citizenship by first becoming domestically successful, and African Americans did precisely that—while writing and reading black domestic romance novels that reflect and reinforce the community's preoccupation with success. Frances E. W. Harper's *Iola Leroy* (1892) and Pauline Hopkins's *Contending Forces* (1900) are representative of the genre,[1] and they make community conversation a key part of their formal structure. That is, while emphasizing that black communities have no shortage of stable, loving, nurturing homes, these works also thematize and enact the practices of racial self-affirmation that fueled community conversation via literary salons and other intellectual gatherings. Furthermore, while both representing and contributing to dynamic discussions, these texts insist upon straddling slavery and freedom in order to demonstrate that African Americans created homes worthy of the domestic romance genre even before they had recognized households.[2] A general awe at the dignity of those held in dehumanizing circumstances permeates these works, and although written decades after slavery was abolished, they bear witness to the power slavery continues to exert over the nation's imagination. These authors refuse to downplay how regularly white people remind African Americans that they believe bondage to be blacks' most appropriate condition. Black domestic novels feature loving black homes, spotlighting the painful circumstances under which African Americans nevertheless nurture romantic and familial bonds.

Living and writing at the Nadir, in the midst of lynching, these authors saw that black nuclear families were often attacked, not because their members were criminals but because they were successful. As historian Crystal Feimster has shown, a "rape-lynch scenario" shaped mainstream American responses to black nuclear families. Black men could be lynched for embodying a manhood that would be respected in white men,[3] and black women were said to lack the virtue of true womanhood. Because black women were not to be viewed as women, they purportedly could not be raped; supposedly, they were sexually insatiable (Freedman 80–83). With racist rhetoric as their shield, white men would sexually assault black women to terrorize them as well as the men in their lives who knew they would be killed for trying to protect black women and girls. In other words, black success of all kinds attracted hostility, but the achievement represented by a heteronormative nuclear family proved especially enraging. Whether physical or discursive, post-Reconstruction white violence constituted what Rosen calls "terror in the heart of freedom." African Americans living and writing at the turn into the twentieth century left evidence that their communities understood that dominant discourses and practices have always worked to ensure that black accomplishment will not translate into respectability or safety.

Dignified Black Futures

Because African Americans continued pursuing greater and greater success, the repressive violence of night riding and Black Codes intensified, ultimately producing a Jim Crow social order, and Frances E. W. Harper's 1892 novel, *Iola Leroy*, provides an access point to the community conversation that kept African Americans striving. The text depicts victories during slavery, which led to triumphs during the Civil War, creating opportunity to face the cruel obstacles of freedom[4] and overcome yet again. While straddling slavery and freedom, the plot of *Iola Leroy* aims to teach African American readers[5] the best way to create a future that both honors forebears and empowers successors. In surveying the slave past, Watkins Harper[6] finds endless evidence of black love and, while celebrating it, she also notes that black love often strengthened slavery's hold. Mapping a future in freedom therefore requires grappling with a question so key that answering it becomes the animating impulse of the novel: *How do we ensure that our love is a source of strength that benefits the race, not an easily exploited resource for those in power?* Answering this question is crucial because the text insists that homemaking is the key to racial uplift. As both an access point to the post-Reconstruction community conversation and as a text that makes that conversation part of its narrative structure, *Iola Leroy* asserts that racial uplift is best understood as practices of making-oneself-at-home on an explicitly collective scale.

The action begins with a spotlight on enslaved people who make themselves at home by inventing a language to share news about the Civil War. Speaking in code constitutes an embodied practice of belonging. They know they are part of the community because they understand the language, and they confirm their desire to be in community by using it. As the enslaved character Robert Johnson makes his way home from the market, the narrator emphasizes the energy that speaking this way gives to everyone encountered:

"Good mornin', Bob; how's butter dis mornin'?"

"Fresh; just as fresh, as fresh can be."

"Oh, glory!" said the questioner, whom we shall call Thomas Anderson. . . .

His informant regarding the condition of the market was Robert Johnson, who had been separated from his mother in his childhood and reared by his mistress as a favorite slave. She had fondled him as a pet animal, and even taught him to read. Notwithstanding their relation as mistress and slave, they had strong personal likings for each other.

As [Robert Johnson and Tom Anderson] passed along, they were met by another servant, who said in hurried tones, but with a glad accent in his voice:

"Did you see de fish in de market dis mornin'? Oh, but dey war splendid, jis' as fresh, as fresh kin be"

"That's the ticket," said Robert. . . .

"'Good mornin', boys," said another servant on his way to market. "How's eggs dis mornin'?"

"Fust rate, fust rate," said Tom Anderson.

"I thought so; mighty long faces at de pos'-office dis mornin' . . ."

[The narrator concludes:] "Surely there was nothing in the primeness of the butter or the freshness of the eggs to change careless looking faces into such expressions of gratification. . . . What did it mean?

"During the dark days of the Rebellion, when the bondman was turning his eyes to the American flag, and learning to hail it as [a sign] of deliverance, some of the shrewder slaves . . . invented a phraseology to convey in the most unsuspected manner news to each other from the battle-field." (Harper 67–8)

Harper uses this embodied practice of belonging to emphasize the solidarity forged among strata of the community. Favored and educated, Robert cherishes his connection to those far less literate. *Iola Leroy* reminds readers that even among the enslaved, there are different ways to pursue and gauge achievement. Many assume being treated well by one's enslaver represents success, but Robert defines his own aspirations. After having escaped slavery and served in the Civil War, Robert visits Aunt Linda, who had known him as a child. She remembers how well his mistress treated him and wonders if he has any regrets about having run away. She prods, "Now, own up, Robby, didn't you feel kine ob mean to go off widout eben biddin' her good bye?" She continues, "Didn't yer feel a little down in de mouf when yer lef' her?" Robert does not hesitate: "Not much" (180). Many expected good treatment to produce contentment, as it did for the anonymous woman in *Incidents in the Life of a Slave Girl*. Indeed, while in bondage, Robert explains why he knows his mistress does not suspect his plans: "She is just as sweet as a peach to her Robby" (85). Sure enough, when he visits Miss Nancy years later, she confesses to never having thought he would leave her. She asks, "Wasn't I always good to you?" and Robert answers, "You were good, but freedom was better" (164). Harper consistently acknowledges that, even in slavery, African Americans have their own conceptions of success and make decisions accordingly.

Because *Iola Leroy* often defines achievement in domestic terms, the novel's opening scenes highlight not only coded language but also the homemaking that takes place in slave cabins. The narrator emphasizes, "while numbers deserted to join [Union] forces, others remained at home, slept in their cabins by night and attended to their work by day; but under this apparently careless exterior there was an undercurrent of thought which escaped the cognizance of their masters" (68). Harper thereby suggests that African Americans who do not run toward Union lines to attain freedom may seem to accept bondage, but they actually engage in practices of making-oneself-at-home. They affirm their right to self-definition and support each other in doing so, even while enslaved. Harper's text demonstrates that some deemed escape to be success and others considered it an achievement to stay near their enslaved loved ones while carving out spaces of community on the plantation. In other words, they make homes in cabins that seem to reconcile them to servitude, but their activities reinforce their sense of belonging in families and communities even as the United States assures them that they do not, and can never, belong. They call on an authority beyond the nation in order to act on the belief that they belong *in* the country, not *to* it. They cultivate homemade citizenship while grappling with the violent ways in which they are encouraged to understand themselves only as chattels. The narrator would have readers notice the victory inherent in appearing to be content while preserving a sense of self that can withstand everyday toil as chattel without internalizing that status.

The text suggests that those who leave slave cabins to help the Union and those who stay are more alike than different when Robert Johnson and others await their chance to escape, and Uncle Daniel explains why he will not accompany them. His story seems to be about loyalty to his enslaver, but his every decision is driven by familial ties, just as *Incidents* and *Behind the Scenes* emphasize how some adjust to slavery because they focus on family. In short, Uncle Daniel remains focused on his own homebuilding success. His story begins with his fondness for "Marse Robert," but that fondness is based on the fact that he had facilitated Uncle Daniel's marriage to Aunt Katie, the woman of his choice. Marse Robert convinces Katie's enslaver to allow them to marry. He does not agree to cohabitation, creating another opportunity for Marse Robert to help, when Aunt Katie's mistress treats her cruelly—by disregarding her bond with her dead child. Uncle Daniel recalls, Marse Robert had gone to Gundover "tearin' mad" and "foun' out he war hard up for money," so he "bought Katie and brought her home to libe wid me" (81). Uncle Daniel says he will not leave because "I promised Marse Robert I would stay, an' I mus' be as good as my word," but the reader's view into the cabin reveals he is motivated by attachment to his wife. In fact, because Marse Robert was good to the couple, Uncle Daniel was always by Aunt Katie's side, even on her deathbed. She grabbed his hand, made him promise to meet her in heaven, and she "went ter hebben in a blaze ob glory" (168).

Similarly testifying to the strength of black family bonds, Ben Tunnel explains he will not leave the plantation because he refuses to abandon his mother. He declares, "while I love freedom more than a child loves its mother's milk, I've made up my mind to stay on the plantation. . . . I can't take her along with me an' I don't want to be free and leave her behind in slavery" (83). White Southerners had been equally aware of the power of familial ties. The slave-owning Eugene Leroy claims, "I would willingly free every slave on my plantation if it didn't mean expatriating them. Some of them have wives and children on other plantations, and to free them is to separate them from their kith and kin" (115). By representing this self-serving stance in a text that contributes to the community conversation, Harper underscores African Americans' awareness that slaveholders did not see enslaved people as so different from themselves that they assumed familial bonds meant nothing to them. Not only did they know kith and kin mattered; they used that knowledge to enrich themselves, whether in this seemingly benevolent way or by keeping servants submissive via threats about their families.

Strikingly, definitions of black success often revolve around loyalty to mothers. Characters work to maintain affection for their mothers and testify to the white-authored violence that seeks to destroy intimate attachments. As Frederick Douglass had explained in his 1845 narrative, enslaved children are kept from their mothers as a matter of course: "It is a common custom . . . to part children from their mothers at a very early age. Frequently, before the child has reached its twelfth month, its mother is taken from it, and hired out on some farm a considerable distance off, and the child is placed under the care of an old woman, too old for field labor. For what this separation is done, I do not know, unless it be to hinder the development of the child's affection toward its mother, and to blunt and destroy the natural affection of the mother for the child. This is the inevitable result" (13). Within a system that profits from destroying it, sustained affection constitutes a victory. Loyalty to his mother keeps Ben Tunnel from escaping to Union lines with Robert Johnson. Likewise, throughout the narrative, Robert is fueled by his mother's memory. She had been sold away from him when he was about 10 years old. During slavery, he does not hesitate to leave the mistress who treats him well because "I ain't forgot how she sold my mother from me. Many a night I have cried myself to sleep, thinking about her, and when I get free I mean to hunt her up" (85).[7] Toward the end of the Civil War, Robert is wounded, and he lands in the hospital and in Iola's care. During his periods of delirium, "he sometimes imagined that she was his mother, and he would tell her how he missed her" (157).

Harper places in the archive of the community conversation evidence of African Americans' sense of belonging, the strength of their familial bonds, and the violence that answers both. After all, Robert's mother had been sold away from him because she had dared to protect herself from bodily harm. Aunt Linda explains to an adult Robert that the mistress made the sale out of fear. Robert's mother had "snatched de whip out ob her han' and gib her a lickin'" (169). Aunt Linda continues, "we women had ter keep 'em from whippin' us, er dey'd all de time been libin' on our bones" (ibid.).[8] In short, maintaining a belief in one's right to avoid violation would always be answered with violence.

Meanwhile, the text draws a parallel between defending oneself from a beating and preserving a bond with one's child; both represent success that white supremacy seeks to destroy. When Robert reiterates his mission to find his mother, Aunt Linda offers a portrait of the homemaking that had been accomplished in slave cabins. As many slave narratives had testified, women worked such long hours that children were often asleep when they could be present. Aunt Linda recalls, "many a time hes she set in my ole cabin an' cried 'bout yer wen you war fas' asleep" because "she lub'd you as she lub'd her own life" (180). Harper presents Robert's mother, whom neither he nor the reader has encountered, as a woman who engaged in practices of making-oneself-at-home, who cultivated a sense of self and a sense of belonging that was answered with relentless violence.

Iola Leroy also demonstrates that making-oneself-at-home can involve crafting a sense of belonging outside individual homes. When Robert serves in the Civil War, he makes himself at home by claiming a place in the military force whose victory will lead to acknowledging that black people belong in the nation, not to it. He also records others' practices of making-oneself-at-home. For instance, he tells a commanding officer about Tom Anderson, a man who—while enslaved—used ingenuity to learn how to read. Specifically, he "got a book of his own, tore it up, greased the pages, and hid them in his hat. Then if his master had ever knocked his hat off he would have thought them greasy papers, and not that Tom was carrying his library on his head" (92). Robert also shares the experience of a 19-year-old who was found with a book when his day's work was complete; his owner reacted by threatening 500 lashes and increasing his daily work quota (ibid.). The young man had a desire to pursue success, which involved traditional literacy; while pursuing that, he was attacked. The 19-year-old then identified the American tendency toward know-your-place aggression, concluding that "there must be something good in that book if the white man didn't want him to learn" (ibid.). Thus, the teenager finds even more innovative ways to develop as a reader and writer, but his doing so is not in protest to his master's violence so much as his master's violence responds to his focus on accomplishment. After sharing these stories with his captain, Robert admits that Tom Anderson had not gotten far with his reading ability[9] but that Robert had shared what he read in newspapers with him and others so that a lack of traditional literacy did not shut people out of the community conversation. Robert notes, "And our owners thought we cared nothing about what was going on" (ibid.).

Robert's testimony regarding other community members highlights that which is there all along but is overlooked, and the scene gestures beyond the text to suggest that scholars have repeated the tendency to assume that enslaved people "cared nothing about" defining and pursuing success. The captain with whom Robert shares these stories declares, "I hope that the time will come when some faithful historian will chronicle all the deeds of daring and service these people have performed during this struggle, and give them due credit therefor" (149). This commentary about historians is striking because the passage highlights women's roles. Another Union officer shares that "a colored woman managed admiringly to keep us posted as to the intended movements of the enemy. She was engaged in laundry work, and by means of hanging sheets in different ways gave us the right signals" (ibid.). Enslaved people's practices of making-oneself-at-home register on several levels as Harper's text contributes to the community conversation. The woman who helped the Union while doing laundry asserted her right to belong in the nation, not to it; the relatively privileged among the enslaved later shares others' stories out of a spirit of community and belonging; and the author presents all these examples in a text designed to affirm African Americans in the 1890s present and to preserve a legacy for posterity. Evidence that enslaved men, women, and children always focused on achievement is everywhere.

When readers understand African Americans' preoccupation with success and the nation's determination to rob them of it, the importance of *Iola Leroy*'s representation of loyalty to mothers and to military service becomes clear: both are about pursuing achievement. The title character, Iola, and her brother Harry grow up unaware that they have a drop of "African blood" and that their father owns their mother, Marie. They discover the truth only once their father dies, and his cousin has the courts invalidate the marriage, making the widow and her children into property. The news reaches Harry at school before he has come home, where he would have been declared chattel. He decides to join the Union Army because his definition of success involves maintaining a bond with his mother. As Harry pursues his goals, he faces the result of white supremacist violence, that his mother's marriage has been nullified and that she and Iola are now enslaved. He therefore cannot continue to treat home as the emblem of accomplishment; he must pursue accomplishment via military service. He cannot use the home as a source of fulfillment because know-your-place aggression targets his family as soon as it is not considered white. Harper's text highlights what scholars have been slow to recognize in the archive and repertoire of African American literature: Americans with "African blood" constantly pursue their ideals, and their cultural expression documents that focus. However, when those who are not considered straight, white, and male undertake their pursuit, they are attacked; they then continue their quest while acknowledging the various assaults. Harry's definition of success centers on military service with the hope of later creating a home. The aim is achievement, whether he must invest in the military or in domesticity. While making progress, attacks arise; he identifies them while forging ahead.

Iola's journey follows a similar pattern; her orientation toward success inspires service in the war before domesticity can become a priority. Despite the expectations of the domestic romance genre, Iola cultivates a sense of belonging via vocation before trying to create a home life. She is a nurse for Union soldiers during the war. Once the war ends, she pledges to find her mother. She also pledges to join the "new army that had come to supplant ignorance with knowledge" by becoming a teacher (160, 159). While searching for her mother, Iola teaches the newly freed, and the narrator declares, "Iola had found her work, and the freedman their friend" (160). With this, Harper demonstrates that, once no longer considered white, Iola pursues success in her work and helps freedman to do the same. Together, they cultivate a sense of belonging, despite routine rejection from the nation and from white Americans. Reuniting with her family to make a home does not become less important, but because white violence has dismantled her household, she cannot always place home life at the center of her conception of success. She moves from slave cabins to Union hospitals, then to schools, and only eventually to a home of her own.

While depicting African Americans' aspirations, *Iola Leroy* foregrounds slavery no less than freedom, and this representational strategy results from Harper's investment in recording the community conversation's preoccupation with black love. The presumed rupture of Emancipation's momentousness can hardly be felt because black love—familial and romantic—creates continuity. When the text represents the years immediately following the Civil War, readers see African Americans fiercely devoted to reuniting their families. Iola is determined to find her mother, but she is not unique; similar quests are undertaken by her confidante Robert Johnson and others. As African Americans laid claim to freedom, they sought the right to keep their loved ones close without being attacked. For example, when Robert encounters John Salters[10] in freedom, Salters is sharing his life with Aunt Linda, and Robert asks if they married after the war. Salters explains he and Aunt Linda had been married long before the war but had been separated by sales. Once free, Salters managed to locate his now-adult daughter and then returned to the plantation and found Aunt Linda. "She hedn't married again, nuther hed I;

so we jis' let de parson marry us out er de book; an' we war mighty glad ter get teggeder agin, an' feel hitched together fer life" (174–75). Harper uses even this minor character to underscore how much the bonds of love remained.

Because *Iola Leroy* highlights the continuity (created by black love) between slavery and freedom, its commitment to recording practices of making-oneself-at-home honors African Americans' preoccupation with achievement even when they would be justified to place emphasis elsewhere. For instance, they routinely put aside the pain of dealing with those who played God with their lives. Fulfilling their notions of success proves to be far more important than responding to white aggression or protesting its injustices. As such, Robert explains that he will "gather all the information possible from those who sold and bought my mother. I intend to leave no stone unturned in searching for her" (163). This brief statement reveals what most determines decisions. Harper shows that African Americans had to look beyond their significant pain and justified anger in order to have any chance of finding their scattered loved ones. There was no time for revenge—or even an unkind word. The novel acknowledges that buying and selling people constitutes violence; it is the mundane brutality that made slavery profitable. These white-authored attacks answered the achievement of the enslaved who held on to their humanity and to their affection for each other. Harper suggests that just as those in slave cabins focused on affirming each other more than on reacting to white people, African Americans making their way in freedom maintain community-centered priorities.

Given that African Americans will bring love into the future, even if slavery has robbed them of everything else, Harper's novel suggests that the strength of the race's future will correspond to its homemaking success. However, because black love had strengthened slavery's chains, the challenge in freedom is to find ways to make homebuilding not simply a response to familial and romantic connections but also a locus of strategies for building dignified black futures. That is, the community conversation encourages continued refinement of the definitions of black success, and *Iola Leroy*'s contribution to the discussion argues that African American domesticity needs both to reflect and reproduce blueprints for ensuring that familial and romantic ties will not simply constitute weaknesses through which the race can be exploited.

Harper therefore uses her heroine's marriage prospects to instruct readers on how to create a future of possibility for the collective, which is clearly a concern of the community conversation that fuels African American achievement in hostile environments. Iola receives proposals from Dr. Gresham, a white man with an abolitionist upbringing, and Dr. Latimer, who, like Iola, could pass as white but refuses to do so. Iola rejects Dr. Gresham because marrying him would mean being absorbed into his family, giving up the search for her mother, and thereby ignoring her connection to African Americans, but Harper does not make this an easy choice. Though Iola initially rejects his overtures by saying that "neither gratitude nor friendship is love," the narrator reveals: "Iola was not indifferent to Dr. Gresham. She admired his manliness and respected his character" (137). In fact, "She had learned to enjoy his presence and to miss him when absent, and when she began to question her heart, she found that unconsciously it was entwining around him" (ibid.). As they worked together during the war, Iola recognized that Dr. Gresham "had power to call forth the warmest affection of her soul; but she fought with her own heart and repressed its rising love" (138). As Gabrielle Foreman reminds us, Harper was "never interested in 'stories about white men marrying beautiful quadroon girls, who, in doing so, are lost to us socially'" (80). Nevertheless, Iola must work to keep her feelings in check, especially because they developed while she and Dr. Gresham read magazines and books together (101). By noting that "reading matter" could encourage love, Harper underscores her belief in the power of the text she has produced to steer the community conversation in ways that will empower African Americans.

By highlighting Iola's genuine affection and the difficulty of her decision, Harper's novel makes a strong statement about what kind of coupling will produce homes that benefit black communities,[11] especially given that households based on romantic love are considered the most valuable (as discussed in Chapter 1) and therefore meant for whites only. When describing Iola's feelings for Dr. Latimer, the race man whose proposal Iola will accept, our narrator explains, "In their desire to help the race, their hearts beat in loving unison" (241). Furthermore, "they esteemed it a blessed privilege to stand on the threshold of a new era and labor for those who had passed from the old oligarchy of slavery into the new commonwealth of freedom" (244). Serving those who have passed from slavery into freedom means helping those who know well that love connects the past and present. Because this community knowledge shapes the text, when Iola chooses the relationship that benefits the entire race, her union demonstrates that love, which creates continuity between slavery and freedom, can indeed be made to facilitate possibility for African Americans, not just limitations. It is because their union gestures toward a home that will uplift their people and demonstrate the power to transform black love into an asset for African Americans that Iola and Dr. Latimer serve as the hero and heroine of a "good strong book" that will be "of lasting service to the race" (238).

Though white violence most intensely targets black homes built on the foundation of marriage, black domestic success will attract white violence, whether the ties are romantic or not; Harper's domestic romance therefore spotlights households based on heredity. Because love creates continuity between slavery and freedom, many characters search for long-lost siblings and parents. As searches conclude, the narrator proffers a chapter titled "Delightful Reunions," which revolves around Iola's and Harry's mother, Marie. It begins, "Very bright and happy was the home where Marie and her children were gathered under one roof. . . . Into that peaceful home came no fearful forebodings of cruel separations" (194). However, even if free from fear of the kinds of separations that characterized the slave past, this home is never truly peaceful for the black woman whose love inspired its creation. It is in "Delightful Reunions" that Marie admits to worrying that her son Harry will be killed: "He is so fearless and outspoken that I am constantly anxious about him, especially at election time" (196). When Harry enters the room, she shares her concern directly: "I am afraid that you will get into trouble and be murdered, as many others have been" (197). Harry offers no assurances; he says that if he dies serving the poor and needy, he will have died at his post. "Could a man choose a better place to die?" he asks rhetorically (ibid.).

Understanding that Harry will not leave the South, Marie agrees to go North with Robert, and once there, she is so worried about Harry that it makes her sick. Because she refuses to seek medical care, Robert asks Dr. Latimer to visit the house, and he concludes, "her failing health proceeded more from mental than physical causes" (222). Harry should arrive in one week, so Dr. Latimer says, "his presence will do you more good than all the medicine in my chest" (223).

If the narrative is shaped by the question of how to make black love an asset and not a source of vulnerability, how does Marie's fear fit into the novel's answer?

Marie's anxiety underscores the fact that African Americans have always made themselves at home in the midst of violence; homemade citizenship has become a mode for living as well as a trope in cultural production because white violence answers any measure of black success and any assertion of black belonging. Indeed, the novel's next chapter sheds important light. Titled "Friends in Council," it features a conference convened to discuss the problems that the race faces and exemplifies the novel's overall design, which foregrounds debate and community conversation. One speaker, the Hon. Dugdale insists, "the men who are acquiring property and building up homes in the South show us what energy and determination may do even in that part of the country. I believe such men can do more to conquer prejudice than if they spent all their lives in shouting for their rights and ignoring their duties" (228). Several speakers tout the need for solid homes that will be the race's salvation. Iola herself says, "If we would have the prisons empty, we must make the homes more attractive" (233). Thus, the novel highlights the belief among African Americans that they have the power to change their conditions—that if they simply make good decisions, they will be safe. While promoting black self-determination, however, the text also acknowledges all that negates community efforts, suggesting that the race's current situation did not result from poor decisions. Another conference speaker notes, "there is an undue proportion of colored people in prisons" and someone answers, "this is owing to a partial administration of law in meting out punishment to colored offenders. I know red-handed murderers who walk in this Republic unwhipped of justice, and I have seen a colored woman sentenced to prison for weeks for stealing twenty-five cents. I knew a colored girl who was executed for murder when only a child in years. And it was through the intervention of a friend of mine, . . . that a boy of fifteen was saved from the gallows" (ibid.).[12] By representing diversity within the community conversation, the text insists that educating African Americans to discipline themselves might be productive, but it also highlights the racist violence of unjust legal outcomes. Those gathered for the debate literally embody black achievement themselves, but that fact has not interrupted the unfair treatment of the race. If black children must be saved from the gallows, know-your-place aggression does not seek simply to dwarf black accomplishments in the present; it seeks to stifle the race's future.[13]

While the novel insists that "we must instill into our young people that the true strength of a race means purity in women and uprightness in men" (ibid.), it also contends with how routinely African Americans embody purity and uprightness and are attacked nonetheless. Another attendee later explains, "I also fear that in some sections, as colored men increase in wealth and intelligence, there will be an increase in race rivalry and jealously. It is said that savages, by putting their ears to the ground, hear a far-off tread. So, today, I fear that there are savage elements in our civilization which hear the advancing tread of the Negro and would retard his coming" (236).

The novel records the community's laser focus on success even as it acknowledges the vulnerability of black individuals, families, and communities. After proposing to Iola and feeling confident that they will make a productive home life together, Dr. Latimer tries to convince her to be less preoccupied with the injustices she sees. He says, "I think you brood too much over the condition of our people." She answers, "Perhaps I do, but they never burn a man in the South that they do not kindle a fire around my soul" (243). Still trying to calm her, he relays information shared in educated circles. Iola's fiancé assures her: "I have heard several of our ministers say that it is chiefly men of disreputable characters who are made the subjects of violence and lynch-law" (ibid.).

Again, the novel gives voice to different perspectives, but statements like this must be understood in the context of Marie's concern for her son Harry's life. She worries herself sick about Harry, not because he has a "disreputable character," but because he is an outspoken asset to his community. The black home that has been reassembled after the ravages of slavery may not be torn asunder by slave auctions, but lynching has emerged to achieve similar results. Given these realities, Iola has little reason to believe that her home with Dr. Latimer will be safe. Like Harry, and like Iola herself, her husband has chosen to cast his lot with people who are often attacked because their prosperity and productivity inspire white people's "race rivalry and jealously." Indeed, the vulnerability that hovers over this couple recalls that experienced by Minnie and Louis in Harper's 1869 novel *Minnie's Sacrifice*, in which Minnie is lynched. These community-oriented couples make homes while never ignoring their countrymen's tendency toward using violence to keep African Americans from claiming success and asserting that they belong.

As African Americans acknowledge the odds against them, while achieving nonetheless, their practices of making-oneself-at-home include cooperative economics. After Iola marries Dr. Latimer and they settle into a life of uplifting the race, her uncle Robert sells his northern business and moves with his mother and sister (Harriet and Marie) back down South. He buys "a large plantation . . . which he divided into small homesteads, and sold to poor but thrifty laborers" (250). The focus on achievement is both individual and collective. The narrator reports that Robert's "heart has been gladdened by [the poor but thrifty laborers'] increased prosperity and progress. He has seen the one-roomed cabins change to comfortable cottages" (251).

Watkins Harper records the community's investment in domesticity. She depicts African Americans who have built successful homes because doing so allows her text to show who and what the people in black communities have been and will continue to be: men and women of ingenuity and determination, love and commitment. Still, as Harper offers that picture, the reminder remains: achieving their goals may bring violence as often as it brings praise.

Contending Forces, Community Conversation

Like *Iola Leroy*, Pauline Hopkins's first novel, *Contending Forces*, enters the community conversation on success by addressing both the slave past and the race's future and by building dynamic discussion into its narrative structure. Set during post-Reconstruction, it engages the antebellum era to contextualize current action. Its resonance with *Iola Leroy* continues as it underscores the necessity of honoring the past in order to build a future, and it gestures toward what African Americans should prioritize as they work for the race's greater good. Indeed, while promoting racial uplift, the novel defines it as the pursuit of collective success, secured through community-wide practices of making-oneself-at-home. The subtitle identifies it as "A Romance Illustrative of Negro Life North and South," so the text often uses marriage and home life to gauge achievement. It encourages the creation of black homes that are distinct from slave cabins—an accomplishment that primarily depends on black women being empowered to choose their mates, as articulated in *Incidents* and *Behind the Scenes*. Just as a question drives *Iola Leroy*, *Contending Forces* revolves around a query that the text uses the long, painful journey of its protagonist, Sappho Clark, to answer. Sappho has been living a secret life. Raped in the South at age 14, she bore a son; she has taken the name Sappho to make a new start in the North. She cares financially for the boy but does not claim him. He lives with her aunt, Madame Frances, and though he often sees Sappho, he does not know she is his mother. In this new life in Boston, Sappho continues to feel shame about her secret, but finally relinquishes it long enough to accept a marriage proposal from the man she loves, Will Smith. However, because she had done so without his knowing about her past, she assumes he would abandon her once he knows. Under duress,[14] she reveals her secret in a farewell letter to her fiancé, leaves her life in Boston, and returns South. When Dora, her closest friend and her fiancé's sister, discovers that Sappho has left (and why), she asks the text's framing question: "Terrible curse of slavery! shall we never lose the sting of degradation?" (Hopkins 330).

Contending Forces provides an access point to the community conversation on success, so by structuring the novel around that key question, Hopkins insists that shedding degradation is possible but only when black women are empowered to make decisions about love and domesticity, completely free of shame. A future of possibility depends on the life chances of the race's women. Hopkins's text thereby offers an artistic rendition of Anna Julia Cooper's declaration, "when and where I enter without special pleading . . . then and there, the race enters with me" (*Voice* 31). Black achievement cannot be gauged without attending to black women's quality of life.

Contending Forces argues that black success will depend on black women's agency in choosing their mates, and it makes this point by emphasizing the power and importance of community conversation. Indeed, the novel all but declares that developing a racial future requires community conversation, partly because black women do not claim their birthright if exposed only to dominant discourse. *Contending Forces* highlights discussion and debate—through the sewing circle that Sappho attends with Dora, for example. Hopkins demonstrates that critical exchanges about success are not merely the province of men in purportedly public spaces. In the sewing circle gathering about which readers learn the most, Mrs. Willis speaks about "the place which the virtuous woman occupies in upbuilding a race" (149). The text does not represent Mrs. Willis's speech, but it registers Sappho's astonishment with a point made: "Did I understand you to say that the Negro woman in her native state is truly a virtuous woman?" (148). Mrs. Willis assures her of the accuracy of her understanding.

Claims about black women lacking virtue should be seen as discursive violence that emerges because they have successfully embodied exactly what the nation claims to respect in womanhood. As activist Fannie Barrier Williams put it in 1893, "It is sufficient for us to know that the daughters of women who thirty years ago were not allowed to be modest, not allowed to follow the instincts of moral rectitude, who could cry for protection to no living man, have so elevated the moral tone of their social life that new and purer standards of personal worth have been created, and new ideals of womanhood, instinct with grace and delicacy, are everywhere recognized and emulated" (704). Ensuring that a reputation of promiscuity clings to African American women regardless of actual behavior constitutes know-your-place aggression, and it persists long after slavery has ended.

As Mrs. Willis contributes to the community conversation on success within the text, gesturing toward such conversations outside the text, it is significant that she quickly shifts her audience's focus in a remarkably affirming way. Mrs. Willis insists, "Our ideas of virtue are too narrow. We confine them to that conduct which is ruled by our animal passions alone. It goes deeper than that—general excellence in every duty of life is what we may call virtue" (149). While not detracting from her point about how different black women's reputations would be if they had not been subjected to slavery, Mrs. Willis insists that their self-worth need not depend upon a pristine sexual past. If one can exhibit virtue in realms other than the sexual, then there are many ways in which women can be virtuous. With this, Mrs. Willis offers Sappho a perspective that could free her from shame, but, understandably, Sappho remains preoccupied with definitions of virtue related to sex. She asks if Mrs. Willis believes God will hold black women responsible for "the illegitimacy which our race has been obliged, as it were, to flood the world?" (ibid.). Mrs. Willis remains unequivocal, declaring that responsibility can exist only where one has a choice (150).

Emphasizing choice, Mrs. Willis gives Sappho, who was kidnapped, raped, and impregnated at age 14, plenty of reason to relinquish guilt and shame. Sappho persists, however, asking how one might overcome passion and embrace Christ's purity (154). Once again, Mrs. Willis's answer gestures toward the importance of living without shame. She insists, for example, that ridding oneself of passion should not be the goal: "All work of whatever character . . . needs a certain amount of absorbing interest to become successful" (ibid., 154). Just as virtue applies to much more than sexual matters, passion is not inherently dangerous; it is required for a productive life. In fact, "All desires and hopes with which we are endowed are good in the sight of God, only it is left for us to discover their right uses" (155).

If every desire becomes good when one discovers its constructive use, then the desire to marry must be brought under the guidance of a righteous purpose. In *Contending Forces*, no less than in *Iola Leroy*, that purpose is uplifting the race. Indeed, Mrs. Willis says that an unnamed woman who kept silent about her past so that she could marry the man of her choice had been wise. If left to his own judgment, the man would have bypassed the gift of this woman as his wife, and no one (neither the couple nor the community) would have benefited from that. Mrs. Willis concludes, "I think in her case she did her duty" (156).

In other words, this woman succeeded in making a home and she claimed her right to belong, and when the community conversation affirms her choices, her actions broaden the horizon for other African Americans. The novel offers a truly stunning philosophy. Namely, a black woman's duty does not, by definition, have to revolve around sacrifice; women should pursue greater and greater success.

Hopkins also uses the venerable Mrs. Willis to assert that racial uplift (collective practices of making-oneself-at-home) should involve romantic love and pleasure! An apparently incredulous Sappho remains confounded and asks longingly, "What is our duty? . . . It is so hard to know our duty" (157). Again, Hopkins insists upon infusing the community conversation on success with a progressive, life-affirming message usually deemed irrelevant to black women. Mrs. Willis gives a surprising answer: "Your duty is not to be morbid. . . . Your duty is, also, to be happy and bright for the good of those about you. Just blossom like the flowers, have faith and trust" (ibid.).

Mrs. Willis articulates a life-affirming, possibility-creating philosophy and marks the difference between a slave cabin and a home of one's own. Slaveholders no longer directly steal black women's choices, but options can be limited when one accepts dominant discourses meant to keep women, especially black women, in their "proper" place. Shame only serves to constrain, not to uplift. Because racial uplift is best defined as making-oneself-at-home collectively, the entire race suffers when black women bend to shame. Thus, a home is a space in which black women have the power to choose, the importance of which Jacobs and Keckley made painfully clear. Though the slave past has left an imprint on their lives, forcing many of them to become rape survivors, black women should have the freedom to enjoy their lives—not simply endure it, but actually blossom. As suggested by Sappho's difficulty with internalizing Mrs. Willis's words, these are unexpected answers to the most pressing questions of the post-Reconstruction present, and Hopkins deliberately uses a revered messenger to articulate these ideas.

Though Sappho struggles to accept this possibility, the novel uses her journey to assert that success must be defined so that romantic love is a key component of the future that the formerly enslaved and their descendants create. *Contending Forces* suggests that African Americans must understand love to be their birthright . . . that they deserve love, especially romantic love. Romantic love is prioritized even as dominant discourses and practices most relentlessly attack this type of bond.

Sappho begins as a shame-ridden woman (living in secret and without her child) and becomes a proud mother and wife, and while this transformation starts with her acceptance of her child, it depends on her belief that she deserves a lover of her choice. *Contending Forces* makes motherhood the mechanism through which Sappho sheds the shame that will keep her from happiness, but the novel refuses to suggest that motherhood can right all wrongs. Sappho begins to see herself as a decent person only when she accepts her role as Alphonse's mother. When she flees Boston, abandoning her fiancé Will Smith, the narrator explains, "innocent or guilty, our deeds done in the flesh pursue us with relentless vigor unto the end of life" (341). In other words, Sappho cannot escape her past, so her conception of accomplishment must involve learning to live with her past in a way that makes a dignified and productive future possible.

As Sappho strives to make a home that can facilitate success for her and her son, she must walk the path carved by the violence of rape and dominant discourses and practices that encourage shame. Claiming her child is part of how she must live with her past rather than flee from it, but accepting this reality is difficult; in fact, acceptance comes only after several other stages. First, Sappho dwells on her desire for revenge against both her rapist and John Langley, the politician who used her victimization to shame and terrorize her (ibid.). Soon, this desire is washed away in a flood of tears that "relieved the overcharged brain and saved her reason" (342). At this point, she begins to focus on her own sin rather than that of others: her neglect of her child, the fact that she "felt nothing for the poor waif but repugnance" (ibid.). Soon, she decides, "come what would she would claim the child and do her duty as his mother in love and training. . . . They would nevermore be separated" (ibid.). Upon sharing her plans with her aunt, Madame Frances, her aunt affirms her impulse, saying, "in doing your duty, happiness will come to you, the greater and more abiding for the trouble which has preceded it" (344). However, when Sappho reveals that she will immediately take the boy and "never part with him again on earth," her aunt is clear: "Well, my dear child, I see no necessity for you to become a martyr in order to do your duty" (ibid.).

When Sappho begins truly claiming the son, she realizes shame had robbed her of "the joys of motherhood, of pride of possession in her child" (345), but the text soon reveals that mother-love is not only insufficient; it is also, as her aunt's caveat suggested, an insufficient reward for all she has suffered. For a short time, Sappho feels "mother-love chased out all the anguish that she had felt over his birth," and she wonders how she had remained separated from Alphonse for so long. Suddenly, "in this new and holy love that had taken possession of her soul was the compensation for all she had suffered" (347). Indeed, on the trip South, her son functions as an anchor. The narrator notes, "mentally and physically, she was overtaxed, and but for the child she would have broken down" (ibid.).

Sappho is now defining success in terms of claiming her son and making a home for him, and she must work toward her goals by navigating violence and its aftermath. However, by the time they reach New Orleans, she faints. She is therefore rushed to the hospital and her child to an orphanage (348).

Placing Sappho in the care of nuns, the text again insists that she should not expect her life to be complete when she learns to love the child she bore out of rape. The nuns uplift the race while operating within alternative domestic configurations, but Hopkins nonetheless uses them to reinforce the significance of the heteronormative nuclear family, given the hierarchy of homemaking (discussed in Chapter 1). Their actions suggest that, without having a life partner, it is not feasible for Sappho to live with her son. The Mother does not believe she should keep the child with her at all times and at all costs. When Sappho pledges to do precisely that, the Mother counters. The convent will present Sappho as a widow to lend respectability to her situation and thereby increase her employment opportunities. Sappho again resists, wanting there to be "no more deception" (352). The sister is unequivocal, though; she says, "I am glad to see that you are ready to bear all things in meekness for His sake. But you are not called upon to make too many sacrifices" (ibid.). The nun's solution is to employ Sappho as governess to a widower's daughters and have Alphonse live at the convent, where Sappho can visit him weekly.

Through the nun's practicality, the text suggests that making a home with her child requires Sappho to have a partner, but it also insists that motherly love does not bring complete happiness and that Sappho deserves romantic love. The narrator reports, though Sappho's life "now bade fair to be tranquil and monotonous enough, she nevertheless found herself asking, 'Why could she not be happy?'" (354). Despite her attempts to forget Will, the fiancé she left, "when night came she lay awake hungering for the sight of a face, the touch of a hand, the glance of an eye. Sometimes the craving grew almost too powerful to be resisted, and once she started to dress, resolved to return to Boston, find Will, and trust all to his love" (ibid.). In these moments of yearning, she would calm herself by remembering that she would "die at his feet" if he rejected her. She therefore "told herself that life was done and nothing remained but patience. So she sat dumb and submissive beneath her martyrdom" (ibid.).

Sappho has become exactly what her aunt insisted was not required, a martyr for her child, and the text highlights the injustice of Sappho's struggle. When trying to create a home and a sense of belonging, she grapples with the consequences of the violence American society heaps on black women. However, she encounters people who try to lighten her load. In fact, even the person for whom she thinks she is sacrificing does not want her to do so. When she tries to assure her son, Alphonse, that she is not unhappy, he responds, "Oh, yes, you are. When I am a big man I shall find the tall, handsome gentleman who gave you flowers at the fair" (356). She then urges Alphonse not to speak of the past, and it becomes clear that she has gone from fleeing a past of shame about her rape to fleeing a past of love and happiness with Will.

Clearly, the challenge to be met is living with one's past in a way that creates possibility. Avoiding her role as a beloved romantic partner is no more admirable than avoiding her role as Alphonse's mother. Showcasing the range of Sappho's true desires, *Contending Forces* suggests that having a home of her own involves dignity and pleasure as both a mother and wife.

To confirm that giving up romantic love in order to care for her child represents a cruel and unwarranted sacrifice, the narrator shares that when Monsieur Louis, the widower who employs her, proposes marriage, "about Sappho's heart there was a strange feeling of suffocation, a feeling such as a martyr might have experienced at the stake" (358). In other words, accepting his proposal would constitute the final step in closing off the possibility of reuniting with her true love. The fact that she would be doing it for her son's benefit, providing him with a stable home and honorable name,[15] will not diminish the pain of denying her desire for a life not defined by having given birth to her rapist's child.

Sappho's definition of success requires fulfilling one's duty, but she struggles to believe that the duty of racial uplift includes joy and pleasure. The message that Sappho should not embrace martyrdom is as clear as the guidance she could not accept earlier from Mrs. Willis. The venerable woman had assured Sappho that virtue comes in many forms, that passion is not inherently evil, and that being happy is an actual responsibility. If Sappho had been able to absorb these ideas, she might have believed herself worthy of a home of her own, consecrated by the romantic love of the man of her choice—exactly what Jacobs and Keckley show was so important to enslaved forebears. Fortunately, Will finds her before she answers Monsieur Louis's proposal, so she ultimately gains all that Hopkins believes black women deserve, but her joy was delayed because she had not been able to follow others' advice and free herself of shame. Because Sappho marries her beloved and will have a home of her own with him, Hopkins casts the rape survivor's journey as proof that the race can indeed "lose the sting of degradation." To lose that sting is to live free, in precisely the way that enslaved forebears must have imagined as they envisioned making the transition from a sexually vulnerable servant to a woman with a home of her own.

The community conversation maps the route from house slave to homemaker for women whose lives have been touched by slavery's legacies, and *Contending Forces* suggests that homemaking clears the path if it is based on choice, consecrated by love, and marked by pleasure. Black women, as a group, must be able to take their deserved positions as cherished wives and mothers. As the novel ends with Sappho married to Will and poised for a future of possibility, their domestic success indicates for readers not only that Sappho and her family will be happy but also that the race will benefit from this union that has brought so much joy to an African American woman's life. As Sappho creates a home that benefits the community, Hopkins joins Harper in defining racial uplift as the practice of making-oneself-at-home on a collective scale.

The fact that Sappho encounters many characters who try to show her that she is cheating herself and the world by not being happy underscores the value of community conversation, but Hopkins also uses such conversation to remind readers that, as much as African Americans deserve to enjoy domestic success, other Americans will not likely leave their homes intact. *Contending Forces* consistently acknowledges white violence and its role in the national project of keeping black men, women, and children in their "proper" place. In fact, know-your-place aggression drives the portrait readers receive of Luke Sawyer, the character who enters the narrative to define the novel's title, *Contending Forces*, and to fulfill a promise made in its opening pages. Hopkins's preface explains, "I have presented both sides of the dark picture—lynching and concubinage—truthfully and without vituperation" (15), and it is Luke who most directly bears witness to the impact of these thoroughly intertwined phenomena.

Luke's life story exposes the nation's investment in keeping African Americans from choosing romantic partners and creating the kinds of households that are said to command respect and bring safety. He is a male counterpart to Sappho in that his past must be faced, not fled. However, though readers do not know exactly how Luke's personal story ends, he stands as a reminder that even if Sappho's journey eventually inspires optimism, readers must remember that whenever African Americans claim belonging and maintain optimism, they must do so while grappling with the injustices that the United States insists upon inflicting.

Luke enters the narrative because the American Colored League of Boston, which is devoted to racial uplift, sponsors a gathering to address the lynchings terrorizing African Americans. The large church is "filled to overflowing" because "today a condition of affairs confronts us that [the great abolitionists] never foresaw: the systematic destruction of the Negro by every device which the fury of enlightened malevolence can invent" (244). That is, decades after slavery, black success continues to be targeted, and lynching proves to be one of the "devices" used.

The community has gathered to discuss strategies for confronting the lynching crisis in a way that will benefit the race, that will keep it moving toward success. Naturally, there is disagreement. Early on, the crowd hears from Dr. Lewis, who considers his own to be the gathering's most important opinion because he operates a school in the South, where most lynchings occur. He advises extreme caution and argues that even if white men do not change, their children will have a more favorable view of African Americans "if we are patient, docile, harmless" (250). The narrator registers the crowd's disappointment: "Some among the audience began to grow restless. Was this what they came to hear—an apology, almost an eulogy upon the course pursued by the South toward the Negro?" (251). Because accommodationist arguments from black speakers continue, Luke's emergence proves to be explosive. Specifically, local politician John Langley tells those gathered, "let us not offend the class upon whom we depend for employment" (253). Before John Langley has taken his seat, Luke Sawyer rises, uttering "the solemn protest of Patrick Henry, so famous in history: Gentleman may cry 'Peace! Peace!' but there is not peace!" (254). The crowd responds favorably, demanding that Luke be allowed to address them. Luke begins by defining the "contending forces" of the novel's title. He declares, "the contending forces that are dooming this race to despair" are "conservatism, lack of brotherly affiliation, lack of energy for the right and the power of the almighty dollar which deadens men's hearts to the sufferings of their brothers" (256). In other words, those in power reward people for conforming to dominant values, so whenever one prioritizes material comfort, there will be incentives for not intervening as others suffer—even if they suffer from the racial violence that sparked this meeting.

Though Luke is never portrayed as a traditional head-of-household himself, his testimony highlights the pervasiveness of what Hopkins calls "lynching and concubinage" and what historian Crystal Feimster calls the "rape-lynch scenario." Indeed, his not being a head-of-household makes his testimony more powerful because it underscores white people's commitment to using violence not only to destroy but also prevent black (domestic) success. Sawyer's first experience with this sort of violence occurred when he was 10 years old. Because his mother was slightly better educated than his father, she encouraged him to become an entrepreneur. He did so, his business fared well, and he soon had "as much money as any man in the county" (ibid.). He avoided politics, understanding "that that might be made an excuse for his destruction" (ibid.). Seeing Luke's father's success, a white man opened a store on the same street. Without Luke's father saying a word to sway his customers, they remained loyal, so the competing store would soon need to close. Suddenly, Luke's father began receiving threatening letters, and his wife suggested they leave town. He was preparing to do so, but he wanted to sell his stock and thereby not lose everything. One night, a mob smoked his family out of the house, hung him from the nearest tree, "whipped [Luke's] mother and sister, and otherwise abused them so that they died next day" (257). Luke's twin brothers were babies; the mob "took them by the heels and dashed their brains out against the walls of the house! Then they burned the house" (ibid.). A traumatized 10-year-old Luke "crept into the woods to die" (ibid.).

Luke bears witness to the fact that black success beckons the mob and that lynching and rape are interdependent. His father had become a target, not for being a criminal but for being a success. His "crime" is participating in the economy as something other than an exploited laborer. Furthermore, Luke's testimony highlights his parent's "crime" as a couple: they were partners creating a self-sufficient home. When threatened for being successful, they decide leaving together is more important than keeping the store they had worked to create, but that willingness does not save them any more than this black entrepreneur's decision to avoid politics (the strategy promoted in Dr. Lewis's speech). Rather than insist upon political rights or defend himself against market competition, Luke's father had said nothing. His costumers continued to shop with him of their own volition. He had sought nothing more than fair participation in the economy. Still, he and his infant sons were lynched, and his wife and daughter were likely raped before they died.[16]

Though 10-year-old Luke had expected to perish in the woods, he survived, and his doing so translated into experiencing more of the nation's commitment to know-your-place aggression; his countrymen forced him to confront lynching and concubinage again. A colored planter named Beaubean from a nearby town found the traumatized, prepubescent Luke and took him in. Coming of age in Beaubean's family, Luke watched his daughter Mabelle grow up; he admired her and developed undying gratitude toward her father. When she was 14 and Luke was 19, she spent a school holiday in the city. Her friends returned without her, reporting that she had gone into a store with her father's brother. Luke and Mr. Beaubean searched all night for her, to no avail. They then enlisted the help of a detective. After three weeks, "we found her a prisoner in a house of the vilest character in the lowest portion of the city of New Orleans—a poor, ruined, half-crazed creature in whom it was almost impossible to trace a resemblance to the beautiful pet of our household" (260). Luke himself carried her home. Mr. Beaubean was distraught. When Mr. Beaubean confronted his half-brother, a state senator, his brother added insult to injury: "'What does a woman of mixed blood, or any Negress, for that matter, know of virtue? It is my belief that they were a direct creation by God to be the pleasant companions of men of my race. Now, I am willing to give you a thousand dollars and call it square'" (Hopkins 261). Because Beaubean swears to "carry [his] case into the Federal courts," his house was mobbed "that night" (ibid.).[17] Luke managed to escape the burning house with Mabelle, and he took her to a convent (ibid.). Mabelle turns out to be Sappho.

In "a romance illustrative of Negro life North and South," Luke's testimony reminds readers that, as African Americans pursue their goals, they must do so with full knowledge that white violence will likely accompany them every step of the way. Luke's testimony reveals that having a home of one's own attracts brutality more often than respect and safety. Long before he can become a head-of-household himself, Luke's experiences expose the links between "lynching and concubinage," given the violence that stalks African Americans when they embody all that the nation claims to respect. The targeting of black manhood via lynching, and of black womanhood via rape, serve the same *know your place!* purpose. Contrary to mainstream claims, homemaking success does not yield civic inclusion or even safety. Yet, in the midst of this violent reality, Luke's parents loved each other and made a home for themselves and for him, and Mr. Beaubean's home was so full of love that he adopted Will, nurturing him alongside his daughter. The United States opposes their every achievement, so African Americans pursue success while knowing that they are all but inviting injury. White violence is relentless, but as long as they can draw a breath, black people find ways to make home and create a sense of belonging nonetheless.

*   *   *

Like many black domestic novels, *Iola Leroy* and *Contending Forces* center on admirable black families and their households because African American communities have never had a shortage of them. Black authors did not focus on domestic success to counter mainstream distortions so much as they aimed to represent an historical reality. Yet, the historical reality of black achievement, especially traditional domesticity, has always been accompanied by vigorous attempts to destroy it while claiming it never existed. In slavery, even before they had recognized households, black couples and families loved and nurtured each other. Dominant discourse attacked their bonds by asserting that their familial connections were not particularly strong, thereby justifying the separation of families via sales, but enslavers used those very bonds to control those who supposedly felt little attachment. During post-Reconstruction decades, as the descendants of the formerly enslaved worked to build a future, acknowledging the love of their forebears helped them make sense of their present. However, African Americans also saw that love had intensified their ancestors' vulnerability, and it could do the same to them. Aware of the dangers, communities continued to achieve and to affirm belonging. Their victories, as had been the case for their forebears, inspired violence.

In this climate, Frances E. W. Harper offered her pedagogical narrative *Iola Leroy* to encourage readers to define success in ways that prioritize traditional homemaking for the purpose of racial uplift, and she insisted that love cannot be the only factor when making decisions about romantic coupling because racial uplift requires an orientation toward the collective. One must put love in service to community; only then will having a home of one's own become worthwhile. Accordingly, Harper placed a spotlight on Iola's romantic decisions, leaving no question in readers' minds that Iola's future home will benefit the race. Iola's choice inspires optimism, but that optimism is complicated by the context Harper provides. As discussed, Marie has created a home for her reassembled family, and slave auctions will not intrude upon it, but the novel cannot ignore the validity of her worrying herself sick because her son Harry is an asset to the race. His vulnerability therefore hovers over any victory represented by Iola's decision to marry Dr. Latimer rather than Dr. Gresham. After all, their homemaking success will likely beckon the mob just as sales and auctions seemed to be irresistibly drawn to the love of the enslaved. To similar effect, *Contending Forces* spotlights the northern home of Ma Smith, which pays homage to the self-determination of her husband, who had been "a free-born Southern Negro—a Virginian" (82). His death has left the home to his wife and children, Dora and Will, who are now model adults. The household also nurtures many more than those related to him by blood. Sappho is one of the many boarders who constitute a chosen family that Ma Smith brings together for "musical evenings or reception nights" (102), which prove to be embodied practices of belonging. This chosen family, and the people who enter Sappho's life because of it, put in her path community kin (such as Mrs. Willis of the Sewing Circle) who love her with life-giving words rather than the shame-inducing platitudes of dominant discourse. Far from a superwoman impervious to the messages with which the nation bombards her, the black woman (who is too often a rape survivor) searches for sources of resiliency. Her odds of thriving increase when community members help her feel worthy of all that the nation wants to deprive her of, including romantic love and pleasure.

In the repressive post-Reconstruction era, defining success revolves around engaging the present in ways that take lessons from the past as one eagerly looks to the future. By depicting not only black households but also a dynamic community conversation—of which these artistic works themselves are a part—novels like *Iola Leroy* and *Contending Forces* represent the diversity of opinion in African American communities facing constant attack from white Americans. In such conversations, there is no escaping the need to address challenges to black achievement. Black citizens acknowledge that they face a crisis that they do not deserve because their accomplishments inspire aggression. Whether literal night riders or not, African Americans' white counterparts seek to destroy black success while claiming it never existed.

New Negroes, New Homes

From the 1890s to the 1930s, African Americans remained intent on claiming greater and greater success; generations that had not been enslaved were determined that slavery's legacies would not limit them. Meanwhile, many white Americans continued their efforts at keeping their black counterparts in their "proper" place. As African Americans created more expansive lives than their forebears had eked out in slave cabins, their victories were answered with a forceful blow from the United States Supreme Court in *Plessy v. Ferguson*. This 1896 decision sent a message that reverberated nationally, that providing separate accommodations for white and black people was appropriate and that if African Americans viewed it as a slight, they were choosing to do so.[1] There was nothing inherently degrading about segregation, and there was nothing in racial separation, the court argued, that violated the citizenship protections of the Thirteenth Amendment. The Supreme Court basically declared that African Americans have a proper place. Further, if they do not appreciate having to occupy that place and are vocal about it, then their behavior is not dignified and it proves they should not be respected.

This know-your-place aggression from the Supreme Court joined violence from both powerful and ordinary white people, and it set the stage for additional attacks, thereby countering black efforts to gain all that should accompany freedom.[2] African American migration, which intensified in 1914 and 1915 and again in the 1920s, should therefore be seen as not simply migrants' pursuit of "the warmth of other suns,"[3] but as another example of black people securing success and being answered with white violence. Mobility was considered a feature of modern citizenship,[4] so white Americans wanted to exclude black people from it. Whites tried to terrorize blacks into staying in place. Indeed, it was linking mobility to citizenship that made transportation—or, as historian Blair Kelley puts it, the *Right to Ride*—a crucial site of struggle.

White Americans attempted to prevent the victory of black mobility, and when it was secured nonetheless, they answered with even more violence by rioting in cities that had an influx of African Americans. The physical violence of lynchings and race riots was facilitated by the discursive violence of depicting African Americans as immoral and criminal while depicting the Ku Klux Klan as a saving grace. In the 1910s and 1920s, the organization "spread into areas that had previously shown few bold manifestations of race hatred" and "in many communities candidates for public office feared defeat if they were not on good terms with the Klan, preferably as members" (Franklin and Moss 384). Know-your-place aggression also took the form of making lines between racial groups more rigid, with "mulatto" ceasing to be a census category after 1920. During slavery, the assertion that familial bonds meant little to black people manufactured a difference between them and their oppressors; now, insisting on a strict racial dichotomy bolstered continuing declarations about black inferiority.

Black achievement inspired the violence of enforcing "natural" distinctions between black and white people, so the investment in portraying African Americans as immoral intensified. Ida B. Wells realized in the 1890s that the claim that black men were natural rapists was actually "an excuse to get rid of Negroes who were acquiring wealth and property and thus keep the race terrorized" (qtd. in McMurry 143), but the black rapist myth remained quite effective. The 1906 Atlanta riot, during which white mobs killed 30 African Americans and injured hundreds more, began with unfounded newspaper reports about black rapists, and "after a false interracial rape accusation in 1908, white mobs in Springfield, Illinois, burned the black business district and lynched two black men" (Freedman 231).

In other words, race riots often began with lies about black men attacking white women, and it is no coincidence that mobs targeted not simply successful individuals but entire communities in which African

Americans were known to be self-sufficient and dignified. In 1921, the section of Tulsa, Oklahoma, known for its thriving businesses as "Black Wall Street," was decimated in two days of brawling that began with a rumor of a black male teenager assaulting a white female teenager. Likewise, the prosperous black town of Rosewood, Florida, was annihilated in 1923. A white mob from a neighboring village flew into action based on a white woman's false rape accusation. "By 1924 lynchings declined to fewer than twenty per year, but a higher proportion of these resulted from allegations of sexual offences" (Freedman 231). Because the goal was always to put successful black people back in their "proper" place, the discursive violence of labeling black men rapists always proved a convenient and effective partner. Given the reactionary nature of know-your-place aggression, blacks must have been meeting the standards of dignified manhood that the nation claims to respect but only celebrates in white men.

Noticing this pattern is crucial, as is remembering what Frances E. W. Harper and Pauline Hopkins made clear in the 1890s, that lynching facilitated rape. Constantly stoking fears about black men's supposed obsession with white women made a nonissue in national discourse of the actual rape of black women by white men. Yet, it was white men's violation of black women that had made slavery profitable for 250 years, and the practice did not end after Emancipation.[5] Racial violence (both physical and discursive) denied black citizenship, and the form corresponded to the gender of the person whose belonging it negated. African American women were cast as natural whores to justify rape, and black men were declared to be natural rapists to justify lynching. These depictions, as well as the physical and legislative aggression they fueled, answered black success. Black people had to be cast as whores and rapists because they so routinely proved to be anything but.

Rape might be muted today in most Americans' memory of migration and race riots, but the community conversation on success engaged it at the time as an example of the white violence designed to interrupt black people's journeys toward achievement. While the victory of mobility sparked riots and black rapist labels, it equally inspired declarations that "it is not the same thing for a white man to assault a colored woman as for a colored man to assault a white woman, because the colored woman had no finer feelings nor virtue to be outraged" (South Carolina newspaper qtd. in Wells, *Red* 127). Marita Bonner asked in 1925, "Why do they see a colored woman only as a gross collection of desires, all uncontrolled, reaching out for their Apollos . . . with avid indiscrimination?" (1267). The answer was clear: such ideas encouraged aggression toward black women wherever they went, including white homes where black housekeepers could never assume sexual safety.

Casting black women as whores also justified their being put in their "proper" place according to *Plessy v. Ferguson.* As black club women continued their commitment to "lifting as we climb," they viewed being relegated to segregated railcars as an attack that only encouraged more attacks. Namely, "the womanhood of the race" encountered "every outrage and insult" in such accommodations (*Woman's Era* qtd. in Freedman 118). As Wells made clear in 1887, portraying black women as immoral amounted to an attempt to obliterate the accomplishments of African American "mothers, wives and maidens who have attained a true, noble, and refining womanhood" ("Our Women," 564).

Domestic success is the most jealously guarded achievement in a nation committed to know-your-place aggression, so black artists have always honored the degree to which house slaves and housekeepers were also homemakers. As demonstrated in Chapter 1, black women's efforts on behalf of their own families proved life-affirming in the midst of slavery's violence. During post-Reconstruction, as discussed in Chapter 2, black men, women, and children searched for the loved ones that slavery had taken out of their lives and they supported community members with similar goals. As they helped others find happiness, black women were grateful that their bodies were no longer literally owned, but often had to be convinced that they deserved pleasure. Believing in one's right to pleasure therefore constituted a victory that artists like Pauline Hopkins wanted more community members to claim. New Negro women novelists such as Nella Larsen and Zora Neale Hurston continued Hopkins's crusade. Their works place a spotlight on protagonists whose practices of making-oneself-at-home involve mobility, which white violence always answered. Furthermore, Larsen's Helga Crane and Hurston's Janie Crawford enter the community conversation to explore how unattractive marriage and motherhood can be because they prioritize pleasure while seeking success. To believe in their right to pleasure required disregarding the discursive violence of the whore stereotype and the sexual harassment and assault it justified. Black women could not avoid the know-your-place aggression that countered their freedom of movement, but Larsen and Hurston preserve evidence of women whose definitions of success nevertheless prioritized pleasure.

Because literature offers an access point to the community conversation, the similarities and differences between black domestic romances of the 1890s and New Negro novels of the 1920s and 1930s shed light on the ongoing discussion of how to define black achievement in environments designed to discourage and destroy it. As cultural historian Marlon Ross argues, novels written by the first generations not to experience slavery adopt a narrative form that isolates the protagonist in order to establish a level of "agency that can out-maneuver Jim Crow restraints" (5). As these novels focus on individuals rather than entire communities, the women who produce such works put pressure on the consensus forming around how best to define success in the new century. Women authors of the 1920s and 1930s remain focused on racial uplift, but while predecessors had defined it as *collective* practices of making-oneself-at-home, their texts begin insisting that more individualized journeys must be examined in order to test definitions of black achievement, determining whether those definitions affirm the women who comprise half the community.

Putting forth female protagonists whose practices of making-oneself-at-home veer away from marriage and child-rearing was bold at a time when the community conversation was privileging *race motherhood*. As historian Erin Chapman explains, "Race motherhood was never explicitly stated in New Negro publications but was everywhere implied by the nearly absolute absence of commentary on black women's personal experiences and lives independent of black men or children" (57). Whereas black women of the 1890s used their domestic roles to legitimize their demands for political participation,[6] New Negro women were encouraged to claim space only in service to a revised race agenda that made black men's ability to be patriarchs its primary goal. The black mother had fueled racial uplift efforts of the 1890s, but the black male laborer was deemed the most accurate gauge of racial progress by the 1920s. Indeed, mothers were more likely to be blamed for the race's problems, so black women needed to be redeemed and embracing race motherhood brought redemption. Questioning expectations would make women vulnerable to harsh criticism and possible ostracism. Nevertheless, fiction by women such as Larsen and Hurston reveals the degree to which race motherhood was interrogated, even as its influence proved inescapable.

The work of New Negro women novelists reveals black women's investment in questioning how the community was defining success. In particular, Larsen and Hurston put forth protagonists whose conceptions of achievement revolve around pleasure, rather than marriage and traditional homemaking.[7] These protagonists succeed at holding on to the belief, which Hopkins would have encouraged, that they deserve pleasure, that their aspirations should reflect that, and that the entire community's definition of success should reflect it, too.

Success without Pleasure?

Nella Larsen's *Quicksand* appeared in 1928, in the cultural moment of the New Negro and the New Woman. As African American women gained increasing access to the public sphere, not only because the race was moving away from slavery but also because women were entering a wider array of professions, black women registered concerns while contributing to the community conversation defining accomplishment. Larsen offers a complex protagonist, Helga Crane, and uses a third-person narrator to reveal Helga's intense self-reflection. Above all, Larsen offers Helga as a protagonist who defines achievement in terms of enjoying both pleasure and the stability of inclusion, but she is constantly put in her "proper" place. In environments shaped not only by white investments in countering black women's success but also by the belief among African Americans that women must uplift the race through submission, pleasure and inclusion seem to be mutually exclusive. *Quicksand*'s plot is driven by the opposition Helga encounters when pursuing success by working to grasp both pleasure and community inclusion.

Larsen's portrait of Helga begins with an emphasis on her appreciation for beauty and makes it a sign of her status as a New Negro woman, the apparent opposite of a race mother. Larsen characterizes Helga's New Negro womanhood as an insistence upon beauty and pleasure and the right to meditate on, and dwell within, both. Helga's "craving" and "urge for beauty" lead her to spend most of her money on clothes, books, and furnishings (10). Indeed, readers meet Helga as she is surrounded by the beauty of her room and weighing her decision to leave her teaching position at the famous school for African Americans in Naxos.[8] This professional decision will also mean ending her engagement to James Vayle. Their relationship began with the comfort they found in each other when neither felt at home in Naxos as new faculty members. However, James soon began to fit in and Helga did not, which allows Larsen to suggest from the start that marriage to a race man requires accepting a specific role. Helga had not conformed the way James had, leading her to recall, "How her maladjustment had bothered him!" (11). As the child of a white woman impregnated and abandoned by a black man, Helga does not have a respected family name, so she had initially gravitated toward James because his social standing allows her smoother entry into a black community whose uplift mission she shares. However, just as she learns that the school's structure creates barriers to trust and intimacy between teacher and student,[9] it becomes clear that marriage protocols could squelch the feelings she had hoped would flourish with her future husband. Black domestic novels of the 1890s had offered uplift as uniformly edifying, but Larsen suggests a closer look at individual journeys, especially those of women, reveals harmful outcomes.

Claiming the success of mobility, Helga leaves Naxos because its regimented schedule and insistence upon conformity prevent what she considers crucial to making-oneself-at-home: individuality, self-expression, and pleasure. She believes the institution has become less a school and more a machine. In Helga's view, "life had died out of it"—it was "now only a big knife with cruelly sharp edges ruthlessly cutting all to a pattern, the white man's pattern" (8). Conformity is required in order for the school's existence to send the only message deemed acceptable, that white people are magnanimous and black people are grateful (ibid.). The constraints that define the school parallel those of marriage, so Helga flees both, wanting simply to be accepted for who she believes herself to be. Essentially, Helga has always felt lonely and isolated because her white mother had married a white man who despised her, so she had hoped to achieve a sense of belonging in Naxos. Once that fails, she seeks it in Chicago because the only relative who had always been kind to her lives there. When she visits, he is not home but his new wife is, and she rejects Helga. Making clear that the brown woman is not welcome, Helga's uncle's wife ends their exchange with: "And please remember that my husband is not your uncle. No indeed! Why, that, that, would make me your aunt!" (31).

This rejection does not change Helga's focus on achievement, however, so she seeks employment because the pleasure of beautiful things remains a priority. Finding a job in Chicago is frustrating. Black women are relegated to domestic work, but even if willing to do it, as a former teacher, she does not have housekeeping references. Fortunately, a black woman lecturer who needs an assistant and traveling companion contacts the agency with which Helga is registered. After an interview, Helga and Mrs. Hayes Rore agree that Helga will accompany the widow from Chicago to New York City. Helga intends to remain in New York to (like so many real-life migrants) make a new start, so Mrs. Hayes Rore uses her connections to secure for Helga a job and place to live. However, she tells Helga not to mention to others, as she had with her, that her family is white (44). This advice reinforces the isolation Helga has always felt. Her being black had been a problem for her stepfather; now her having a white mother is assumed to be a problem for the black community in Harlem where Helga is looking forward to making a life. She had thought of New York as more sophisticated and therefore more accommodating than Naxos, but this advice suggests otherwise.

Though Helga's smoldering shame about her origins is reinforced by her benefactor's advice, this feeling initially remains submerged, so for about a year, Helga enjoys the success she seeks. She feels a strong sense of belonging among her new friends and loses herself in the pleasures of like-minded acquaintances, the aesthetics of her surroundings, and the joy of feeling confident that both happiness and stability are within reach. Mrs. Hayes Rore introduces Helga to Anne Grey, whose house is big enough to accommodate a guest, and in time, she invites Helga to remain as a roommate. Helga is pleased because "Anne's home was in complete accord with what she designated as her 'aesthetic sense'" (47). With this, as well as a circle of friends whose interests and tastes she shares, Helga "lost that tantalizing oppression of loneliness and isolation which always, it seemed, had been a part of her existence" (48).

In fact, Helga feels so content that mainstream acceptance completely falls out of her list of aspirations; she has no interest in "white New York." The narrator reports, "Of that white world, so distant, so near she asked only indifference" (ibid.). In this year of contentment, Helga views Harlem thusly: "Everything was there, vice and goodness, sadness and gayety, ignorance and wisdom, ugliness and beauty, poverty and richness. And it seemed to her that somehow the goodness, gayety, wisdom, and beauty always there was a little more than of vice, sadness, ignorance, and ugliness. It was only riches that did not quite transcend poverty" (49). Invigorated by Harlem's abundance, Helga becomes convinced her absolute ideal is attainable: both pleasure and a stable sense of belonging. She now expects to marry a "brown or yellow" man who is well established. She thinks, "already financially successful, any of them could give to her the things which she had now come to desire, a home like Anne's, cars of expensive makes such as lined the avenue, clothes and furs . . ., servants, leisure" (ibid.).

Her ideal future is free of race motherhood. It does not come with the bothersome "visionary uplifting plans of Dr. Anderson" (ibid.). Dr. Anderson was the principal at Naxos, so Helga had been required to meet with him before resigning, and he had nearly convinced her to stay. As he had spoken with her about racial uplift, a "mystifying yearning . . . sang and throbbed in her" (23). Dr. Anderson's passionate words made Helga feel again "that urge for service, not now for her people, but for this man who was talking so earnestly of his work, his plans, his hopes. An insistent need to be part of them sprang in her" (ibid.). The only reason Helga had not remained mesmerized by Dr. Anderson's uplift speech is that he had mentioned her "dignity and breeding," inadvertently arousing her shame about the "illegitimate" circumstances of her birth. His well-intentioned comments had provoked an anger so intense that Helga had stormed out of his office, having "missed the import of his words" (24), only to feel "shameful contrition" later (25). In other words, Helga had been attracted to Dr. Anderson; it was desire and potential pleasure that drew her. Only that trance could make race motherhood seem appealing.[10]

Because pleasure remains central to Helga's definition of success, but she allows shame to ruin it, Harlem loses its charm. Helga frequently wonders, "why . . . should she be yoked to these despised black folk?" (57). She fails to recognize that African Americans need not be despicable to be despised; they need only to achieve what the nation claims they cannot. Duped by dominant discourse, Helga begins to dislike her friends, including her roommate Anne (50). Having decided to leave Harlem, the conviction emerges more and more: "She didn't, in spite of her racial markings, belong to these dark segregated people. She was different. She felt it. It wasn't merely a matter of color. It was something broader, deeper, that made folk kin" (58). These thoughts rob Helga of pleasure. In fact, it is when Helga feels most connected, and feels the most pleasure, that she insists upon distance. When dancing at a club among friends, Helga is "lifted, sustained, by the extraordinary music. . . . The essence of life seemed bodily motion. And when suddenly the music died, she dragged herself back to the present with a conscious effort; and a shameful certainty that not only had she been in the jungle, but that she had enjoyed it, began to taunt her. She hardened her determination to get away. She wasn't, she told herself, a jungle creature" (61). Belonging to black people and black culture brings pleasure, but Helga turns it against herself, just as know-your-place aggression would have it, and the joy of belonging becomes a curse.

Leaving Harlem, Helga continues her quest and believes she achieves more than what is possible in the United States by going to Denmark. In contrast to what she suffered from her uncle's new wife in Chicago, Helga is warmly welcomed by her Danish aunt and her aunt's husband. Her time with them therefore initially feels like a dream come true. It seems Helga will be free to enjoy life because she has found a sense of belonging, which comes with the material pleasures she has always desired. The narrator conveys, "Always she had wanted, not money, but the things which money could give, leisure, attention, beautiful surroundings. Things. Things. Things" (69).

Only after having so much of what she wants in Denmark does Helga realize that the pleasure she values requires something less tangible. Though Denmark brings her all the things she desires, the Danes require her to play the role of someone else's desired object. In short, she is more on display than living a life. She resists this realization, but it presses in as she must consider the possibility that race is the reason she has not received a marriage proposal from her apparent suitor, the artist Axel Olsen. The narrator reports, "But in spite of his expressed interest and even delight in her exotic appearance, in spite of his constant attendance upon her, he gave no sign of the more personal kind of concern which . . . she had tried to secure" (79).

Helga's realization is upsetting because, in her pursuit of success (recognizable for its accompanying pleasure), she has been insisting upon fundamental differences between Denmark and the United States that she now doubts. When it occurs to Helga that Axel has not proposed because she is Negro, she "frowned on this thought, putting it furiously from her, because it disturbed her sense of security and permanence in her new life, pricked her self-assurance" (ibid.). Her sense of security had been based on believing Danish culture to be the exact opposite of American culture. Helga had convinced herself that the United States was the place "where they hated Negroes!" and "where Negroes were not people" (83). It was "where Negroes were allowed to be beggars only, of life, of happiness, of security" (84). The United States, she insists, is "where if one had Negro blood, one mustn't expect money, education, or sometimes even work whereby one might earn bread" (ibid.). The

United States is where black people cannot pursue, in a word, success, so it is disconcerting to admit that Denmark may not be different. After all, she has been secure in the thought that "the Danes had the right idea. To each his own milieu. Enhance what was already in one's possession. In America, Negroes sometimes talked loudly of this, but in their hearts they repudiated it. In their lives too. They didn't want to be like themselves. What they wanted, asked for, begged for, was to be like their white overlords. They were ashamed to be Negroes, but not ashamed to beg to be something else. Something inferior. Not quite genuine. Too bad!" (76).

Despite this assessment, not receiving a marriage proposal shows Helga that a welcome from Danish people does not translate into true belonging and community, and the text soon suggests that Helga's belief that African Americans do not want to be themselves applies more to her than to anyone else. When black dancers perform on a Danish stage, and everyone in Helga's party is captivated by them, she feels "shamed, betrayed, as if these pale pink and white people among whom she lived had suddenly been invited to look upon something in her which she had hidden away and wanted to forget" (85). She feels that "all along they had divined its presence, had known that in her was something, some characteristic, different from any that they themselves possessed" (ibid.). Most damning of all, "they had admired it, rated it as a precious thing, a thing to be enhanced, preserved. Why? She, Helga Crane, didn't admire it. She suspected that no Negroes, no Americans, did" (85). In this moment, Helga's discomfort derives from her inability to conceive of uniquely black qualities as admirable. Once again, she is aware of her desires, but she clings to ideas that rob her of joy.

Helga values pleasure, but her ideal is both satisfaction and the stability of belonging, so it pains her to realize that she has had only diversion in Denmark, not inclusion. The reality does not press upon her, though, until she learns that her Harlem roommate Anne Grey is getting married; at that point, she truly feels her "peacock" status. Earlier observations now become poignant. For example, her aloofness has been enhancing her allure in Denmark while that same "air of remoteness . . . had been in America so disastrous to her friendships" (76). It suddenly becomes clear that what she has in Copenhagen are not actual friendships. From her earliest days among her aunt and uncle's friends, the narrator highlights what Helga does not seem to grasp, that the women are kind despite the attention she draws from men because they feel "no need for jealousy"

(72). Helga is "not to be reckoned seriously in their scheme of things. True, she was attractive, unusual, in an exotic, almost savage way, but she wasn't one of them. She didn't at all count" (ibid.). In other words, Helga is a display piece, not an eligible woman.

No doubt, Helga had been attracted to Axel partly because a relationship with him would never come with the burdens of race motherhood. However, when deprived of a marriage that she could enjoy because it would be free of such obligations, she wonders what it really takes to secure her ideal of success, both pleasure and belonging. Nothing about Helga's circumstances had changed, but receiving Anne's letter about her upcoming nuptials brings clarity. The letter "added, somehow, to her discontentment, and to her growing dissatisfaction with her peacock's life" (83). Escaping uplift is quite appealing, but now, her peacock life offers much less pleasure. The letter is also upsetting because it mentions Dr. Anderson, now Anne's fiancé, and thoughts of him have always made Helga angry, though she does not understand why.

Even without clarity about her feelings for Dr. Anderson, Helga realizes in her letter-induced anguish that she has never stopped asking herself why she couldn't "be happy, content," and an answer begins to form. Namely, she has never ceased wondering if she should have given herself to marriage and race work, if she should have become a race mother. Trying to free herself of regret, she thinks, "Yes, if I hadn't come away, I'd be stuck in Harlem. Working every day of my life. Chattering about the race problem" (ibid.). Yet, the question of whether race motherhood is a life worth securing haunts her, even as she tries to assure herself that she has made the best decision. Ultimately, as much as she believes she deserves pleasure, she cannot shake the suspicion that having it requires accepting race motherhood because pleasure outside that paradigm will not last.

When Denmark no longer brings Helga pleasure and a sense of belonging, Larsen's text boldly demonstrates that black women's definitions of success could easily thrive if marriage were taken out of the equation. Indeed, *Quicksand* consistently reveals that women find marriage compelling only because race men cannot acknowledge desire without feeling shame, so a woman must conform to a "proper" relation if she wants shared sensuality. Larsen's text insists that black men committed to uplift see themselves in a particular light and simply cannot bear to have the image disturbed.

Quicksand demonstrates that black men devoted to uplifting the race remain focused on achievement, but the community conversation has shifted to define achievement more in terms of propriety than pleasure. Often robbed of access to propriety during slavery, Reconstruction, and post-Reconstruction, African Americans let intimacy and true connection guide them. Indeed, as discussed in Chapter 2, they sometimes encouraged each other to temper that impulse to prevent love from becoming an exploitable resource for white supremacy. However, by embracing race motherhood and elevating the black male worker, discussions among African Americans had become invested in propriety to a degree that sacrifices women, which is what earlier community conversations had worked to *prevent* Sappho from doing.

Black women characters' aversion to marriage becomes clear as they navigate race men's rigidly patriarchal agendas. For instance, if Helga had married James Vayle, it would have been because he could not deny his passion despite his commitment to propriety. Though James had easily agreed to postpone their marriage because he had been unhappy with Helga's failure to conform to Naxos, "something held him, a something against which he was powerless" (12). True, "the idea that she was in but one nameless way necessary to him filled her with a sensation amounting almost to shame. And yet his mute helplessness against that ancient appeal by which she held him pleased her and fed her vanity—gave her a feeling of power" (ibid.). Especially because Helga had not been in love with him but simply "expected to love him, after their marriage" (ibid.), their union would not have been dangerous in the way her mother's surrender had been. "Certainly, she had never loved him overwhelmingly, not, for example, as her mother must have loved her father" (27), but the personal power Helga had gained from this dynamic could not change the broader context, so fearlessness had not been an option, and Helga remained "subtly aware of possibilities she herself couldn't predict" (12). Marriage would have primarily addressed James Vayle's simultaneous inability to ignore his desire for Helga and his refusal to acknowledge it without a proper relation. Realizing how little her own feelings would factor, Helga prioritizes her own desires enough to avoid the trap of propriety that would only make her feelings less and less relevant. Not unlike Naxos itself, James Vayle could offer stability, but the rules he values would leave no room for Helga's individuality and pleasure.

Larsen similarly suggests the widowed Anne Grey would have happily remained unmarried, but because Dr. Anderson is rigid, marriage is the price for having gotten close to him. Anne understands that "it was the voice of Robert Anderson's inexorable conscience that had been the chief factor in bringing about her second marriage—his ascetic protest against the sensuous, the physical" (96). If she wants to experience sensual, physical intimacy, which she clearly does, then recognizing the circumstances that would put Dr. Anderson's mind at ease allows her to have agency while grappling with constraints she would rather avoid.

When dealing with race men, New Negro women will have to confront race motherhood, but Larsen suggests that even if they must play the role of race mother to some degree, New Negro women are not exactly happy about it. Furthermore, the artists among them are committed to arguing for the importance of questioning the community's apparent consensus. Anne sees that, especially in Helga's presence, "underneath [Dr. Anderson's] well managed section . . . was another, a vagrant primitive groping toward something shocking and frightening to the cold asceticism of his reason" (ibid.). Anne therefore becomes determined to "carry out what she considered her obligation to him, keep him undisturbed, unhumiliated" (97). Essentially, Anne marries Dr. Anderson because she knows he cannot with dignity share his sensuous side with her unless their relationship is proper. Once married, she continues to focus on protecting him from his own desires. Anne proves to be a New Negro woman who takes on some characteristics of the race mother, but Larsen underscores her reluctance to do so. The idea that women should happily sacrifice for and submit to men is questioned, suggesting that those in the community conversation who insisted that such sacrifices are natural and right were challenged as black women believed their desires—their full humanity—should factor into conceptions of black achievement.

After identifying through James Vayle and Dr. Anderson the achievement-focused race man's struggle with balancing passion and propriety, Larsen presents it once more, and because Helga yields to propriety enough to become entangled, this struggle irreversibly changes the course of her life. Though he is married to Anne and Helga is *not* pursuing him, Dr. Anderson grabs Helga at a party one night and kisses her. She resists, but not for long. Afterward, she cannot put the encounter out of her mind. She is absorbed in thinking "not so much of the man whose arms had held her as of the ecstasy which had flooded her. Even the recollection brought a little onrush of emotion that made her sway a little" (106). She therefore decides to explore "to the end that unfamiliar path into which she had strayed" (107). Having thus decided, she feels "an odd sense of elation," which only increases after they have arranged to see each other. In fact, "it had seemed to her that she hadn't been so happy, so exalted, in years, if ever. All night, all day, she had mentally prepared herself for the coming consummation; physically too, spending hours before the mirror" (ibid.). However, once they meet in the lobby of her hotel, Dr. Anderson apologizes for having kissed her and blames his behavior on the "rotten cocktails" he drank at the party (108). Helga feels "belittled and ridiculed," and after trying to hide these feelings, she "savagely" slaps him. Upon reflection, she comes to appreciate what Anne had already understood about her husband. Helga realizes she had been silly "to close her eyes to all the indications that pointed to the fact that no matter what the intensity of his feelings or desires might be, he was not the sort of man who would for any reason give up one particle of his own good opinion of himself. Not even for her" (109).

Authentic feelings do not matter to a race man; only propriety does. Race men treat pleasure as an enemy to progress; they have taken it out of their definition of success. New Negro women must allow awareness of this fact to help them navigate relationships with such men. Anything less is not smart, Larsen warns, and can lead to "possibilities she herself couldn't predict" (12).

Still eager to achieve her ideal of both pleasure and stability, but with greater clarity about uplift men, Helga makes the life-changing decision to forge a permanent connection from a spontaneous intimate encounter. Frazzled after Dr. Anderson's rejection, Helga finds herself caught in a rainstorm. Seeking refuge, she stumbles into a church and eventually surrenders to the ecstasy of religious experience, which leads her down an unfamiliar path that brings her to a destination she would not have chosen. She has a conversion experience in the church and goes unconscious. Once she recovers, Reverend Mr. Pleasant Green walks her to her hotel. She notices that he, like James Vayle and Dr. Anderson, has a desire for her with which he is not comfortable, and she knows it gives her some power over him. In fact, she could sense in him "a mind striving to be calm." Still, it is also "a mind that was certain that it was secure because it was concerned only with things of the soul, spiritual things, which to him meant religious things" (116). While recognizing her power, she also wonders if she had in previous situations "missed the supreme secret of life" (117). As her mind races, she is appalled at what she is on the verge of considering and where it might lead, so she "deliberately stopped thinking" (ibid.). The next morning, after she has consummated her relationship with the reverend, she feels good and wonders if religion is the reason for this pleasure. She then becomes anxious because happiness and serenity never seem to stay for long. She then realizes, "all I've ever had in life has been things—except just this one time" (ibid.). The narrator suggests Helga has greater clarity: "Things, she realized, hadn't been, weren't, enough for her. She'd have to have something else besides. It all came back to that old question of happiness. Surely this was it" (ibid.). Almost immediately, Helga questions "her ability to retain, to bear, this happiness *at such a cost as she must pay for it*. There was, she knew, no getting round that" (ibid., emphasis added). The issue to face is black male propriety: "The man's agitation and sincere conviction of sin had been too evident, too illuminating" (ibid.). Helga therefore consoles herself that "it was a chance at stability, at permanent happiness, that she meant to take. She had let so many other things, other chances, escape her. And anyway there was God, He would perhaps make it come out all right" (117–18). Helga decides she will be married that very day, and she knows she will not fail to secure her desired outcome. "How could he, a naive creature like that, hold out against her? If she pretended to distress? To fear? To remorse? He couldn't" (118).

Helga is not interested in marriage, but she sees it as a "chance at stability, at permanent happiness." That is, she considers it a gamble, but she has never gambled deliberately to secure pleasure and stability at the same time. She now believes she has always pursued one and lost sight of the other. This time, she lunges for both, convinced the sensual pleasures of the previous night represent the something-deeper-than-things that has always eluded her. Furthermore, she assumes permanent access to it requires paying the price set by propriety. Given the death-in-life her marriage to Reverend Green ultimately brings—the story ends with Helga in a cycle of childbirth and illness—the novel suggests that marriage may indeed be the only way to enjoy certain pleasures, but it is an incredibly dangerous access route. The benevolent patriarch comes with baggage that makes his partner's desires (and sometimes his own) irrelevant. Larsen therefore ensures that the archive bears the imprint of the New Negro woman's substantial questions about whether stability, propriety, and marriage are worth it.

Larsen foregrounds Helga's desires throughout the narrative, and this emphasis proves significant because the novel intervenes in the community conversation on success while it disregards black women unless they devote themselves as facilitators for black men and boys and forsake their own pleasure. It is important that, by the time Helga marries Reverend Green, she has decided to conform in precisely the ways she had refused to do for James Vayle. The difference? With Green, she has allowed herself erotic pleasure, which she believes constitutes happiness beyond "things." Helga seems to prize sensory satisfaction more than material possessions, and she experiences such satisfaction, it seems, only with physical intimacy.[11] When Helga gambles by submitting to marriage to gain lasting access to these pleasures, Larsen underscores Helga's determination to have both pleasure and stability. Despite the community's insistence that she settle for one or the other, she had not relinquished the belief that she deserves both, that truly making oneself at home requires both.

Unfortunately, Helga gambles and loses. She ends up convinced that she has "ruined her life" and that "she had . . . been a fool. The damnedest kind of a fool" (134). As she endures her misery, she is especially resentful of the woman whom the townspeople had always expected Reverend Green to marry and who shamelessly flaunts her desire to be his wife. The narrator reports, "And more than all the rest [Helga] hated the jangling Clementine Richardson, with her provocative smirks, because she had not succeeded in marrying the preacher and thus saving her, Helga, from that crowning idiocy" (135).

Race motherhood emerged in the community conversation to preclude such questions, but black women's cultural production nevertheless asks, *How would black success be defined if women's desires were taken into account?* Larsen's *Quicksand* suggests that true success involves exactly what American society most withholds from women, especially women of color: pleasure. Yet, while placing in the archive a text shaped by questions about whether women can have both pleasure and stability, Larsen above all offers caveats. Throughout the novel, Helga wonders why anyone would bring children into the world only to be mistreated,[12] so she is not delighted when she contributes "the fourth little dab of amber humanity . . . to a despised race" (128). She is therefore relieved when one of them dies shortly after birth (132). Still, the narrative closes thusly, "And hardly had she left her bed and become able to walk again without pain . . . when she began to have her fifth child" (136). Helga lands in these miserable circumstances because she had always believed in her right to pleasure, and she eventually wagers that she would not have to forsake stability for that pleasure. These are bold New Negro woman beliefs, and Larsen suggests that holding them means wrestling with race motherhood. *Quicksand* insists upon the validity and importance of the New Negro woman's resistance to becoming a race mother—even if the battle leaves her feeling defeated. Without her presence, the archive and the repertoire of the community conversation on success is incomplete.

A House Is Not a Home

African Americans meet stated standards, but the nation robs them of the material security that matches their achievements, so they have often developed nuanced definitions of success. As historian Deborah Gray White and others have shown, being middle-class in black communities has gestured more toward a "style of life" than income (*Too Heavy* 70). African Americans with middle-class aspirations formed an "aristocracy of the soul," perhaps highlighting the denigration of their achievements in the United States as well as the erasure of their African heritage as "kings and queens."[13] Noting the investment in cultivating culturally specific standards for success, literary historian Robert Reid-Pharr has argued that nineteenth-century African American literature is marked by the idea that creating and sustaining black identities requires building black homes. Many intellectuals insisted that, if the race was to succeed in shedding the degradation and shame of slavery, their brethren must "sever their sexual, romantic and familial ties to whites" (116). In the 1930s, while engaging the cultural implications of the New Negro and the New Woman, Zora Neale Hurston's most famous novel *Their Eyes Were Watching God* continued the tradition of nineteenth-century works structured around the creation of "purely" black homes. Though most scholars examine the narrative as a love story in which the female protagonist comes to voice, the novel contributes to the community conversation on black success by following a protagonist who identifies and grapples with the distinction between having a marriage and experiencing love and the tension between having a house and making a home. Appreciating the differences, Janie defines success in terms of pleasure and connection. That is, she pursues love and home, despite the nation's investment in preventing black women from attaining either one . . . and violently pouncing when they achieve both. Indeed, the journey taken by the dialect-speaking Janie is especially revealing because, like those around her, she remains driven by her definition of success. As she engages in practices of making-oneself-at-home in both working-class and middle-class enclaves, her quest reveals how similar they can be, given all African Americans' preoccupation with achievement.

Protagonist Janie Crawford's investment in pleasure and connection first becomes evident not with her romantic relationships but her relationship with her grandmother "Nanny." Readers learn of Janie's journey through three marriages when she returns to Eatonville and shares her story with her friend Phoeby, but in recounting all that has brought her to this point, Janie begins with her childhood. Not knowing her father or mother, Janie was reared by her grandmother, who encountered domestic constraints that shaped Janie's experiences.

With their house in the backyard of her grandmother's white employers, "Ah never called ma Grandma nothin' but Nanny, 'cause dat's what everybody on de place called her" (8). Janie also remembers, "us lived dere havin' fun till de chillum at school got to teasin' me 'bout livin' in de white folks' back-yard" (9). The novel gestures toward community definitions of success as African Americans believed this living arrangement to be too similar to slavery. Even at play time, outside of school, the children would pretend that "they couldn't play wid nobody dat lived on premises" (ibid.). Janie's grandmother had acknowledged the logic of such responses by working to secure a house not located in whites' backyard, even if they were "quality" white people (Hurston 19, 8).

Yet, as she looks back on her life while speaking to Phoeby, Janie seems to wonder if Nanny's effort had been motivated by respectability or by the barriers to intimacy that the living arrangement created between her and her granddaughter. The more she recalls having been forced to marry Logan Killicks, the more she believes her grandmother had always prioritized respectability over love and connection. Janie is determined to engage in practices of making-oneself-at-home against the odds the nation stacks against black women, but she will adopt strategies that differ from those modeled by Nanny.

Nanny tells Janie that black women serve as the mules of the world, and though this scene is often referenced, many have overlooked its narrative function: marking the moment Janie begins defining success in terms of pleasure. Rather than accept the role of mule of the world— a working-class version of race motherhood (so prominent in *Quicksand*)—Janie prioritizes her own desires. In defiance of the know-your-place aggression of the whore stereotype and the sexual harassment and assault it justified, Janie joins Larsen's Helga in exemplifying the New Negro woman's aversion to becoming a race mother. Especially because the nation's racism and sexism have prevented her from becoming the influential preacher of her dreams, Nanny invests in her ability to guide Janie away from pleasure and toward propriety. From Nanny's perspective, propriety is more available to her granddaughter than it had been to earlier generations, but even as a teenager, Janie has her own ideas about what constitutes a good life, so she questions what "proper" domesticity will achieve for women. Still, Janie's problems with her grandmother's worldview become clearest, not in her relationship with Logan Killicks, whom Nanny forced her to marry, but in her relationship with her second husband Joe Starks, because he is exactly the kind of man her grandmother would have chosen for her.

By the time Janie leaves Logan Killicks to elope with Joe Starks, her definition of success is firmly rooted in pleasure and connection. She is determined to inhabit a home that prioritizes intimacy over propriety, but through Joe, Hurston continues the presence in Janie's life of Nanny's philosophy. Nanny's decisions had been based on her desire to be a powerful voice in the world, and Joe is driven by the same goal, so when he meets Janie, he is on his way to the newly formed black town of Eatonville, Florida. Once there, Joe becomes mayor and builds a store before building his and Janie's house. This decision proves to be telling, as Joe's definition of success revolves around propriety, often at the expense of pleasure and intimacy. Voicing concern, Janie says she looks forward to when public obligations end because they keep the couple "in uh kinda strain" (45). Their intimate connection suffers from their public connection. She says more directly, "it keeps us in some way we ain't natural wid one 'nother. You'se always off talkin' and fixin' things, and Ah feels lak Ah'm jus' markin' time" (43). Joe's concern with propriety, which emphasizes outside appearances, does not waver. He responds by reiterating his definition of success: "Ah told you in de very first beginnin' dat Ah aimed tuh be uh big voice. You oughta be glad, 'cause dat makes uh big woman outa you" (ibid.). Janie's problem is not that Joe is away doing things but that the assumption that her place is in the home means they cannot be true partners, busy "talkin' and fixin' things" together—as readers have every reason to believe couples in *Iola Leroy* and *Contending Forces* do.

By representing several situations in which Joe excludes Janie from activities because she is a woman, Hurston highlights both characters' preoccupation with pursuing success as well as the stark difference in how they define it. For instance, the townspeople make a ritual of telling stories about Matt Bonner's neglected mule. It is entertaining, it allows individuals to showcase their creativity and storytelling skill, and it bonds the community. Yearning to be a part of the community and not simply a spectator from atop Joe's pedestal, Janie has always wanted to participate, but Joe forbids it. He intones, "You's Mrs. Mayor Starks, Janie. I god. Ah can't see what uh woman uh you' *stability* would want tuh be treasurin' all dat gum-grease from folks dat don't even own de house dey sleep in" (51, emphasis added). With this, Joe reveals his assumption that the external aspects of being his wife matter most; the love connection to which Janie's title refers is secondary. Her being his wife is more about the status it brings, not the intimacy they share. One might say it is more about the house they inhabit than the home they make within it. Joe's comment also reveals that, of the things he can provide, he believes the most valuable have little to do with him and his love. He assumes his most treasured offerings are status and the "stability" that comes with material wealth. If he could see that intimacy means more to Janie, he might have recognized the importance of investing in the pleasure of connecting to each other, rather than in appearances.

Because his sense of accomplishment depends on his wife's "proper" relation to him, Joe makes a habit of publicly disrespecting Janie. She then begins "thinking about the inside state of her marriage" and realizes that what Joe wants most is her submission (67). Not ready to end the relationship, "she pressed her teeth together and learned to hush. The spirit of the marriage left the bedroom and took to living in the parlor. It was there to shake hands whenever company came to visit, but it never went back inside the bedroom again" (ibid.). For Joe, this shift away from the bedroom is not as disturbing as deterioration of their parlor relationship would have been. In his conception of achievement, which resembles Nanny's, propriety takes precedence. If intimacy does not take the "proper" form, it is nearly useless. It's not enough to have a wife; he must have a submissive wife.

The tension between propriety and pleasure, between having a house and making a home, becomes clearest when, after twenty years and the deterioration of their union, Janie speaks from her heart at Joe's death-bed. She explains, "Ah run off tuh keep house wid you in uh wonderful way. But you wasn't satisfied wid me de way Ah was. Naw! Maw own mind had tuh be squeezed and crowded out tuh make room for yours in me" (82). As when Helga Crane flees Naxos and her fiancé, the black woman novelist demonstrates that New Negro women recognize that men who see themselves as race leaders invest in marriage because it conveys respectability, not because it brings joy to the individuals within it. Joe's insistence upon Janie's submission may have served outside appearances—keeping neighbors envious and in awe—but it did not nurture their bond. Insisting that the parlor be maintained in certain ways ultimately kills what could have flourished elsewhere in the house to make it a home.

Hurston has Janie acknowledge that the propriety that aligns with race motherhood damages the head of household as much as those made to submit to him. Quite compassionately, Janie declares upon Joe's death, "Dis sittin' in de rulin' chair is been hard on Jody" (83). The rules he worshipped applied to him as much as to his view of her. He would not have thought himself a good mayor, good husband, or real man if he had not prevented her from participating in certain activities. After all, it was his duty to "pour honor all over her" (58) and to make sure he owned the house in which they sleep. If he could not do that, how could she love him? The patriarchy shaping his definition of success made no room for the possibility that she could.

Ultimately, Janie has compassion for Joe because she sees the violence done when one defines accomplishment in ways that forsake pleasure. She can pity Joe for all that his rules had robbed him of, because she sees that the destruction amounted to "what had happened in the making of a voice out of a man" (83). As with Nanny, wanting to become a public voice leads to an underappreciation of private bonds and intimacies. Nanny and Joe both invest more in having a house than in making a home.

Their Eyes acknowledges the logic of being house-focused while pursuing success, but it also highlights the need to find room outside of that logic when Janie becomes a widow. Having inherited the house and the store, Janie is approached by would-be suitors and would-be matchmakers, including her most trusted friend Phoeby, who encourages a union with a funeral director from a nearby town. At nearly 40 years old, Janie has been enjoying a relationship with the poor, 25-year-old Tea Cake, and Phoeby assumes it is harmless because she is confident about her own matchmaking efforts. However, her husband explains how vicious the talk in town has been, and Phoeby decides to intervene (106).

Because Phoeby's genuine concern is based on common conceptions of accomplishment, Hurston places a spotlight on just how much one must question community wisdom to value intangibles, such as love and pleasure. Being honest about why she thinks Janie should marry the funeral director, Phoeby explains, "He got somethin' tuh put long side uh what you got and dat make it more better" (108).[14] In addition to what he can offer materially, "he's endurable," Phoeby insists (ibid.). Noting the importance of pleasure, she does not pretend he is desirable, but "endurable" should approximate "desirable" when combined with material comfort and the stability of social status. Indeed, what most concerns Phoeby is the risk Janie is accepting with Tea Cake. His lack of financial resources to "put long side" of Janie's only increases the likelihood that he is after her heart for what he can get from her bank account. Janie has considered these issues but insists she is not gambling any more than anyone does when getting married.[15] Besides wagering one's heart and material possessions, marriage is risky because it "always changes folks." In fact, it sometimes "brings out dirt and meanness dat even de person didn't know they had in 'em theyselves" (ibid.). Aware of these possibilities, Janie is willing to try marriage with Tea Cake because he is no Joe Starks, and that fact gives their union a chance. Ultimately, "Dis ain't no business proposition, and no race after property and titles. Dis is uh love game. Ah done lived Grandma's way, now Ah means tuh live mine" (ibid.). With this, Hurston establishes the clearest link between Nanny and Joe Starks and the degree to which Janie pursues success in terms of what their philosophies discounted: pleasure, individuality, love, joy, partnership, companionship. Making a home that facilitates pleasure and connection remains her goal.

Janie joins Tea Cake in Jacksonville, and they marry immediately, as planned, but their life as husband and wife truly takes shape once they move to the muck in the Florida Everglades (111, 123) and make a home with limited resources. There, they live as Tea Cake can provide, agreeing to forget that Janie has a house in Eatonville and money in the bank. Only what they do and have together matters, so homemaking is put in the service of intimacy and pleasure. Housing for workers is available on a first-come, first-served basis, and they arrive early enough to claim space in "the quarters." Quite happily, "Janie fussed around the shack making a home while Tea Cake planted beans" (124). When his workday ends, they go fishing together. Later, while waiting for the work of picking season, Tea Cake plays his guitar for Janie, but this is not enough to fill the time, so he suggests they hunt together. As is their pattern, Janie is willing to learn new skills, and Tea Cake has no rules (as Joe had) about what she should not do because she is a woman, so he teaches her how to shoot a pistol, a shot gun, and a rifle, and "she got to be a better shot than Tea Cake" (125). Together, they hunt and "besides having fun together," they gather items to sell in Palm Beach (ibid.). In short, their homemaking on the muck includes not only making the shack cozy but also spending time together and strengthening their connection while providing for their sustenance. Money and material possessions are not ignored, but they serve the partnership, not appearances. Their life together is characterized by the elements of success that Janie's experience has taught her to value most.

Confirming the centrality of their bond as Janie makes herself at home, when harvest season starts and Janie spends her days in the shack, she takes joy in preparing Tea Cake's favorite meals and desserts. And, "sometimes she'd straighten out the two-room house and take the rifle and have fried rabbit for supper when Tea Cake got home" (126). "She didn't leave him itching and scratching in his work clothes, either. The kettle of hot water was already waiting when he got in" (ibid.). Tea Cake begins coming home at all hours, admitting he misses Janie when they are apart all day. He asks if she would work in the fields too, "lak de rest uh de women" (127). He had worried that she would think he was trying to get out of taking care of her, but she is happy to join him. Working together allows them to have fun throughout the day, and the adjustment to their routine includes Tea Cake helping with dinner (ibid.). Their homemaking shifts, but labor is not rigidly divided based on gender. They also make the shack a home because it is full of their mutual, storytelling friends at night (ibid.). Janie is part of the community and enjoys it, and this fact only strengthens the bond with her husband.

Janie has every reason to believe she has achieved her ideal of pleasure and connection, but Hurston uses Tea Cake to reveal that middle-class race men are not alone in defining success in ways that value women's subordination more than connection. A neighbor becomes determined to set Janie up with her brother. Tea Cake overhears the woman's disrespectful plan as well as Janie's rejection of it, but that does not settle the issue for him. Without knowing Tea Cake overheard the rude neighbor, Janie soon pays for the affront. Tea Cake beats Janie, "not because her behavior justified his jealously, but it relieved that awful fear inside him. Being able to whip her reassured him in possession" (140). According to the narrator, it was "no brutal beating at all. He just slapped her around a bit to show he was boss" (ibid.). He clearly defines achievement as Joe had, caring more about outside appearances than the quality of their connection.

Hurston's narrator notes the public function of the beating, making unmistakable the corruption of true partnership and intimate connection. The beating becomes the talk of the town the next day, and "it aroused a sort of envy in both men and women. The way he petted and pampered her as if those two or three face slaps had nearly killed her made the women see visions, and the helpless way she hung on him made men dream dreams" (ibid.). With this, there is a clear understanding that men should be dominant and women dependent and submissive. This is a working-class environment, but the logic aligns with race motherhood and its elevation of black men and boys. If this were a well-to-do setting, rather than the muck, the same ideas would manifest as an investment in ensuring higher wages for men and encouraging women to take pride in being provided for financially.

With the community condoning the dynamic expressed by Tea Cake's slaps and Janie's helplessness, Tea Cake becomes even more invested in defining success in terms of a masculinist posture, and the effect on their relationship proves enduring. When the beating becomes the talk of the town and men openly envy him, Tea Cake further paints himself as king of the castle. He reveals that he met Janie while she was living in "uh big fine house" and that she has plenty of money in the bank. Nevertheless, she works on the muck because "Janie is wherever *Ah* wants tuh be. Dat's de kind uh wife she is and Ah love her for it" (141). Unfortunately, her being that kind of wife is not enough; he insists upon showing to others (through Janie's bruises) the kind of wife she is. It had not mattered that he heard her affirm her loyalty to him to the rude neighbor. Hurston thereby demonstrates that even a loving union like Janie's and Tea Cake's is vulnerable to the tension created by the pressure to care more about the outside appearance than the inside quality of a marriage.

Janie's eventual separation from Tea Cake must be understood as the result of capitulating to patriarchal ideas about how men and women should relate. Janie ends up shooting Tea Cake in self-defense because he is hallucinating from having been bit by a rabid dog, and these circumstances arise from his increasing refusal to make decisions with Janie as a partner. When a dangerous storm is heading toward the muck, Janie notices the Seminoles migrating, but she is never consulted about whether she and Tea Cake should leave. A friend stops by and asks Tea Cake about his and Janie's plans, given that "De Indians gahn east," but Tea Cake is dismissive: "Indians don't know much uh nothin', tuh tell de truth. Else dey'd own dis country still" (148). Then, when the storm is bad enough to scare Tea Cake and he insists they try to outrun it, not only does he feel defeated when they cannot, he is also dogged by the fear that Janie is wishing she had stayed in her big house and not married him. She assures him that she is simply a woman in a storm with her husband (151), but clinging to expected roles prevents Tea Cake from believing her. His inability to find comfort in her loving words sets the stage for his confrontation with the rabid dog. Feeling like less than a man because he has not provided the fine house he is sure she now misses, he pushes himself to exhaustion, trying to be her hero in other ways.

Being her hero perpetuates a pattern of not being her partner. After enduring a grueling journey through the storm, they rest in a house, but Tea Cake believes it might flood, so they should venture out again. Reaching the Six-mile Bridge into Palm Beach becomes their goal. Once there, the shelter they find is good for sleeping but not for living, and Tea Cake wonders if Janie regrets being with him. Once again, she reassures him; this time, she more forcefully articulates her dependence to express her love. Before meeting him, Janie says, she had expected to stand still but "you come 'long and made something outa me. So Ah'm thankful fuh anything we come through together" (158). As much as she highlights the importance of going through things together, Tea Cake's need to maintain a masculinist posture prevents him from fully absorbing her words. She tells him not to go into the streets because whites will force him to work without pay. Here, Janie shows awareness of how the small black victory of having survived will attract white aggression; meanwhile, Tea Cake seems oblivious to the ongoing violence that structures the nation whose disregard for the Seminoles he had mimicked. She explains, "Dey claims dey's after de unemployed, but dey ain't bein' too particular about whether you'se employed or not. You stay in dis house" (161). He leaves anyway. As predicted, he is forced at gunpoint to bury dead bodies. Finally, he runs away, knowing Janie must be worried sick.

It is within the context of his making decisions for them, rather than in partnership with Janie, that readers must understand Tea Cake's descent into rabid hallucinations. It all arises from his feeling that he must be a hero after making so many mistakes. When Janie must shoot him in self-defense, Tea Cake not only breaks their bond but also places her in the position of being arrested and appearing in court, where jurors pass judgment on their relationship (176).

Because abiding by traditional ideas about the role one should play in romantic relationships leads to the most damaging decisions, Hurston suggests that valuing propriety over pleasure places unnecessary limits on love. There is consistently a tension between a house and a home, between marriage and love, and this tension centers on how intensely rules factor into decision-making. Thus, because Janie's second husband Joe (in concert with Nanny) had particular ideas about what makes a proper home, those ideas create dynamics in which a certain kind of dwelling feels required, but the bonds inside suffer. However, because Janie's definition of success leads her to care less about the structure she inhabits than about the bonds nurtured within it, she makes a home of a shack. Ultimately, the difference between a house and home is whether the opinions of those outside matter enough to affect the experiences of those inside—if "they" take priority over "we." The same proves true of the difference between marriage and love. Are the couple's decisions based more on how "they" see the union or how "we" do?

Hurston ends the novel as Janie offers the clearest articulation of the damage done by propriety. Janie tells Phoeby that others may judge the love she shared with Tea Cake because it did not resemble theirs or because it did not look the way people believe love should, but she has found that love is not like a grindstone—doing the same thing to all it touches (182). If love is not like a grindstone, marriage certainly is. Marriage insists upon putting all women in a subordinate position and all men into a dominant one. As a result, as Janie learned with Joe, it damages those who claim the "ruling chair" as well as those they expect to rule. This pattern holds with Tea Cake as well. He begins the relationship without rigid ideas about what a woman should and should not do, but he remains aware of the dominant role men "should" have, and he bows to the insecurity that not fitting that mold produces in him. The more he adopts a masculinist posture, the more Janie submits to reassure him, and the more they let the grindstone of marriage determine how they relate to each other.

Marriage is like a grindstone, but love is not. Janie declares that love is like the sea; it changes with each shore it touches. That is, love would have honored each individual in the relationship, allowing them to build together whatever serves their bond best. Hurston offers a glimpse of this possibility via Janie's and Tea Cake's homemaking on the muck. Because it does not last, Hurston's text places a warning in the community conversation, encouraging African Americans to continue questioning how they are defining success. Just as a house must fit certain structural criteria visible to outsiders, but a home can be made in a house, a tenement, or a shack, only certain configurations are considered marriages, but love can thrive in all kinds of unions. Indeed, being legible as a marriage—because it brings outside standards of accomplishment even more to bear—can damage the emotional connections that might otherwise simply ebb and flow and gain strength like the sea. Like love, a home can seem less tangible and measurable because its configurations are not predetermined. However, its freedom from rules (that have nothing to do with the individuals inside it) can make it stronger—if those individuals can manage to keep the grindstone of propriety at bay.

*　*　*

Nella Larsen's *Quicksand* and Zora Neale Hurston's *Their Eyes Were Watching God* feature protagonists who pursue success in terms of creating lives that include pleasure and emotional connection, not just propriety and community service. In other words, Larsen's Helga Crane and Hurston's Janie Crawford are New Negro women who do not find race motherhood compelling. Larsen's and Hurston's investment in writing novels acknowledging the New Negro woman's importance to the community conversation on black success suggests that they shared their characters' conviction about black women's right to pleasure. To hold on to their belief that they deserve pleasure constitutes a defiant victory in the face of the whore stereotype that facilitated black women's sexual vulnerability. And this vulnerability was designed to answer various achievements, including basic survival and self-regard as well as mobility and migration. To black women's victories (big and small), the United States always has an answer: *you are nothing.*

Larsen and Hurston offer protagonists who refuse to forsake pleasure. They represent women who internalized Hopkins's message even if Sappho struggled to do so. Importantly, because they offer such intimate portraits of individual women, these texts demonstrate that the know-your-place aggression that answered black women's successes did not emanate from outside the community alone. These texts insist that the apparent consensus about race motherhood being a woman's highest achievement must also be examined.

While previous generations embraced homemaking efforts that allowed them to reclaim what slavery took, the ideology of race motherhood helped create hierarchies within black communities that some women authors insisted needed interrogation. In particular, some encouraged skepticism regarding definitions of success that hinge on the creation of homes based on traditional marriage. Whereas domestic novels like *Iola Leroy* and *Contending Forces* highlighted the joys of legitimizing marriages, simply emphasizing the need to put love in service to the race, New Negro–era texts exhibit less faith in the correlation between love and marriage. While love's undeniable role in sustaining communities from slavery to freedom infused black domestic novels with faith about the compatibility of love and marriage, the possibility that marriage could be based on something other than love shaped later works. Complex questions therefore permeate black women's novels of the 1920s and 1930s: *Is marriage desirable in itself? Or does its desirability depend on certain characteristics, such as romantic passion or egalitarian partnership?* While romance and partnership were assumed for the couples portrayed in black domestic fiction,[16] New Negro novels question this inevitability, especially because they feature women negotiating relationships with men committed to uplifting the race *by being patriarchs*. Perhaps most powerfully, these texts wonder, *might black success be defined differently if communities acknowledged women's desires to be something other than mothers and wives?* Claiming her position as a beloved wife was empowering for Sappho, but New Negro women characters yearn for other options.

Larsen's Helga Crane breaks her engagement to James Vayle because it is clear that their union will make no space for her individuality and because joy and pleasure will not be factors. She tries to give herself the beauty and pleasure she seeks by working in Chicago and New York, but her pleasure is fleeting, so she continues her quest in Denmark. Again, she succeeds in grasping pleasure but becomes increasingly committed to having both pleasure and permanence. Because she miscalculates as she lunges for both by marrying a preacher, Larsen makes her journey into an urgent warning. Especially because propriety and marriage might produce absolute misery, why not give oneself the chance at pleasure? Surely, there cannot be real success without it. Hurston also offers a character who gives traditional domesticity a serious try, given Janie's twenty-year marriage to Joe Starks. While they enjoy social status, Hurston seems to acknowledge the reward precisely in order to highlight what was lost in attaining it. Janie and her husband have outside respect but no inside quality of connection. The unmistakable message of Janie's story is that propriety, and the social stability that may come with it, are nothing compared to the intangibles that cannot be so easily measured. After all, men who adopt the belief that they are nothing without dominance cannot feel the love and acceptance the women in their lives offer.

Together, Helga and Janie survive in the archive to gesture toward the dangers of placing more emphasis on propriety, "things," and houses than on joy and a love-filled home. They do not always assume that their happiness and worth depend on "subordination to strong, benevolent, capable patriarchs" (Chapman 57). Yet, despite having resisted the role, both Helga and Janie spend time devoted to race motherhood, so their stories urge the community to consider more complex definitions of success. These authors encourage community members to develop conceptions of achievement that can accommodate black women's whole selves, not just that which places them in service to others, as mules of the world.

Home as Human Right and Black Power

African American migration represented the success of mobility, so white Americans recommitted to know-your-place aggression throughout the 1910s and 1920s by answering black accomplishment with race riots in urban centers. World War II began in 1939, and supplying other countries with military material pulled the United States out of the Great Depression. African Americans again migrated in remarkable numbers, partly attracted by well-paying war industry jobs. White Americans responded by attacking black people throughout the 1940s for enjoying access to employment, housing, and recreation.[1] With the majority of African Americans living in urban spaces by the 1950s and 1960s, they had once again survived (and sometimes thrived), despite the violence they faced. White brutality continued, and as always, it took many forms. Because hostility emerged in every arena providing access to accomplishment, historian Carol Anderson calls it *White Rage*.

Corroborating Anderson's insight, I contend that know-your-place aggression is the best lens through which to view the years following the 1954 *Brown v. Board of Education* decision. The court's ruling to end school segregation was a hard-won victory for black attorneys, who often faced verbal and physical violence for being out of their "proper" place.[2] It overturned *Plessy v. Ferguson*, whose "separate but equal" logic had created the climate in which racial violence flourished since 1896. Securing their desired decision in *Brown* required black lawyers' exceptional intellect, steadfast labor, and optimistic goodwill, but besides enduring abuse on the way to this victory, these lawyers and their communities saw *Brown* answered with more aggression, as many states simply did not comply.

In May 1955, the court issued *Brown II*, which called for states to act with "all deliberate speed," and this set the stage for more opportunities to remind African Americans of their "proper" place, because the only thing deliberate and speedy was the denial of black people's right to the resources enjoyed by citizens. As historians Robert Harris and Rosalyn Terborg-Penn explain, "The Ku Klux Klan used violence and intimidation, while the White Citizens Councils that were organized in the mid-1950s often employed economic retaliation against African Americans who tried to vote or to send their children to previously all-white schools" (27). The *know your place!* message was clear: "White Citizen Council members turned down mortgages, called in loans, denied insurance, and even refused medical care to African Americans who tried to enjoy their rights" (ibid. 27). Matching the actions of ordinary white citizens, politicians signed the "Southern Manifesto" in 1956, promising to prevent integration. At the same time, national rhetoric added insult to injury by insisting that black people were citizens while discrimination continued in education, employment, and housing. Indeed, any progress African Americans made despite these barriers was used to deem the country a model worth emulating, unlike the Soviet Union.[3] National declarations about equal opportunity notwithstanding, while federal programs promoted home ownership, African Americans were opposed in their every effort to secure desirable (or even decent) housing.

Still focused on securing their definitions of success more than on the opposition meeting them at every turn, African Americans in the 1950s and 1960s kept working toward their goals. Doing so continued to make them targets. Historians and cultural critics easily recognize the violence African Americans face for failing to conform to dominant values—for example, when they suffer for being "punks, bulldaggers, and welfare queens"[4]—but those whose ambitions align with mainstream values are no less attacked.

What happens when one understands the pursuit of so-called "integration" not in terms of protest or resistance but in terms of accomplishing goals and claiming resources? After all, "integration" is really about getting white people to stop hoarding everything desirable. What happens when what scholars have called "civil rights" are viewed as human rights, pursued not for "equality" with white people but as an assertion of clarity about one's due? There is nothing better than proximity to white people for convincing others that being equal to them is *not* worthwhile. And that is exactly what black women's proximity as house slaves and housekeepers taught them. Surely, the same could be said of black men's proximity as chauffeurs, porters, and servants. As Mildred, the domestic worker protagonist of Alice Childress's newspaper columns from 1951 to 1955, makes clear, working for countless white individuals reveals a commonality: they hold themselves and each other to low standards.[5]

So, even when African Americans' aims were conservative, like wanting to fight in integrated military units or to move to the suburbs, the community conversation of the 1950s and 1960s continued the work of defining and redefining black success in a country hostile to it. Scholarship has often been shaped by the belief that African Americans simply internalize mainstream standards, but that requires ignoring community awareness of the violence that success brings to anyone who is not white. Rigorous engagement with black culture requires seeing how misguided it is to assume that African Americans primarily respond to "dominant" ideologies . . . and to assume that they often do so out of remarkable naiveté about the country's investment in fair play.

The community conversation of the 1950s and 1960s centers on a range of goals—from those based on conservative definitions of success that align with stated American values to those based on radical definitions that don't—and two important dramas highlight both ends of the spectrum: Lorraine Hansberry's *A Raisin in the Sun* (1959) and Alice Childress's *Wine in the Wilderness* (1969). These canonical plays highlight self-affirming cultural practices within domestic spaces, even as those spaces remain key sites of know-your-place aggression. A black household can be evidence of one's assertion of human rights (as in *Raisin*) or a representation of the power of self-determination (as in *Wine*).

Hansberry's groundbreaking drama engages the fact that—via laws, public policy, and employment discrimination—the United States has inflicted violence on people of color by denying them access to the basic building blocks of home. While the federal government encouraged "all" Americans to pursue home ownership, the Federal Housing Administration (FHA) enacted bloodless violence by ensuring that whiteness determined access to basic resources, to say nothing of those that might yield the American Dream.[6] Even the labor movement's "family wage" campaign empowered white heads of household while excluding non-white people (Reddy 359–61). Employment and housing discrimination prevented most citizens of color from organizing their homes according to the ideal—a male breadwinner and his financially dependent wife and children—but the few who did had achieved a level of success that would not go unchecked. White Americans attacked families of color who dared to move into "their" neighborhoods. Thus, mainstream declarations about the nation's preferred domestic configuration amounted to discursive violence that encouraged physical violence.

Given its 1959 Broadway appearance, *Raisin*'s cultural impact emerged alongside the sentiments that would soon coalesce in the Black Arts and Black Power movements of the 1960s. Alice Childress's 1969 drama *Wine in the Wilderness* takes place in an apartment in Harlem, a segregated neighborhood. The audience encounters *Wine*'s characters in the middle of a "riot,"[7] so their accommodations are no more comfortable than those of the Younger family in *A Raisin in the Sun*, but unlike the Youngers, the characters in *Wine* do not focus on relocating. Instead, articulating Black Power ideals, they define achievement as an empowered mentality. They engage the community conversation on success by embracing the independence that comes with black nationalism, even if it does not come with a house.

Though these plays differ significantly, both Hansberry's *Raisin* and Childress's *Wine* amplify the voices of single women whose experiences complicate conceptions of African American achievement. Whereas Nella Larsen and Zora Neale Hurston featured migrating female protagonists whose individual definitions of success drive the action, Hansberry and Childress portray unmarried black women who seem trapped in domestic spaces where they are denigrated. According to theater historian Soyica Colbert, Hansberry situates "a migration narrative in an apartment" in order to emphasize confinement (*Theatrical Body* 33). When Childress's *Wine* joins *Raisin* in contributing to the community conversation, both highlight the damage done in black households by prevailing ideas. The rhetoric of the black church in the 1950s and that of Black Power in the 1960s vilified single women's goals. The affirmation offered by African American Christianity and Black Power routinely fails to reach single black women, even in intimate spaces. Hansberry and Childress therefore center those very women when engaging the archive and repertoire of the community conversation. Confident debate will continue, these playwrights insist upon influencing its direction and which community members are assumed most relevant to it.[8]

Moving In Does Not Mean Moving Up

Despite every indication that their fellow Americans will not welcome them, by the end of Hansberry's play, the Youngers claim their definition of success and move to the suburbs. Given the attempt to buy them out, they surely understand that to cling to their suburban definition of success is to invite injury. They reach for precisely what white Americans will attack them for securing. The Youngers refuse to let the threat of violence distract them from their goal, so they do not seem to pursue white acceptance; they are motivated by what they believe to be their due,[9] regardless of violent assertions to the contrary. The Youngers' suburban house gestures toward practices that cultivate homemade citizenship, a sense of belonging that does not rely on civic inclusion. Members of the Younger family make themselves at home in the United States, a place that wants to convince African Americans that they will never be at home, even as the country's leaders use them to proclaim that the United States is superior to the Soviet Union.

Playwright Amiri Baraka declared *A Raisin in the Sun* to be the "quintessential Civil Rights drama,"[10] and this interpretation has seemed appropriate because the action revolves around not just a sense of home but a particular sort of house. As a result, the family's quest resonates with assumptions about the aims of the Civil Rights Movement, which is identified with the black church, its respectable preachers, and its congregants' Sunday-best ethos. Yet, the play brings audiences into the Youngers' cramped living quarters in order to reveal an impassioned conversation about accomplishment, which each character believes will be more within reach if they can occupy another space. As a conversation in which many voices are heard, there is plenty of debate, but the most accepted arguments skew toward the belief that achievement depends on women taking a back seat to men. In this way, the Youngers' discussions echo those in the black churches that provided leadership to the so-called Civil Rights Movement.

Mama Lena and her (now deceased) husband define success in terms of adherence to patriarchal values, whether their family inhabits an enviable domestic structure or not. African Americans engage in practices of making-oneself-at-home in squalid tenement quarters no less than in the spaces they presumably value only because white people inhabit them. Still, when defining achievement, the Youngers prioritize the material aspects of their domestic space because they believe these can dramatically affect intimacy and joy. For instance, Ruth and Walter Lee argue constantly, but when they try to repair their bond, they find common ground through a particular image of home. Walter Lee admits to sometimes not knowing how to be close to Ruth, and she responds, "Honey . . . life don't have to be like this. I mean sometimes people can do things so that things are better. . . . You remember how we used to talk when Travis was born . . . about the way we were going to live . . . the kind of house . . . (*She is stroking his head*) Well, it's all starting to slip away from us" (Hansberry 89). As Ruth and Walter Lee bond over a shared vision, stage directions indicate, "*He turns her to him and they look at each other and kiss, tenderly and hungrily*" (89). Up to this point, their exchanges have been antagonistic, reflective of the stress of their working lives and living conditions. The glimmer of something better is caught up in "the kind of house" they had imagined for their family.

Ruth and Walter Lee are not alone in holding this vision; when Lena makes a down payment on a suburban house, she is motivated by a yearning for intimacy that she believes has been stifled by apartment living. She confesses, "I—I just seen my family falling apart today . . . just falling to pieces in front of my eyes. . . . We couldn't of gone on like we was today. We was going backwards 'stead of forwards—talking 'bout killing babies and wishing each other was dead. . . . When it gets like that in life—you just got to do something different, push on out and do something bigger" (94). Here, Hansberry's work helps audiences appreciate that Lena does not simply adopt dominant values, persuaded by FHA loans and Own Your Own Home campaigns. Rather, her aspirations illuminate a community conversation shaped by the black church more than by the economically oriented patriotism of mainstream rhetoric. Indeed, because she is guided by the morality of the church, she knows her way of pushing out to "do something bigger" will disappoint Walter Lee. Convinced he deserves the economic benefits the nation withholds from nonwhite men, he has been insisting that his dead father's insurance money be used to open a liquor store. Having made her case, Lena appeals to Walter Lee: "I wish you say something, son. . . . I wish you'd say how deep inside you you think I done the right thing—" (ibid. 94). She focuses on Walter Lee because she wants to see him become the head of a "proper" household. She wants him to step into this role so badly that, after he accuses her of emasculating him by investing in a down payment rather than in his dreams, she puts the remaining money in his hands (106–7), including that which had been designated for his sister's education. In no time, he loses every dime.

When it becomes clear that Walter Lee has lost all the money she had entrusted to him, Lena's hopes of salvaging the family remain tied to their physical surroundings. She resigns herself to staying in the apartment, insisting it can be made homier. She says, "Been thinking 'bout some of the things we could do to fix this place up some. . . . Why this place be looking fine. Cheer us all up so that we forget trouble ever come" (140). Again, central here is the logic that material domestic surroundings can generate intangible (but palpably life-affirming) benefits, facilitating family members' sense of belonging. As important, they see a decent home as their due. Deprived of her material ideal, Mama Lena encourages her loved ones to transcend their surroundings by investing in that which is within reach, the symbolic resources of patriarchy. The Youngers keep striving, adjusting strategies and refining definitions as needed. Though they cannot easily change their financial situation to gain access to a house, they can inhabit their current residence "properly" by living according to the patriarchal values espoused by the black church.[11]

Guided by this philosophy, Mama Lena becomes a proxy for patriarchy, convinced traditional gender roles will secure her family's success. Early on, Ruth says that Lena spoils Travis by making his bed for him, thereby discouraging him from learning to do a decent job of it himself. Lena responds, "Well—he's a little boy. Ain't supposed to know 'bout housekeeping" (40). If this seems insignificant, Lena's acceptance of male versus female roles becomes glaring the more she shares about her late husband. When Ruth declares the injustice of paying so much rent for their "rat trap" of an apartment, Lena admits it has indeed become a "rat trap," but it was supposed to be a temporary stop along the road to success. In a *suddenly reflective mood*, Lena tells Ruth of her deceased husband's love for his children. She recalls,

And then, Lord, when I lost that baby—little Claude—I almost thought I was going to lose Big Walter too. Oh, that man grieved hisself! He was one man to love his children. . . . I guess that's how come that man finally worked hisself to death like he done. Like he was fighting his own war with this here world that took his baby from him. . . . Crazy 'bout his children! God knows there was plenty wrong with Walter Younger—hard-headed, mean, kind of wild with women—plenty wrong with him. But he sure loved his children. Always wanted them to have something—be something. (45)

She continues, "Big Walter used to say, . . . 'Seem like God didn't see fit to give the black man nothing but dreams—but He did give us children to make them dreams seem worth while'" (45–46). Clearly, Lena had made peace with her husband's wild ways with women and accepted that she was less important to him than his children. As cultural historian Kristin Matthews points out, Lena's maiden name was Eggleston. She had offered Big Walter eggs, access to familial resources in a country that deprived him of material ones. She had been more a vessel for what he treasured than a treasure in herself.

Even in her husband's absence, Lena values Walter Lee and Travis more than female members of the household, just as the conservative black church does with men and women in the House of God. She pins all hope on Walter Lee, despite evidence that she should not, and she diminishes her daughter Beneatha—who, because she is not male, is made to symbolize all that must remain "beneath" (a woman's "proper" place). Lena operates from the belief that, because he is a man, Walter Lee must be able to step into the head-of-household position left vacant by his father. Walter Lee shows little sign of being a leader, but because he is male, leadership presumably lies dormant within him, and Lena is determined to awaken it. She does not believe her proper place is head of household; she is not leading the family by choice.[12]

By configuring her home to align with patriarchal values, Lena embodies her conception of a successful woman, and she sees no irony in her definition. Indeed, because it is shaped by a conservatism that would make most black preachers proud, she believes her achievement will yield benefits; but no matter how conservatively it is defined, black success inspires white aggression because the nation equates blackness with "valuelessness." As literary historian GerShun Avilez explains, "There is a fundamental understanding that 'a change in color leads to a change in value' and vice versa" (Avilez 137). As such, black people's tendency to fulfill mainstream standards only intensifies white Americans' insistence upon black valuelessness, motivating its violent reinforcement. For instance, when real-life African Americans (like Hansberry's family[13]) integrated neighborhoods, white residents marked these potential neighbors as fundamentally different from themselves and redefined as undesirable the domestic structures they mortgaged. Thus, when a black family moved into a suburb in California's San Fernando Valley in 1959, residents spray-painted their garage, "Black Cancer is Here. Don't Let it Spread" (Wilkerson 331). This vandalism functioned as a violently performative speech-act that imposed a rigid distinction between black and white residents and marked domestic space associated with African Americans as contaminated, though the exact same space would remain attractive and valuable if inhabited by white people. Similarly, when a black family beat the odds by buying and moving their furniture into a home in a neighborhood near Chicago in 1951, flyers were distributed that read: "Keep Cicero White." Even more forcefully, when "teenagers got out of school" and "husbands returned home from work" one day, "all of them joined housewives who had kept a daylong vigil," growing the mob to 4,000. "They chanted 'go, go, go, go.' They hurled rocks and bricks. They looted" (ibid. 374). By destroying property, the white mob ensured that any structure or area that came to be seen as "black" would, in fact, have less value. As Avilez explains, "raced 'valuelessness' becomes an integral element in the delineation of Black domestic structures" (138). Valuelessness does not inhere; it is imposed. And its imposition would be unnecessary if African Americans were failing. African Americans' accomplishments inspire their white counterparts to destroy evidence of black success while insisting it never existed.

Mama Lena faces the violence of having valuelessness attached to her family—first by relegation to a rat-infested apartment and then by white opposition to her family's access to better housing in the suburbs—but she remains focused on her goals, which she believes patriarchy will yield. Lena's strategies for pursuing success have led many to label her a "matriarch," but as suggested earlier, "the patriarch's proxy" is much more accurate.[14] Her proxy function becomes clearest in how she relates to Walter Lee, whom she feels should replace her deceased husband as head of household. Once she knows Ruth is pregnant and considering abortion, Lena urges Walter Lee to talk to Ruth, but he is more concerned with influencing decisions about the insurance money. She tries to redirect Walter Lee's attention by settling the issue; there will be no investing in liquor stores, she says. He shoots back with accusations that her decision will continue their financial hardships. It will keep Travis sleeping on a couch and will relegate him to watching his wife attend to other people's children and watching his mother work in other people's kitchens (Hansberry 71). When Lena again urges him to talk to his wife, he prepares to leave and rejects Ruth's offer to accompany him. He then insults Ruth; she returns the venom and leaves the room, prompting Lena to ask with intense motherly concern, "Walter, what is the matter with you?" (72).

Lena's view of accomplishment is so rooted in patriarchy that she sees herself as anything but the proper head of household; making herself at home despite the nation's hostility therefore revolves around empowering Walter Lee. First, she tries to empower him by nurturing him; she and her son have an exchange that acknowledges the frustration he has been feeling. She says he gets "all nervous acting and kind of wild in the eyes," and he seems always to be "tied up in some kind of knot about something" (ibid.). He admits she is right: "I want so many things that they are driving me kind of crazy" (73). He also feels his work as a chauffeur "ain't no kind of job," so when he looks toward the future, he sees "a big, looming blank space—full of *nothing*" (ibid.). Here, Hansberry spotlights African Americans' preoccupation with achievement via Walter Lee's confession about feeling like a failure. In response, Lena offers another standard by which Walter Lee can still grasp success; she reveals what he had not given Ruth a chance to share, that Ruth is pregnant. He is stunned. Lena continues, "I think Ruth is thinking 'bout getting rid of that child" (75). Walter Lee insists: "No—no—Ruth wouldn't do that." His mother responds poignantly: "When the world gets ugly enough—a woman will do anything for her family. *The part that's already living*" (ibid., original emphasis).

When Ruth reenters, she confirms Lena's suspicions about considering ending the pregnancy, and there is a shift in how Lena relates to Walter Lee. No longer operating as his mother, she conjures Big Walter's image and directs Walter Lee to animate it. She declares,

MAMA: *(Presently)* Well—*(Tightly)* Well—son, I'm waiting to hear you say something. . . . *(She waits)* I'm waiting to hear how you be your father's son. Be the man he was. . . . *(Pause. The silence shouts)* Your wife say she going to destroy your child. And I'm waiting to hear you talk like him and say we a people who give children life, not who destroys them—*(She rises)*. I'm waiting to see you stand up and look like your daddy and say we done give up one baby to poverty and that we ain't going to give up nary another one. . . . I'm waiting. (ibid.)

When he does not step into the role and cannot tell Ruth to bring the pregnancy to term, Lena responds "*bitterly*": "You . . . you are a disgrace to your father's memory" (ibid.). Because Walter Lee has not embodied the patriarchal role Lena respects and wants to preserve in the family, she steps into the head-of-household position herself by leaving to put a down payment on a house in Clybourne Park.

Far from a matriarch, Lena so profoundly invests in male leadership that she serves as the patriarch's proxy while trying to make a patriarch of her son. She believes Big Walter worked himself to death in a futile battle against the world that took his baby son, Claude, but she strives to continue all that Big Walter represented through Walter Lee. She wants him to "look like your daddy" and say what he would say.[15] When he cannot, she financially commits to Clybourne Park. If they move, they will continue Big Walter's legacy of working themselves to death. Long before making the down payment, Lena had predicted that a mortgage would require her to "take on a little day work again, few days a week—" (44). Later, when Lena seems to have given up on the plan to move, Ruth pleads, "I'll work . . . I'll work twenty hours a day in all the kitchens in Chicago . . . I'll strap my baby on my back if I have to and scrub all the floors in America and wash all the sheets in America if I have to—but we got to MOVE! We got to get OUT OF HERE" (140). Moving will inaugurate a life of even more toil, but they march toward their goals, even if they must face mobs to do so. Believing the family will fail only if it loses the guiding light of patriarchy, Lena keeps the Younger household aligned with Big Walter's ideals, his way of making success and citizenship despite the nation's hostility.

When not trying to resurrect Big Walter through Walter Lee, Lena functions as a proxy for God. Again, her definitions prove to be shaped by the black church, not so much by potential acceptance from a country that has always excluded African Americans. At one point, Lena slaps Beneatha for saying God is an idea she does not find interesting (51). As she enforces her view of God's will, Lena is not being a matriarch; as Beneatha rightly points out, her mother is being a tyrant (52). Tyranny accurately characterizes what Lena enacts. After all, traditional domesticity is based on the assumption of men's ordained right to "rule" their households (Coontz 9, 142, 238–41), and while Lena wishes she did not have to play the man's role, she feels obligated to channel her husband's patriarchal leadership. Understanding Lena's violence within the framework of tyranny therefore clarifies her conception of God as the supreme patriarch.

Because men are prioritized when defining household success, women are made to shoulder responsibility for all that goes wrong. Lena blames herself for Big Walter's demise (Hansberry 106–7). Likewise, Walter Lee accuses Ruth: "That is just what is wrong with the colored woman in this world. . . . Don't understand about building their men up and making 'em feel like they somebody. Like they can do something" (34). Later, when frustrated with both Ruth and Beneatha because they insist the insurance money is his mother's to manage, Walter Lee says, looking at them "*from the door, very sadly*": "The world's most backward race of people, and that's a fact" (38). In this moment, he locates the race's supposed shortcomings in its women. When a frustrated Ruth asks, speaking of her husband and his prospective business partners: "Why don't you all just hurry up and go into the banking business and stop talking about it?" Walter Lee shoots back: "Why? You want to know why? 'Cause we all tied up in a race of people that don't know how to do nothing but moan, pray and have babies!" (87). In adding "have babies," Walter Lee blames Ruth for being pregnant. If the race should be judged for pregnancies, both men and women are at fault, but the blame lands squarely on women's shoulders when the problem is framed as "having babies."[16] Not only does such rhetoric illogically indict women; it also corrupts any domestic success they have eked out of tenement living.

Still, what is most striking about Walter Lee's characterization of the community's problems is that it ignores the nation's violence against African Americans, suggesting that financial hardship is of their own making, not a result of the aggression of U.S. policies that deny access to the "family wage." Whereas homemade citizenship results from practices of making-oneself-at-home, which are grounded in understanding that mainstream aggression targets black achievement, Hansberry's text exposes Walter Lee's misguided belief that black women limit his life chances. Not only does this make little sense; it also ensures that the black domestic sphere cannot become a safe haven that affirms those within it.

In harmony with the black church, the Younger household devalues those who do not concede the "natural" rightness of male leadership, so even as Walter Lee fails to measure up to Big Walter's image, he remains the priority. After losing the last of the insurance money, Walter Lee resolves to compensate by accepting the Housing Association's offer to buy the house to keep the family from moving into the neighborhood. Though it means conceding the family's presumed "valuelessness," it will restore some of the lost money. Mr. Lindner, the Housing Association representative, is en route to the Youngers' apartment to finalize the agreement, and when Walter Lee informs his family of that fact, he rehearses the "show" he will put on for the visitor. After previewing his performance of acquiescence to white supremacy, Walter Lee leaves the room. In his absence, Beneatha says in disgust, "That is not a man. That is nothing but a toothless rat" (144). Lena launches into a speech that gains its force from the fact that the man of the house is out of the room. She again serves as a patriarchal proxy, perhaps approximating her dead husband's words. Feeling the moral judgment against her that her mother's defense of Walter Lee contains, Beneatha responds, "Be on my side for once! . . . Wasn't it you who taught me to despise any man who would do that? Do what he's going to do?" (145).

Hansberry uses Beneatha to highlight the danger of operating as if men represent the totality of the community's needs—as if definitions of success should revolve around men. Lena admits that she and her husband had indeed taught Beneatha to hold men to a standard against which her brother's behavior fails, but she insists that one must love another person the most "when he's at his lowest and can't believe in hisself 'cause the world done whipped him so!" (145). The "he" is more important in Lena's pronouncement than she seems to realize. Men can be forgiven for actual mistakes and loved through them, but there is no mercy for women who are perceived to have fallen short. As Lena preaches compassion to the daughter she recently slapped, Hansberry's script highlights the irony of this scenario, even if Mama Lena does not notice it. Shifting responsibility to Beneatha, all Lena wants to know is "Have you cried for that boy today? I don't mean for yourself and for the family 'cause we lost the money. I mean for him: what he been through and what it done to him" (ibid.). Establishing parameters for acceptable answers, this question reinforces the idea that women must sacrifice themselves. Any attention to women's experiences will be considered racial betrayal, which presumably leads to community failure, because everyone knows that men's experiences are the only legitimate representation of African American life. If there is any differentiation, if women face challenges that are not represented when men express their frustrations, then female voices must be silenced and their concerns treated as a distraction from the most important issues facing the race.[17]

As Lena holds Beneatha to this standard while she faces the reality of lost medical school money, Hansberry's text gestures toward an unasked question, *What might be possible if the family did not assume that accounting for Beneatha's desires would yield failure for the collective?* Beneatha's future has been jeopardized because her brother lost the money earmarked for her education, but her mother treats this as a trivial concern in the face of Walter Lee's bruised ego. Lena invalidates any articulation of what Beneatha has lost, and there is to be no accounting of what "the family" has lost. Thus, "the family" is subsumed by its male member; only his losses count.[18] If he is perceived to experience pain, no one else matters. There is a vague awareness of the role "the rest of the world" has played, but accountability falls to the women closest to him, as if their virtues (or flaws) are as powerful as racism.

As Lena subordinates herself and seeks to strengthen Walter Lee, Hansberry's drama places a spotlight on definitions of success and debates about those definitions. Lena enacts the belief that male dominance comes at the expense of women and that this dynamic is natural and right, and Beneatha challenges those beliefs, even as she must stand alone. Beneatha's assessment of her brother is deemed to be as detrimental to the family as racism is; meanwhile, the antiwoman bias that makes this conclusion possible justifies dismissing Beneatha's concerns. Walter Lee lost the $3,000 he was supposed to set aside for Beneatha's medical school aspirations, but Lena insists that no one should cry over that fact. Clearly, then, her mother would not have cared about what Beneatha had articulated earlier to a friend: "While I was sleeping in that bed in there, people went out and took the future right out of my hands! And nobody consulted me—they just went out and changed my life" (134). After all, it was not simply Walter Lee who changed Beneatha's life; it was also her own mother, who placed her future in Walter Lee's hands because she was convinced that, simply because he is male, she should defer to him.

Beneatha's aspirations mean less in this household because they do not align with patriarchy. No one is as blunt as Walter Lee in mocking Beneatha's goals, but no one contradicts the assumptions undergirding his comments. He says, for instance, "Who the hell told you you had to be a doctor? If you so crazy 'bout messing 'round with sick people—then go be a nurse like other women—or just get married and be quiet" (38).

Ruth and Lena offer nothing in her defense. Also, Ruth says Beneatha is odd for not trying to secure the good-looking, wealthy George Murchison (49). When Beneatha finishes her list of reasons for not desperately wanting to marry George by saying, "If I get married at all," Ruth and Lena spew in unison: "If!" (50). It matters, then, that this conversation devolves into the debate about God that ends with Lena slapping Beneatha.

Each exchange involving Beneatha is shaped by the idea that male leadership and female subordination are hallmarks of God-ordained success. As a result, after presenting a united front to support Walter Lee in rejecting Mr. Lindner's offensive offer, the family is back to belittling Beneatha and her ideas (150). The triumph that Lena and Ruth mark by agreeing that Walter Lee "finally come into his manhood today . . . kind of like a rainbow after the rain" hinges on the continued denigration of Beneatha and all that she represents: a simple questioning of patriarchy.

Every step of the way, the Younger household has defined accomplishment in patriarchal terms, so when Hansberry's script places a spotlight on it, it exposes the need to question conceptions of success based in patriarchy, conceptions that lead to devaluing the women who make up half the community. Scholars and readers rarely notice this, however, because most insist upon seeing Mama Lena as the embodiment of triumphant resistance to racism. Even the insightful Imani Perry argues, regarding Lena, "in Lorraine's literary world, mother wisdom is trustworthy though subtle, and paternal inheritances are thorny and overpowering" (138–39). However, when Lena's behavior is examined not as a reaction to white hostility but for its impact on black people, it becomes clear that when family members do not live up to patriarchal ideals, she not only withholds affirmation, she is violent.[19] Besides slapping Beneatha, she "*starts to beat [Walter] senselessly in the face*" (129) for losing the insurance money.[20] As Colbert suggests, such scenes expose "the conditions that enable Mama to create a house" as well as those "that establish Beneatha's homelessness" (43). The Younger household is not a safe haven, especially for women who question (divinely ordained) male leadership.

Hansberry's drama suggests that households structured this way should be questioned as much as the conservative black church on which they seem to be modeled. The black church may be leading the way toward securing so-called "civil rights," but its methods for doing so deserve debate. While Hansberry's play contributes to mainstream conversations by appearing on Broadway, it also contributes to the community conversation, and Beneatha's stances (even if quelled—perhaps especially because they are quelled) complicate debates among African Americans both inside and outside the text. With Beneatha, Hansberry preserves in the archive and repertoire of the community conversation a figure that challenges African Americans to account for the impact on women, especially single women, as they continue the work Hansberry knows African Americans will continue. Namely, defining, redefining, and pursuing black success in a nation hostile to it.

Why Move at All?

People of color who measure success by home ownership often encounter white violence, making poignant the question Mr. Lindner asks the Youngers: "What do you think you are going to gain by moving into a neighborhood where you just aren't wanted?" (Hansberry 119). Might it be better to find contentment in segregated spaces? As Toni Morrison has often noted, integration robbed black communities of many of their resources.[21] Further, as bell hooks has argued, cultivating spaces of affirmation in the midst of dehumanizing circumstances is a victory to be celebrated, a prime example of what this study calls homemade citizenship. hooks notes that creating "homeplace" empowers marginalized people to "be affirmed in our minds and hearts despite poverty, hardship, and deprivation" (hooks 42). That is, homeplace does not obliterate the hostility and injustice of the larger society; it equips communities to survive and thrive while mainstream forces work for their destruction. Alice Childress's *Wine in the Wilderness* acknowledges the "homeplace" function of black-oriented spaces of the 1960s by foregrounding the importance of the "Black Is Beautiful" philosophy. The United States attacked African Americans by erecting innumerable barriers to material resources, but black communities made the homes they occupied spaces of affirmation. In Hansberry's script, Lena's belief in her right to success manifests in her commitment to patriarchal ideals that connect her to the black church, and in Childress's play, characters believe they succeed by embracing "Black Is Beautiful" discourse. Never denying that the characters' chosen ideals are empowering, these works also examine the consequences of the precise ways in which they empower. According to *Wine*, while African Americans have always gained strength by disregarding mainstream standards, "Black Is Beautiful" fails to create a safe space for all members of the race, especially single women. Indeed,

Childress's contribution to the community conversation on success suggests that "Black Is Beautiful" hinders homemaking practices centered on partnership and companionship and the more inclusive racial self-affirmation that these would foster.

Unlike their counterparts in *A Raisin in the Sun*, the characters in *Wine in the Wilderness* do not obsess about a "better" life in suburban single-family homes, but Childress suggests that patriarchy still plays too great a role in shaping their aspirations. Bill, the main male character, reflects and perpetuates the portions of the community conversation shaped by Black Power philosophies. As Margo Crawford makes clear, Black Power ideology was always intersectional; theorists' conceptions of blackness revolved around manhood. Indeed, "their emphasis on black male power often convinced them that the liberation of black men would lead to the liberation of all black people" (Crawford, "Family Affair," 185). With masculinity at the center, Black Power perspectives typically developed in opposition to white manhood, ostensibly rejecting everything set forth by white men because it had all been done in the name of oppression.

Accordingly, Bill believes he is free from white influence, partly because he is not striving to certify his success by becoming a head of household; he sees himself as an independent artist, a countercultural maverick. Bill does not pursue the suburbs because he has come to prefer the more symbolic benefits of patriarchy to the material ones. As the United States government made the suburban house into the most coveted sign of one's patriarchal standing, home ownership made African Americans bigger targets for violence, as white people guarded their turf. Bill avoids this.

Tommy, the female protagonist, accepts the patriarchy undergirding Bill's conception of black self-regard, so when she finally questions it, the action reaches its climax, and Childress's script insists that the community conversation contend with single black women's perspectives. Tommy's acceptance of patriarchy gains significance when the audience learns she grew up in the African Methodist Episcopal (AME) church. This institution is distinct from the Southern Baptist church that seems to guide Mama Lena and what Americans understand to be the Civil Rights Movement because AME congregants embrace an Afrocentric ethos that Black Power adherents would appreciate. However, it clearly leaves masculinism intact. Thus, whether the church acknowledges Christ's bronze skin and wooly hair or simply accepts White Jesus, patriarchal teaching is a commonality that deserves interrogation. Tommy eventually critiques the black nationalism that Bill embraces because she senses its investment in her subordination. Even if not centered on the suburban homes that "The Man" tells him to covet via living wage campaigns and the Federal Housing Administration (FHA), Bill's Afrocentricism requires a gender hierarchy that objectifies women and makes them less than citizens within their own homes, families, and communities. A homeplace that requires black women's subordination is no homeplace at all, Childress's script suggests.

Wine in the Wilderness is set in the apartment of Bill Jameson, an artist who wants to finish a 3-part painting on black womanhood. He has completed the "innocent girl" and the "African queen," and now needs a model to represent the "messed up chick"—the embodiment of what the violence of American racism has done to black women. His friends, Sonny-Man and Cynthia, believe they have found his perfect model in Tommy, a less educated woman who has lost everything to the chaos in the streets. Tommy accompanies these strangers to Bill's apartment because she thinks she will be introduced to a possible boyfriend. Her desire to find a companion, with whom she can weather life's storms, is palpable.

In fact, because Tommy yearns for a life partner, Childress creates a text in which the "Black Is Beautiful" philosophy must be understood in relation to homemaking success and to the intimacies that can strengthen or weaken communities. Just as discussions in the 1890s noted that black love could be exploited by those who would keep African Americans disfranchised, Childress identifies danger. Following the 1920s and 1930s examples of Larsen and Hurston, Childress joins Hansberry in wondering aloud whether black women's desires are shaping community conceptions of achievement, including those articulated in intimate spaces. Childress's characters are no less concerned with achievement than Hansberry's suburb-obsessed Younger family, but the loudest voices in *Wine* define success in terms of rejecting civic inclusion, which they mistakenly believe is a new strategy. That is, they misread their forebears' practices of making-oneself-at-home as internalizations of mainstream values. Ultimately, *Wine* enters the community conversation to critique the masculinist tendencies of the Black Power movement and its manner of declaring "Black Is Beautiful."

Childress sets the action in Bill's apartment, which expresses his investment in cultural recuperation and preservation through art as well as his rejection of traditional domesticity, which he associates with capitulation to white supremacy. The stage directions dictate, "The room is obviously

Black dominated, pieces of sculpture, wall hangings, paintings. An artist's easel is standing with a drapery thrown across it so the empty canvas beneath it is hidden. . . . The place is in a beautiful, rather artistic state of disorder" (345). Just as important, "The room also reflects an interest in other darker peoples of the world . . . A Chinese incense-burner Buddha, an American Indian feathered war helmet, a Mexican serape, a Japanese fan, a West Indian travel poster" (345–46). In line with the décor, Bill sees himself as free from traditional respectability. Trying to discourage Tommy's romantic interest in him and to keep her focused on posing for his painting, he admits to being a divorcée. Furthermore, "she divorced me, Tommy, so maybe I'm not much of a catch" (351). When Tommy's interest does not diminish, he declares, "Tommy, I don't wanta ever get married again. It's me and my work" (ibid.). Thus, Bill's definition of success revolves around contributing to the world, but only through his art; he sees himself as an artist, not a husband or father. In fact, he has altered the apartment by taking it from three rooms to one. He does not aim for the kind of environment he and his ex-wife likely shared, and he refuses to replicate the kind of home in which he grew up. The audience discovers this dynamic when, after enduring Bill's condescension most of the evening, Tommy spills a drink on herself and changes clothes. Bill truly sees her for the first time and is captivated.

At this point, Bill begins confiding in Tommy, and it becomes clear that he despises the domesticity his parents had provided. His parents had apparently attained what Mama Lena aspires to in *Raisin in the Sun*. He says, "Everybody in my family worked for the Post Office. They bought a home in Jamaica, Long Island.[22] Everybody on that block bought an aluminum screen door with a duck on it, . . . or was it a swan? I guess that makes my favorite flower crabgrass and hedges. I have a lot of bad dreams" (358). Stage directions call for Tommy to massage his temples and the back of his neck, but there is no break in his testimony. He continues, "A dream like suffocating, dying of suffocation. The worst kinda dream. People are standing in a weird looking art gallery, they're looking and laughing at everything I've ever done. My work begins to fade off the canvas, right before my eyes. Everything I've ever done is laughed away" (358). Here, memories of the home Bill grew up in merge with his deepest fears.[23]

Bill's artistic drive comes partly from his determination to avoid duplicating the life his family had, which he sees as the height of conformity—everyone had an aluminum screen door. He strives to make a more consequential impact by defining success as the opposite of conformity. He apparently believes pursuing the American Dream made his parents and neighbors content with crabgrass and hedges. He wants to avoid fitting into that mold because, having discovered some of the culture of the "darker peoples of the world," he knows assimilation costs. He cannot conceive of the possibility that, like Lena in *Raisin*, his parents were more likely driven by a community conversation defining achievement than by a desire to assimilate and be "equal" to white people. Bill does not consider this possibility, but Childress must have. After all, she articulated keen awareness of the low standards to which white Americans hold themselves through her housekeeper protagonist Mildred in newspaper columns from 1951 to 1955.[24] The words of her contemporary James Baldwin therefore likely resonated: "there is certainly little enough in the white man's public or private life that one should desire to imitate" (*Fire* 341). Bill's parents no doubt had plenty of experiences that led them to define accomplishment in ways that had little to do with emulating mainstream America.

During this revealing conversation, Bill not only sees Tommy's beauty; he also realizes it is working-class and thoroughly American, altering his view of black women and their relationship to black self-regard. Prior to this moment, Bill had conceived of "Black Is Beautiful" as an aesthetic shift he could not afford to ignore as an artist. He still has a painting of a white woman on display, but he admits, "This is a new day, the deal is going down different. This is the Black moment, doll. Black, Black, Black, is bee-yoo-tee-full. Got it? *Black is beautiful*" (356). This beauty existed only in relationship to the African continent, though. His painting of "Wine in the Wilderness" represents "Mother Africa, regal, black womanhood in her noblest form" (347)—that is, untainted by the United States. Bill's triptych is therefore based on the assumption that American experiences have destroyed black women, have made "messed up chicks" of them all. Because he is invested in rejecting white standards, he gives the United States a victory that the reactionary nature of white violence contradicts. When Bill notices the distorted lens through which he has been viewing Tommy, he declares, "I'm glad you're here. Black *is* beautiful, you're beautiful, A.M.E. Zion, Elks, pink roses, bush flower, . . . blooming out of the slavery of Sweetwater Springs, Virginia" (358). Bill finally sees that black women have preserved some dignity and beauty despite all the injustice and violence they have encountered in the United States. It would be more accurate for Bill to notice that the

United States has abused black women for keeping their dignity, strength, and beauty. Recognizing black women's actual worth, the country has remained devoted to putting them in a subordinate position, declaring it to be their "proper" place. Especially when he cannot appreciate the know-your-place aggression black women face, it makes sense that Bill would assume he must condemn the domestic life his parents provided in order to retain something cultural of which to be proud. Exposing Bill's shortsightedness, Childress's script suggests that art can emerge from crabgrass too.

The 1960s were often seen as the time for the "black male revolutionary" to rise.[25] For many, claiming Black Power meant investing more passionately in patriarchal assumptions, and *Wine in the Wilderness* identifies this tendency in both men and women. In this way, "Black Is Beautiful" is shown to be a reiteration of the New Negro era's preference for the male worker, discussed in Chapter 3. Black Power thereby proves to constitute less of a break with the ideals of earlier decades than those who identify with Bill would readily admit. As mentioned, Tommy has come to Bill's apartment because she believes his friends Cynthia and Sonny-Man are playing matchmaker. The couple had encountered Tommy in a bar when they were kept from their street during the chaos. Sonny-Man explains, "She was breakin' up everybody in the bar . . . had us all laughing—crackin' us up. In the middle of a riot . . . she's gassin' everybody!" Tommy explains, "No need to cry, it's sad enough" (350). Bill wastes no time making his request, and Tommy agrees to let him paint her because she does not realize he wants her only as artistic inspiration. She is hungry, though, so the men leave to get her requested meal of Chinese takeout.

Childress registers the male-centered nature of "Black Is Beautiful" discourse by highlighting the mentality that has allowed Cynthia to secure a husband, as Tommy hopes to do. When the men leave, Tommy asks for Cynthia's advice on attracting a man like Bill. Cynthia soon offers criticism: "You're too used to looking out for yourself. It makes us lose our femininity. . . . You have to let the Black man have his manhood again. You have to give it back, Tommy" (353). Tommy's response is visceral: "I didn't take it from him, how I'm gonna give it back" (ibid.), but she quickly retreats: "What else is the matter with me? You had school, I didn't. I respect that" (ibid.). Tommy senses something disturbing in Cynthia's logic but she sets that aside, assuming Cynthia knows better. This deference is not simply about being less educated, however; it stems from the belief that a woman is worth little without a man. Tommy's father deserted her and her mother and lived with another woman for ten or twelve years. When he died, Tommy's mother was asked to claim the body, and she did. The lesson Tommy still carries from that is: "A woman need a man to claim, even if it's a dead one" (ibid.). Believing this, and proving to be goal-oriented, Tommy defers to Cynthia, whose status as a married woman gives her credibility. If a married woman recommends prioritizing black men's desire for patriarchal standing, then Tommy will not dismiss the advice.

Because Tommy is willing to compromise in order to achieve her goal of becoming an attractive mate, Black Power's gender hierarchy becomes clearest in Childress's portrait of Bill, the object of Tommy's affection. When everyone leaves so he can paint Tommy, he offers a litany of what's wrong with "our women." First, "That's the trouble with our women, yall always got your mind on food" (354). Furthermore, "That's another thing 'bout Black women, they wanta eat 'fore they do anything else" (ibid.). Next, "Trouble with our women, . . . they all wanta be great brains. Leave somethin' for a man to do" (355). Later, "Another thing . . . our women don't know a damn thing bout bein' feminine. *Give in* sometime. It won't kill you" (356). Finally, "That's another thing with our women, . . . they want a *latch* on. Learn to play it by ear, roll with the punches, cut down on some-a this 'got-you-to-the-grave' kinda relationship" (ibid.). Apparently, giving the black man "his manhood back" requires women to be submissive, let him be "the brains," and let him dictate whether relationships are long-term or fleeting.

With Cynthia and Bill advancing similar arguments, *Wine* suggests that within the community conversation, there is widespread acceptance of the notion that the entire race benefits from male dominance. While Hansberry's *Raisin* uses an all-but-silenced Beneatha to illuminate the damage these ideas cause, Childress's play does so by making a single black woman its protagonist. As Crawford puts it, "When we acknowledge that Black Power masculinist discourse was deeply intersectional, the signature difference of Black Power feminism is not intersectionality but the seizure of intersectionality from the male stronghold" ("Family Affair" 186). *Wine* both highlights and critiques black nationalism through Tommy, gesturing toward high-stakes debates in the lived world.

If black nationalism hinges on recuperating black men's "rightful" position of power and leadership, then men's success should be visible in those whom they lead. Accordingly, community conversations inflected by

Black Power emphasized men's responsibility to steer their people away from accepting white supremacist denigration. In the process, community assessments of achievement involved defining an aesthetic believed to denote self-determination, and adhering to this aesthetic was most important for women because their obedience reflected well on men. Specifically, "The new physical beauty standards privileged looking 'natural' and looking 'African.' 'Africa' signified nature, roots, authenticity, and purity within this Black Arts imagination. Clothing and hairstyles that were deemed 'African' became signs of this natural black beauty." Thus, "the short 'afro' hairstyle began to be named the 'natural'" (Crawford, "Natural," 154–55). None of this was taken to be a hollow fashion statement.[26] As Black Arts Movement leader Larry Neal put it in *Ebony* magazine in 1969, "The natural, in its most positive sense, symbolizes the Sister's willingness to determine her own destiny. It is an act of love for herself and her people. The natural helps to psychologically liberate the Sister. It prepares her for the message of a Rap Brown, a Robert Williams, a Huey Newton, a Maulana Karenga" (qtd. in Crawford, "Natural" 155). Clearly, women becoming receptacles for men's ideas cements male leadership as the measure of black success. A woman contributes to the work of loving "her people" not by having ideas herself but by embodying the importance of men's ideas. In this formulation, the movement's body politics made women central primarily as a litmus test; if the race was faltering, it could be best observed in its women.

Therefore, just as black women were pressured to embody race motherhood in the 1920s and 1930s, rhetoric of the 1960s encouraged women's subordination. Many Black Power adherents believed success hinged on "castrating" white power in order to "render it feminine" (Crawford, "Natural," 154). If rendering white power *feminine* signified a victory for the race, then the movement's conception of women's roles deserves attention. In short, African American women were told in explicit, implicit, and ostensibly flattering ways that empowering the community required their subordination and objectification. As Crawford explains, "black women were often objectified as the embodiments of black beauty ('African Queens' and 'natural beauty')" and their bodies were "often imagined as the motherland, the receptacle for the black (male-dominated) nation" (ibid.). Certainly, this is the logic motivating Bill's "Wine in the Wilderness" painting.

However, the play *Wine in the Wilderness* highlights Black Power's patriarchal investments in order to question them, and black beauty is questioned along with those investments, so the script's attention to a black woman's desire for companionship proves significant. Conceiving of Black Power as a "family affair," adherents were encouraged to see each other as "brother" and "sister." Black feminists immediately cautioned that this practice ignored how problematic family dynamics could be (Crawford, "Family Affair"). Asking why those in the movement so seldom spoke in terms of "man" and "woman," black feminists articulated concerns and envisioned possibilities that Childress reflects and advances through her unmarried female protagonist. Therefore, especially when read as part of the community conversation on success, Tommy's investment in romance and egalitarian partnership speaks volumes.

Even while highlighting Tommy's yearning for a mate, *Wine* acknowledges the complexity of domesticity's meanings within the community conversation. There is always diversity of opinion; the community conversation does not settle definitions so much as it traces the contours of conceptions that are in contention. Reminiscent of Hurston's Janie, Tommy's homemaking desires are not about respectability or class mobility but about partnership and companionship. Trying to keep Tommy's mind off of a possible romance with Bill, Cynthia assures Tommy, "you don't want a poor artist." Tommy responds, referring to herself in third-person: "Tommy's not lookin' for a meal ticket. I been doin' for myself all my life. It takes two to make it in this high-price world. A Black man see a hard way to go. The both of you gotta pull together. That way you accomplish" (352). Achievement drives Tommy's impressions of the past and her vision for the future. Soon thereafter, Cynthia cautions, "Tommy, don't be in a rush about the marriage thing" (355), and Tommy has no patience for this counsel. "Keep it to yourself," she says, "I was thirty my last birthday and haven't ever been married. I coulda been. Oh, yes, indeed, coulda been. But I don't want any and everybody. What I want with a no-good piece-a nothin'? I'll never forget what the Reverend Martin Luther King said . . . 'I have a dream.' I liked him sayin' it 'cause truer words have never been spoke" (ibid.). The stage directions call attention to the fact that Tommy is straightening up the room as she continues, "I have a dream, too. Mine is to find a man who'll treat me just half-way decent . . . just to meet me half-way is all I ask, to smile, to be kind to me. Somebody in my corner. Not to wake up by myself in the mornin' and face this world all alone" (ibid.). In a particularly raw moment, Tommy confesses, "I'm so lonesome . . . I'm lonesome . . . I want somebody to love. Somebody to say . . . 'That's allright,' when the world treats me mean" (353). For Tommy, making a home is about companionship and comfort in a harsh world and about partnership in a high-priced world. She wants a home that will provide a homeplace.[27]

Thus, while Bill believes traditional homemaking to be detrimental to success as an artist and black nationalist, Tommy believes it can be beneficial—allowing Childress's text to place in the archive and repertoire of Black Power both domestic and political possibilities not generally associated with it.[28] By likening her dream to King's, Tommy suggests that pursuing one's goals requires refueling, which homeplace can provide. It is even better, Tommy reasons, if one finds a partner who is committed to meeting you "half-way," understanding that "the both of you gotta pull together." Tommy's vision here is limited neither to financial considerations nor to a particular structure, such as the Youngers' single-family house in the suburbs. Though she acknowledges teamwork is necessary because it is a high-priced world, she emphasizes emotional and spiritual support. Furthermore, the connection she draws to King's dream emerges from her investment in political empowerment; she shares that she votes (355). However, voting is insufficient. After all, King's achievements were outside of the realm of voting because the goal of the movement was never civic inclusion alone. Childress thereby uses Tommy to demonstrate the value of the diversity within the community conversation. The AME church has shaped her and so has the Southern Baptist church via Martin Luther King Jr. Thus, the text conveys to community members that dismissing strategies that are not explicitly black nationalist is a mistake. Like the goals of Black Power, the dreams articulated by King and by Tommy require reaching beyond the authority of white Americans and of the nation-state.

As it aligns with black women's long tradition of insisting upon the compatibility of domesticity and empowerment, Tommy's dream revolves around African American couples comforting each other when the United States mistreats them, which it inevitably will. She understands that black achievement will beckon violence, so black men and women need each other *as partners*, as was presumably the case in the 1890s when black domestic novels like *Iola Leroy* and *Contending Forces* entered the community conversation. Tommy's ideal will not provide escape so much as space to recuperate. Childress also uses the tension between Tommy's and Bill's views of homemaking to insist that marching toward success as a community requires relinquishing gender-based hierarchies. Even Tommy shows a desire for gender hierarchy by being willing to alter herself to attract a man, but she has held on to enough self-worth to ultimately want partnership more than leadership.

Given that Tommy yearns for a home based on companionship more than material resources, and on partnership more than hierarchy, the semiotics of her homemaking gestures prove significant. Stage directions call for her to straighten the room several times and her doing so is misconstrued by Cynthia, the play's more educated, middle-class black woman. Having seen Tommy busy herself in Bill's apartment more than once, Cynthia instructs, "Leave the room alone. What we need is a little more sex appeal and a little less washing, cooking and ironing. (*TOMMY puts down the room straightening*) One more thing, . . . do you have to wear that wig?" (353). Tommy's straightening the room conjures a housekeeper image for Cynthia rather than the role Tommy describes while taking these actions: homemaker. Given how often African American women acknowledge each other's investment in moving from servant to autonomous homemaker, what are the barriers to seeing Tommy as lady of the house?

Using both Bill and Cynthia, Childress seems to suggest that black nationalists were hasty in believing they had abandoned the limitations of earlier decades. Assuming that their forebears had been mesmerized by European models for living, black nationalists had elevated African ones, and troubled by the preoccupation with straightened hair, they had insisted upon the beauty of afros.[29] Childress therefore puts Cynthia's judgment about Tommy's room-straightening alongside her critique of the wig. Cynthia could not see Tommy as a possible woman of the house because her aesthetic does not fit the Black Power standard. Thus, an inability to see Tommy as woman of the house because she wears a wig may not be so different from the inability to treasure a black woman because she has full lips, a wide nose, and kinky hair. The community's women are no better off with naturals than with straightened hair if their appearance matters more than their hearts and minds. As Joyce Green put it in the groundbreaking anthology, *The Black Woman*, "But sisters don't have no time to be dumb afros as opposed to dumb blondes" (139).

Childress's text suggests that given how they are deployed to evaluate women, straightened hair and afros are essentially the same, but Tommy comes to this conclusion reluctantly. If it will make her more eligible, she is willing to embrace an aesthetic and a demeanor aligned with class aspiration. That Tommy had been willing to try on false consciousness becomes clear when she no longer cares about Bill's and Cynthia's acceptance—that is, once she feels used and tells them off. Tommy and Bill ended up sleeping together after their conversation about Bill's dreams and Tommy's upbringing. The next morning, Bill's friends return, and Tommy learns not only that this was never meant to be a romantic encounter but also that she was considered a perfect model for "the messed up chick."

Tommy feels used, but she maintains her dignity and speaks her truth: "I don't stay mad, it's here today and gone tomorrow. I'm sorry your feelin's got hurt, . . . but when I'm hurt I turn and hurt back. Somewhere, in the middle of last night, I thought the old me was gone, . . . lost forever, and gladly. But today was flippin' time, so back I flipped. Now it's 'turn the other cheek' time. If I can go through life other-cheekin' the white folk, . . . guess yall can be other-cheeked too. But I'm goin' back to the nitty-gritty crowd, where the talk is we-ness and us-ness" (361). Here, she apologizes for having told off Bill and Cynthia but acknowledges having spoken authentically: when she is hurt, she hurts back. Now that it is time to turn the other cheek, she can forgive them, but she prefers her old self to the persona she had adopted to be welcomed among them. Further, she prefers those who are not educated and middle class because they are more communal; they speak in terms of *us* and *we*. Tommy does not need what Cynthia and Bill offer: hierarchy, Afrocentric respectability, and its promised class mobility.[30]

Presumably, among people who speak in terms of *we* and *us*, black women do not have to submit to black men and do not have to prove themselves by wearing the right hair and clothes. Tommy declares, "And, Cynthia, if my hair is straight, or if it's natural, or if I wear a wig, or take it off, . . . that's all right; because wigs . . . shoes . . . hats . . . bags . . . and even this . . . (*she picks up the African throw she wore a few moments before . . . fingers it*). They're just what what you call . . . access . . . (*fishing for the word*) . . . like what you wear with your Easter outfit" (362). Cynthia helps her, saying: "Accessories," and Tommy continues, "Thank you, my sister. Accessories. Somethin' you add or take off. The real thing is takin' place on the inside . . . that's where the action is. That's 'Wine in the Wilderness,' . . . a woman that's a real one and a good one. And yall just better believe I'm it" (362). With this, Tommy challenges the "revolutionary" logic Larry Neal and many others espoused, that an afro and African garb prove one's freedom from the effects of white supremacist brainwashing and that straight hair is a sure sign of self-hatred.

Ultimately, Tommy believes that among those who speak in terms of *we* and *us*, a black woman need not wait for a man to crown her "Wine in the Wilderness," a woman of which the community should be proud. Placing romance at the center of her definition of success, even if she had to compromise to obtain it, may have brought Tommy to Bill's apartment, but it will not determine her future. Her domestic aspirations had always been about making a home that will help her recuperate from the violence she knows her country saves for her. Now that she sees the problem with trying to win the approval of educated black people with supposedly African-based conceptions of how she should look and act, she may modify her strategies, but she will continue the journey toward her goals. If the community definition of success revolves around "Black Is Beautiful" while denigrating many, then a few are made simply to symbolize accomplishment by looking the part. In contrast, Childress uses Tommy to assert black women's right to actually enjoy success by insisting that they help shape conceptions of it.

*   *   *

The characters in *A Raisin in the Sun* define achievement in ways that seem to align with mainstream values but that actually reflect the community conversation as it was guided by Southern black churches. Even their suburban aspirations might be best understood in terms of a human urge toward, and a conviction about their right to, resources. Having seen earlier generations "escape" apartment living only to be attacked in their suburban houses, many in the next generation became black nationalists who conceived of home less as a structure and more as a space for cultivating independence and black power. Of course, there was nothing new about this, given black people's resourcefulness during slavery, as discussed in Chapter 1. Though characters mistakenly view themselves as innovators, *Wine in the Wilderness* demonstrates how they continued community traditions of creating home in any space where they could determine what would be valued. Rather than invest in the structures most worshipped by a violent white society that reserves living wages and FHA loans for a particular demographic, they claimed a homeplace in which to celebrate the darker peoples of the world and declare their own beauty. While the United States wagered everything on the emasculation of African American men, "home" would be a place where black manhood and leadership would be respected.

While *Raisin* and *Wine* highlight the investment in home as a human right and as black power, they reflect as well as advance the community conversation on success. While home represented a human right for some and black power for others, black women artists urged community members to ask, *Is the racial self-affirmation being cultivated truly benefiting the entire community?* Grappling with that question always required debate, and both *Raisin* and *Wine* honor that truth. In *Raisin*, Beneatha represents those in the community conversation who are outnumbered and even have their goals and dreams discounted, but Hansberry preserves evidence of their success at holding on to their self-conceptions and true desires. As theater historian Carol Davis argues, "despite what can only be called humiliation at the hands of her mother and sister-in-law, Beneatha remains steadfast in her commitment to her own worldview" (36). Black women's aspirations, especially those of unmarried women, must be acknowledged, must be part of both the archive and the repertoire. Undaunted by the odds against them, some African American women stood up for themselves, debating the ideas that most accepted as self-evidently beneficial to the community. When outnumbered in one's own home, speaking up at all is heroic—as is ensuring that posterity knows black women did so. Childress's *Wine* also demonstrates a commitment to acknowledging that the archive and repertoire of the Black Power movement includes women's victories. There is no denying the value of a homeplace born of disregarding mainstream standards. Nevertheless, defining culturally specific success requires accounting for the many ways that the community's definitions impact all of its members, not just men.

In the broadest sense, *Raisin* and *Wine* suggest that black achievement will be attacked when it seems to align with mainstream standards as well as when it deliberately constructs its own. And when one accounts for both playwrights' familiarity with the Communist Party of the United States of America (CPUSA), their scripts demonstrate that African Americans will experience violence whether they embrace capitalism or yearn for other options. When black Americans seem to be conservative capitalists, they will inspire violence for having the temerity to believe they deserve success on its terms; they are supposed to accept it only to yearn, not to attain. When African Americans develop conceptions of accomplishment that turn away from capitalism's tenets and view themselves more as part of a worldwide community of darker races, then they will be punished for having the audacity of not coveting what "belongs" to white men.

With community members so invested in achievement in a country that discourages, destroys, and works to obliterate all evidence of it, supporting each other in the relentless march toward accomplishment requires debate as an embodied practice of belonging. Ultimately, *A Raisin in the Sun* and *Wine in the Wilderness* assert the importance of women's voices in the community's ongoing project of defining its success. Whether African Americans achieve conservative goals or radical ones, their accomplishments will inspire know-your-place aggression. The challenge, Hansberry and Childress suggest, is to resist the temptation to confine one's kith and kin to yet another "proper" place.

Still the Master's House?

The 1960s ended with African Americans continuing to accrue achievements while their fellow citizens and government answered with violence. Tireless activism and collaboration yielded the Voting Rights Act in 1965. Equally strenuous effort motivated the Housing Rights Act of 1968, but it was the assassination of Martin Luther King Jr. on April 4 and the mourning among the disfranchised (in the form of urban rebellions in more than 100 cities) that led the Senate and House to vote quickly in its favor. Of course, discrimination did not lose its life-changing power overnight, so in October 1968, Tommie Smith and John Carlos expressed solidarity with those facing injustice by giving the Black Power salute on the medal stand at the Olympics.[1] The next year, in December 1969, police killed Black Panther Party leader Fred Hampton, who had encouraged black citizens to see police brutality as a violation, not simply a fact of life.

In the 1970s and 1980s, know-your-place aggression at the national level took the form of "benign neglect" based on the advice of Daniel Patrick Moynihan, President Nixon's domestic policy adviser who had made his mark by writing *The Negro Family: The Case for National Action*, the 1965 Department of Labor report that portrayed African American families as dysfunctional. Framed as intense concern for black people's well-being and prosperity, Moynihan's report explained that black families were enmeshed in a "tangle of pathology" because black women were often heads of household. Based on assumptions about the devastating impact of slavery—that it had emasculated black men and made matriarchs of black women—Moynihan's "tangle of pathology" thesis ensured that earlier white violence had a reverberating effect that kept black people in their "proper" place in the present. That is, as African Americans continued to define and pursue success, which often included creating heteronormative nuclear families, American laws, public policies, news coverage, and popular culture erased those achievements with the discursive violence of constantly describing and portraying them as dysfunctional. Furthermore, rather than advocate for equity-producing public policy, Moynihan's 1965 report helped lay the groundwork for opposing redistribution of opportunities and resources. In fact, it argued that the "culture of poverty" among African Americans made society's role immaterial: "At this point, the present tangle of pathology is capable of perpetuating itself *without assistance from the white world*" (47, emphasis added). Thus, by the time the 1968 Kerner Commission Report urged the American government to remedy the damage it had done by keeping opportunity *away* from entire populations,[2] assumptions about the "culture of poverty" (still resonant today) easily stifled political will. The aggression always undergirding Moynihan's policy suggestions became clearest when he insisted in 1970 that the black community's problems "had been too much talked about" (Kihss). African Americans had made "extraordinary progress," Moynihan explained, so "the time may have come when the issue of race could benefit from a period of 'benign neglect'" (ibid.). Here, black success becomes the excuse for disregarding the violence and discrimination that has made "progress" a watchword throughout American history.

With African American families consistently cast as pathological, the stage was set for a national conversation in the 1970s and 1980s fueled by know-your-place aggression against black women. Assumptions about black domestic dysfunction helped Ronald Reagan animate the "welfare queen," which would diminish and destroy black women's success while claiming it never existed. By "condemning 'welfare queens' and criminal 'predators,' he rode into office [in 1980] with the strong support of . . . poor and working class whites who felt betrayed by the Democratic party's embrace of the civil rights agenda" (Alexander 47). One of Reagan's favorite anecdotes "was the story of a Chicago 'welfare queen' with '80 names, 30 addresses, 12 Social Security cards,' whose 'tax-free income alone is over $150, 000'" (ibid. 48). Then and now, this mythic figure eclipses real-life black women,[3] keeping them in their "proper" place no matter what they achieve. Whether a black woman is poor or not, uneducated or not, on public assistance or not, she is easily assumed to be a welfare queen and purveyor of domestic pathology. Meanwhile, the fact that the majority of welfare recipients are white will never lighten the welfare queen's complexion.

National discourse opposed successful black individuals and families by never letting them escape the pall of their supposed pathology, but the community conversation never abandoned its project of defining and re-defining success in hostile environments, and Alex Haley's *Roots* provides an access point to that conversation, which also sheds light on women's contributions. *Roots* was nothing short of a cultural phenomenon. The book, which was categorized as nonfiction, was published in 1976, and a miniseries version aired on television January 23 to 30, 1977. According to ABC, an estimated 130 million people watched at least part of the series, representing 85 percent of all U.S. households (Norrell 167). Almost 9 of 10 black Americans watched some portion of the series, and "by February 1977, 250 colleges were offering credit courses based on *Roots*" (ibid. 168). Also, "*Roots* sold one million hardback copies in 1977" (ibid. 170). However, long before the book saw the light of day, Haley had been writing and speaking about his quest to fill in his family tree, which led to the discovery of Kunta Kinte, the first of his ancestors to be brought to the United States. Having given his "Saga of a People" lecture more than a thousand times, Haley said, "*Roots* was spread all over before it was published" (ibid. 122).

When viewed as part of the community conversation, Haley's story of intense research to locate Kunta Kinte exemplifies the imbrication of the Black Power era and a period of unprecedented integration, which accompanied the height of black nationalism and intensified in the 1970s and 1980s. In 1969, the country saw the first black president of a pre-dominantly white university when Clifford Wharton Jr. took the helm at Michigan State University; in 1970, a Pulitzer Prize in Drama went to Charles Gordon; in 1976, Barbara Jordan became the first African American to keynote a major political party's convention; and in 1982, a Pulitzer Prize went to Charles Fuller for *A Soldier's Play* and in 1983 to Alice Walker for *The Color Purple*. Viewing "integration" as a goal mo-tivated by a sense of one's right to resources, not by hope for "equality" with white people, reveals black firsts to be simply part of the dynamic, multivalent community conversation on success that includes assertions of black nationalism and independence. For instance, in 1970, *Essence* and *Black Enterprise* magazines began publication; in 1972, the first Black National Political Convention was held in Gary, Indiana; and in 1980, Black Entertainment Television was founded in Washington, D.C. The success-oriented nature of the community conversation is also demonstrated by the fact that John Blassingame's *The Slave Community* was published in 1972. This groundbreaking historical study exemplifies the unwavering commitment in black communities to affirming each other while acknowledging white violence. *The Slave Community* demonstrates that, even in bondage, African Americans held on to their dignity and supported each other so that white "masters" did not determine their self-conceptions. Blassingame's racial self-affirmation is powerful when one considers what Alondra Nelson calls the undeniable "yearning for pre-slavery identity" (22) that made *Roots* a cultural phenomenon inspiring countless people to research their genealogies. Because the community conversation always generates various conceptions of accomplishment, the effort to find roots on the African continent coexisted with affirming each other's understanding that, even when considering one's enslaved ancestors, there were victories, big and small, of which to be proud. Accordingly, Haley's text celebrates the community's achievements before enslavement and those secured despite captivity.

While honoring Kunta Kinte and depicting seven generations of his descendants, *Roots* often defines achievement in relationship to black men, keeping black women in passive roles that highlight men's heroism and leadership; so as Haley's epic contribution to the community conversation perpetuated the masculinism of the Black Power era, black women authors continued to offer challenges, not unlike those from Hansberry and Childress, discussed in Chapter 4. To define black achievement in ways that accommodated women still required critiquing masculinism, and Octavia Butler's *Kindred* (1979) and Toni Morrison's *Beloved* (1987) do that work.[4] By nuancing a community conversation being steered by *Roots*, these texts engage in embodied practices of belonging—both debate and "kinkeeping." Alondra Nelson explains, "kinkeeping involves the work of connecting past and present kin with purposeful narrative" (71). Butler and Morrison offer stories of purpose in the 1970s and 1980s about black women's journeys from being enslaved in other people's homes to being women of their own. As I have argued, the heteronormative nuclear family emerges in black cultural production as a sign for the trope of homemade citizenship. Traditional black households remind readers that African Americans have made themselves at home by pursuing success while knowing violence will likely answer their every achievement and assertion of belonging.

Kindred and *Beloved* feature different kinds of traditional homes, but their investment in complicating the discussion overtaken by *Roots* is clear. Placing a spotlight on an interracial couple, Butler reveals how her black woman protagonist Dana defines success, thereby engaging assumptions regarding black women's supposed history of caring more about white families than about their own. Not unlike mainstream assertions about black matriarchs and the resulting "tangle of pathology," community distrust of black women was based on the belief that the brutality of slavery was having a reverberating effect on its victims' descendants. Butler's story of time travel shows why harshly judging female forebears is a mistake. As Dana moves between the 1800s and the novel's 1976 present, Butler offers a fictional version of Angela Davis's scholarly article debunking the notion (often accepted among African Americans) that enslaved women did not resist because they courted white favor.[5] Meanwhile, Butler uses Dana's 1976 experiences to lay bare Dana's definitions of success, exposing her short-sightedness.

With *Beloved*, understanding that nuclear families are shorthand for the cultivation of homemade citizenship empowers readers to focus on success as much as the community conversation always has. As *Beloved* foregrounds achievement and follows characters as they define and redefine its parameters, Morrison addresses the black female passivity that *Roots* circulated. Especially given how Morrison described her inspiration for writing *Beloved*, attending to women's definitions of, and journeys toward, accomplishment proves crucial. Because there existed no memorials acknowledging the slave experience, not even "a small bench by the road," Morrison explained, the "book had to" exist. When success takes its proper place as the framework for examining black cultural production, one sees that Morrison's efforts were clearly less about national recognition of slavery than about how the community conversation—as inflected by Haley's ubiquitous work—was diminishing black women.

Presumed Progress

In the 1969 drama *Wine in the Wilderness*, Cynthia speaks of having given up on dating white men and believing an integrated world is on the horizon. By 1979, Butler suggests integration has become a real possibility. In *Kindred*, the black woman protagonist Dana has recently moved to the suburbs with her white husband Kevin, and they believe their home represents progress for not only their family but also the nation. However, they find themselves haunted by slavery. The question hovering over their life together is whether their new home is still the master's house. Set in 1976, the same year Alex Haley's *Roots* was published, *Kindred* thematizes the nation's bicentennial but refuses to offer simplistic celebration. Haley had articulated what Salamishah Tillet calls "critical patriotism" when describing his intention as a member of President Gerald Ford's Bicentennial Advisory Council: "to make certain nobody overlooks what blacks did to make this country" (qtd. in Norrell 149). Similarly committed to honoring ancestors, Butler's text targets the community out of concern that African Americans were being judgmental of their forebears. Having encountered at least one young man who was convinced that he would have behaved differently if faced with the injustices of earlier decades, Butler likely suspected his views about enslaved predecessors were even less generous. She shared in an interview that, in college, she had

> heard some remarks from a young man who was the same age I was but who had apparently never made the connection with what his parents did to keep him alive. He was still blaming them for their humility and their acceptance of disgusting behavior on the part of employers and other people. He said, "I'd like to kill all these old people who have been holding us back for so long. But I can't because I'd have to start with my own parents." When he said *us* he meant black people, and when he said *old people* he meant older black people. That was actually the germ of the idea for *Kindred* (1979). I've carried that comment with me for thirty years. He felt so strongly ashamed of what the older generation had to do, without really putting it into the context of being necessary for not only their lives but his as well. (Rowell 51)

Butler noticed that community definitions of success engaged the experience of ancestors, but she believed definitions were faulty if they failed to account for the difference between reading about hardships and experiencing or witnessing them. *Kindred*'s protagonist Dana has recently moved with her white husband into a house in the suburbs of Los Angeles. The year is 1976, but she is inexplicably transported to the 1800s whenever the life of Rufus Weylin, her slave-holding white ancestor, is in danger. As the novel examines nineteenth-century U.S. culture through what Dana experiences and witnesses, slavery's horrors are understood above all through how relentlessly white people attack black domestic success. Practices of making-oneself-at-home inside the text allow readers to encounter ancestors who are brutalized whether they inhabit slave cabins or modest shacks away from white-owned plantations. Moreover, as it contributes to the community conversation, Butler's work suggests that even when African Americans lay claim to enviable houses in the suburbs, literally decades after not only Emancipation but also Civil Rights victories, they wonder whether they are still in the master's house.

Dana is transported to the 1800s whenever Rufus Weylin, her great, great grandfather is about to die. It is never clear how or why she travels through time, but Dana assumes she must keep Rufus alive and even facilitate his rape of her great, great grandmother to ensure her own birth generations later. Dana's husband Kevin is transported with her on one of the trips, so they spend time together in both the slavery era and their 1970s present. Because Dana saves Rufus's life several times, she experiences different decades of the 1800s and sees him grow up to become a self-centered man whose conditioning as an enslaver makes him capable of only the most destructive "love."

When pulled into the nineteenth century, Dana is struck by how relentlessly slaveholders work to make black love a curse. On her second trip, Rufus is seven or eight years old and his father Tom Weylin remembers her earlier unexplained appearance. Because Tom Weylin is suspicious and hostile, Dana wants to leave his plantation. Rufus suggests that she go to the home of his friend, Alice, whose mother is a free black woman who might be able to help. Not realizing how close she is to her destination, Dana hides in bushes to avoid eight white men on horses. While hiding, she sees the Greenwood family's home invaded. The white men are patrollers looking for Mr. Greenwood, who is absent without a pass from the Weylin plantation. Greenwood has come to visit his wife and daughter, Alice, who are both free. Dana watches as the man and woman are forced out of the house, the man whipped, the woman stripped (Butler 35). Greenwood will never receive permission to visit his family because Tom Weylin wants him to choose a slave wife whose children will become his property. Against the odds, the Greenwoods love each other and choose each other, so white people attack them in order to reinforce their "proper" place.

Just as white violence answers the Greenwoods' romantic love, it attacks black parental love, aiming to make it nothing but a source of pain.

Sarah, Weylin's cook, shares with Dana that her husband was killed in a tree accident; then, Weylin sold three of her children, letting her keep Carrie only because "she ain't worth much as the others 'cause she can't talk. People think she ain't got good sense" (76). Dana notices the sadness in Sarah's eyes becomes intense anger as she thanks God for her child's disability.

Because black love can be more constraining than chains, Butler honors practices of making-oneself-at-home, even as those practices almost guarantee black heartache. As Dana notes, if Sarah wanted to kill Tom Weylin, she could poison his food and he would never know what hit him, but Weylin's allowing her to keep Carrie—after the heartbreak of losing her other children—encourages her to tolerate the situation (76). Indeed, when Dana tells Sarah that people who had escaped slavery had written books about it, Sarah responds, "Don't want to hear no more. . . . Things ain't bad here. I can get along" (145). Sarah had recalibrated her definition of success. Dana interprets Sarah's reaction thusly: "She had done the safe thing—had accepted a life of slavery because she was afraid. . . . She was the kind of woman who would be held in contempt during the militant nineteen sixties. The house-nigger, the handkerchief-head, the female Uncle Tom—the frightened powerless woman who had already lost all she could stand to lose" (ibid.). Here, Dana notes the contempt of the militant 1960s and seems to identify with it. She soon begins questioning those indictments, however, as Butler underscores the difference between reading about slavery and witnessing it. Engaging the community conversation on accomplishment, *Kindred* highlights not only how easy it is to judge when one has never felt slavery's power; it also notes the profundity of black love, which led Sarah and others to prioritize family when defining success under the cruelest circumstances.[6] There is nothing enviable about the conditions under which enslaved people developed a home life, but Butler's novel insists that their being forced to inhabit slave cabins did not constitute homemaking failure, no matter what the nation intended.

When Dana encounters Sarah's mute daughter Carrie in adulthood, Butler again troubles Black Power indictments of forebears by suggesting that slavery exploits romantic love as easily as parental love. Carrie and Nigel, who is also enslaved on the Weylin plantation, become a couple after Nigel had run away but was caught (139). He is allowed to marry Carrie and is proud that the ceremony had been performed by a free preacher (133). Later, he builds a cabin away from the quarters, declaring,

"Don't have to sleep on rags up in the attic no more" (155). He also builds
a bed and two chairs, and Rufus, his owner, allows him to "hire out" his
time to buy whatever he cannot make.[7] Dana observes, "It had been a
good investment for Rufus. Not only did he get part of Nigel's earnings,
but he got the assurance that Nigel, his only valuable piece of property,
was not likely to run away again soon" (ibid.). Butler emphasizes that
nineteenth-century whites are as aware of black love as Dana is. After
Nigel had run away, Rufus's father had planned to sell him to a trader.
Rufus had gained Nigel as personal property by convincing his father
not to do so. Rufus admits to Dana, "I don't think Daddy relaxed until
Nigel married Carrie. Man marries, has children, he's more likely to stay
where he is" (139). Just as Frances Harper's *Iola Leroy* had, Butler's text
emphasizes white people's awareness of black people's capacity for love;
indeed, they use black love to make slavery more stable and profitable.

As Butler's text revisits slavery, the majority of African Americans that
Dana encounters define success in terms of making a home within the
institution's boundaries because they love other vulnerable people. Mr.
Greenwood risks life and limb disobeying Weylin to maintain his relationship with his free wife; Mrs. Greenwood follows her heart and accepts the
household vulnerability that comes with marrying a slave; Sarah holds
on to the only family she has left, swallowing her contempt for the man
who has sold three of her children; and Nigel buries his desire for total
freedom to accept a measure of freedom within slavery, grateful to build
a cabin for himself and his wife Carrie on Weylin's plantation. Aware
that the nation and their "masters" are determined to strip them of not
only basic rights but also their humanity, African Americans act according to their loving connection to each other.[8] Even if their homemaking
practices looked like what the nation claimed to respect, they could not
have been motivated by dominant standards because the resemblance
only invited hostility and made them targets.

If characters whose practices of making-oneself-at-home within slavery's parameters echo apparently integrationist sentiments in the community conversation of the 1970s, then the black independence strain
finds expression as Dana interacts with a maturing Alice (the child of the
couple Dana had seen brutalized on an early trip). Alice loves Isaac, and
they strive to keep their bodies for each other; it's part of their definition of success. White violence targets this goal; Rufus tries to rape Alice,
and Isaac beats him nearly to death in the woods (118). Dana convinces
Isaac to run ahead and leave Rufus alive, thereby increasing his and

Alice's chances of escape and avoiding the hysteria that a white man's death would cause. Alice and Isaac have four days of freedom together before being caught. Upon learning of their capture, Rufus buys Alice out of the jail. Though she is more dead than alive, Rufus puts her in her "proper" place; he now legally has the control over her that he wants (151). Besides her physical wounds, including dog bites, she is "a very young child again, incontinent, barely aware of us unless we hurt her or fed her. And she did have to be fed—spoonful by spoonful" (153). Alice literally cannot remember who she (or anyone else) is. As Dana nurses her back to health, she believes Dana to be her mother (ibid.), and she does not recall that she is enslaved (156). Further, she does not remember that Rufus had tried to rape her, that she is in love, and that Isaac is missing. In short, she does not hate Rufus. Upon regaining her memory, she not only hates Rufus; she is also furious with Dana. When Dana explains her part in what has happened, Alice asks, "Why didn't you know enough to let me die?" (160). Once Alice is well, she finds ways to carry on, but she never makes peace with her circumstances. She believes in her right to be free of Rufus. She still aspires to the achievement of having a life with a man of her choice.

Butler emphasizes that Alice never accepts as legitimate Rufus's power to dictate how she will experience home and family. Having Rufus's children does not lessen Alice's determination to be free, so most of the time that Alice lives in slavery without her true love, Isaac, she is plotting escape. Rather than settling for benefits within the boundaries set by an owner, as Sarah, Carrie, and Nigel do, Alice's conception of success requires fleeing those constraints. Though it lessens her odds of escaping undetected, she takes her children every time she runs away because she does not trust Rufus to free them. She also believes that, even if she submits, her staying by Rufus's side will not prevent their eventual sale (232). For Alice, achievement means making no compromises with slavery, so she seems to hate herself for the slightest hint of acquiescence. Trying to convince Alice not to run with the children, Dana says, "Goddamnit, Alice, will you slow down? Look, you keep working on [Rufus] the way you have been and you can get whatever you want and live to enjoy it" (234). This is not good enough for Alice. She runs away again and is caught. Rufus beats her, but he also sends her children away to teach her a lesson, leaving her to assume they have been sold. Soon, she dresses herself up in the clothes Rufus provides to indicate her special status among the slaves . . . and hangs herself (248). Like Sarah, Carrie, and Nigel, Alice is committed to having a home with her loved ones, but unlike them, she does not accept slavery's constraints about what that home can be. Both are strategies of making-oneself-at-home. Both tactics emerge from a focus on defining and pursuing success while knowing violence will answer most victories, especially those in the form of black love.

With the striking exception of Alice, Butler features characters who define achievement in terms of traditional domesticity even in the clutches of slavery, and their homemaking practices become an important corollary for Dana and Kevin's tense home life in 1976. After all, *Kindred* refuses to conceive of present-day households as distinct from those of the past. As Dana resumes her 1976 life, now informed by her slavery experience, she passionately invests in domesticity, insisting that her marriage is stronger than ever. However, her efforts are accompanied by a question that is never uttered but nevertheless bounces off the walls of her house in the suburbs of Los Angeles: *Is the home I am creating with my loving husband just the master's house?* The text never allows this question to become irrelevant. Kevin and Dana love each other, but that does not keep them from wondering whether their life together is a modern-day version of a sexualized master/slave relationship, which would shake Dana's confidence about the achievement she believes her marriage represents.

Prior to history's intrusion, Kevin and Dana happily ignore the nation's racial past and present, defining success in terms of transcending race, but once their time-travel experience leads them to more often acknowledge the racial dynamics of their marriage, they confront an unsettling truth. Namely, there is no guarantee that deeper awareness of each other's experiences will yield intimacy and stability, what domestic success should produce. Without question, facing the past helps Dana and Kevin appreciate each other's circumstances more fully, which creates better understanding in the present. For instance, when Kevin must acknowledge Dana's encounters, he realizes that he looks like the white men who brutalize African Americans. *Kindred* thereby suggests that true connection requires such confrontations, and by using time travel, the novel insists that the knowledge gained by reading about something is insufficient. There is power in having embodied knowledge—experiencing a phenomenon, not simply learning about it; nevertheless, one can never take another's place, as Butler demonstrates with Dana and Alice, the great, great grandmother with whom Dana interacts at different points in Alice's life. As much as they resemble each other physically and find themselves in similar situations, Dana and Alice have very different realities. Dana tells herself that she has no choice but to facilitate Alice's rape by Rufus—that she must keep Rufus pacified and that helping Alice submit to him will yield less devastation for Alice herself. However, as literary critic Kelley Wagers puts it, though Dana believes she must encourage Alice to go to Rufus's bed quietly, "the fact that Dana has a choice at all registers an important distance between the two women. Dana's time travel may force her to witness and, to an extent, withstand the conditions of slavery. . . . But she cannot take Alice's place." Thus, Dana can never truly know Alice's reality.

Similarly, *Kindred* demonstrates that even when people love each other, they cannot inhabit each other's experience (Wagers 40), and this reality will either bring Dana closer to Kevin as she revises her definition of success or not. As cultural historian Diana Paulin suggests, even if Kevin feels intense pain and anxiety, "he cannot change history and he cannot live as though he and Dana have the same status" (187). Unequal power relations shape both the past and the present, and even their time-travel wounds underscore this fact. When Kevin returns to 1976 for good, he has a scar on his forehead, but Dana has lost her arm. In a racist and sexist society, Dana's identity brings a very different experience into her life, even as she shares it with a white man, but this is a truth she had avoided acknowledging prior to time travel. As Paulin explains, "the relationship between blacks and whites is mutually interactive [in Butler's view]; yet power and privilege continue to accompany white skin and male gender" (189). Upon their return to the 1970s, Kevin and Dana seem to realize that they must face these truths.

For Paulin and other scholars, the Epilogue makes unmistakable "[Kevin and Dana's] decision to remain together as a more resilient and empowered couple" (ibid.), but I contend that the novel offers no such certainty. Instead, it leaves the couple's future an open question, despite Dana's efforts as narrator to impose closure. Essentially, Butler seems to base *Kindred* on a worldview famously articulated by earlier American authors. For William Faulkner, "The past is never dead. It's not even past."[9] To similar effect, James Baldwin insisted, "History . . . is not merely something to be read. And it does not refer merely, or even principally, to the past. On the contrary, the great force of history comes from the fact that we carry it within, are unconsciously controlled by it in many ways, and history is literally present in all that we do."[10]

Because Butler's novel approaches history as did Faulkner and Baldwin, readers cannot be faithful to the text while treating the past and present separately; the novel's contribution to the community conversation of the 1970s hinges on its recognition of the past's impact on the present. And yet, in subsequent decades, some critics have insisted upon declaring experiences to be fundamentally different because they take place in different time periods. Literary scholar Guy Foster encourages readers to assume that there is a boundary between the nation's history and its current moment, but it simply will not hold. Foster claims that because scholars read *Kindred* according to its supposed parallels with nineteenth-century slave testimonies, they graft "the historical narrative of interracial rape, represented by Rufus and Alice's forced relations" onto Kevin and Dana's marriage, thereby underestimating the importance of their clearly "consensual interracial desire" (148). Foster insists that such readings rely on and perpetuate stereotypical understandings of interracial couples, whereby the white partner is assumed to be racist and the person of color is assumed to be a self-hating race traitor (ibid.). These assumptions arise, Foster explains, because Americans equate interracial sexual relations of the present with those of the past, ignoring the fact that these relationships are forged under very different conditions. However, *Kindred* insists that the world of slave narratives is not separate from the modern moment; slavery is the foundation upon which the present is built.

Time travel forces Dana to face slavery's enduring presence, and her notions of achievement must begin engaging it. She had been working toward integration into the American dream of racial transcendence, which relies on convenient amnesia. Butler's text suggests that this makes Dana as misguided as the young man who said accommodationists should be killed but he would have to begin with his parents. As it highlights Dana's shortsightedness, there is no ambiguity about one aspect of Butler's text: when both members of an interracial couple acknowledge that history cannot be escaped, each *wonders* whether there is any real difference between the circumstances of their modern relationship and the circumstances that defined those of the past. Dana absolutely wonders if she might be a race traitor, and Kevin wonders whether he can ever be more in Dana's eyes than a racist white man. These doubts begin to have an impact on the definition of success that will shape the home they can create together.

Once she begins facing the link between the past and present, Dana acknowledges an uneasiness that she never wanted to believe might be valid because her definition of success had been so centered on transcending race. Early in Dana and Kevin's courtship, Dana's uncle had been hurt by her choosing a white partner. This uncle had always been like a father to her, but "Now . . . it is as though I've rejected him. Or at least that's the way he feels. It bothered me, really. He was more hurt than mad. Honestly hurt. I had to get away from him" (111). When explaining why her uncle felt rejected, Dana had said to Kevin: "I'm marrying you. . . . He wants me to marry someone like him—someone who looks like him. A black man" (ibid.). This is an uncomfortable memory for Dana. In Guy Foster's words, "what 'bothers' Dana is . . . the belief that perhaps he is correct to feel the way he does and that, on some level, she is the one wrong for going ahead with a marriage to someone her uncle so opposed" (153). Foster continues, though Dana "is primarily an individualist, . . . she also appears to harbor some sense of betrayal for her decision to marry 'outside the race'" (ibid.).

Though Foster speaks of Dana's reaction as if it is emotional and illogical, Butler presents her uneasiness as a manifestation of her continued pursuit of success but with the unavoidable recalibration of her beliefs about what characterizes it. She wonders whether she is putting her homemaking efforts in the wrong place. Dana reports that the last thing her uncle had said to her was that he would no longer leave her the apartment houses he owns. Because these properties—"small places, but nice"—belong to the family, "he'd rather will them to his church than leave them to me and see them fall into white hands" (112). Dana muses, "I think that was the worst thing he could think to do to me. Or he thought it was the worst thing" (ibid.). However, if Dana is bothered by these last words, the issue is not that she believes her uncle had been trying to do something to her—she admits he was hurt, not angry—it is that his words make her recognize that those are her family's houses . . . and perhaps she is choosing the master's house instead. Her uncle certainly thinks that is what she is doing—and knowing that "bothers" her. In other words, once she recognizes history's relevance, Dana wonders whether her uncle had been narrow-minded and prejudiced or had simply acknowledged the racial realities of American culture that she and Kevin had always willfully ignored, thereby basing their sense of achievement on the shaky ground of mainstream lies and convenient amnesia.

If her uncle had been simply acknowledging that race matters, then perhaps Dana's choices had been affected by race and racism even as she overlooked these forces. For example, American culture teaches that proximity to whiteness is a prize, no matter what one gives up for it. Not believing this lie, the characters in *Iola Leroy*, even those who can pass, define success without regard to mainstream claims. Their victories, especially their domestic ones, gesture toward homemade citizenship, not an investment in civic inclusion. Dana had scoffed at her uncle's pained declaration about withholding the apartment houses, saying, "Or he thought it was the worst thing [he could do]." Now, perhaps, she wonders if it had not been the worst thing precisely because she defined success by proximity to whiteness so much that she could not even fathom that she had given anything up when she had agreed to "go to Vegas and pretend we haven't got relatives" (ibid.). After Dana has traveled through time and has faced the similarities between the American past and present, she has difficulty dismissing the concerns others express about her relationship. Even if articulated long ago, those concerns haunt her.

Likewise, once unable to ignore the relevance of race and racism to the success of his marriage, Kevin wonders whether the home he shares with Dana is the master's house. He faces this question when Dana returns to 1976 while being attacked by a rapacious patroller. When she comes to consciousness, she does not realize that the man hovering over her is her loving husband Kevin and not the patroller. Panicking, she "scrambled away, kicking him, clawing the hands that reached out for [her], trying to bite, lunging up towards his eyes" (43). Later, Kevin asks, "Do I really look like that patroller?" She says he does not, but Kevin's uneasiness fails to subside and he asks further, "Do I look like someone you can come back to?" (51). Kevin seems to wonder what will become of their union if Dana can no longer distinguish between him and the brutal white men "she encounters in the historical past" (G. Foster 155). If Dana can see no difference, she cannot be with Kevin, and this possibility creates tremendous anxiety for him. As Foster reads it, Kevin's anxiety "spreads to" Dana, and her anxiety "will not be abated until" later, when she "learns, much to her relief, that Kevin had worked closely with the underground railroad" (ibid.). This characterization of their relationship sounds nice, but it requires a linear progression that is far more simplistic than justified, given Butler's representation of history as a persistent presence.

While Dana may be pleased to learn of Kevin's antislavery activities and Kevin is relieved to share them, the novel does not suggest that either one of them ever feels any less anxious because, if success no longer means transcending race, then how will they refine their definition of it? Even while discussing their antislavery beliefs, anxiety is palpable. When Kevin returns to 1976 from being in the nineteenth century alone, he mentions having been accused of helping slaves escape. It does not take long for Dana to ask, "Were you helping slaves to escape?" He snaps back, "Of course I was!" (Butler 193). Dana narrates, "he sounded angry, almost defensive about what he had done" (ibid.). Corroborating this impression, Kevin explains his tone by saying that it had been a while since he had spoken about those activities with someone who understands. Yet, his anger and defensiveness could just as easily arise from the fact that Dana feels the need to ask the question. It is reasonable for readers to notice that Dana did not take for granted that Kevin would have been part of the antislavery cause.[11] Foster's claims notwithstanding, Kevin's sharing that "Around that time, I was accused of helping slaves to escape. I barely got out ahead of the mob" does not keep Dana from asking, "Were you helping slaves to escape?" (ibid.). Therefore, Kevin's and Dana's awareness of it comes and goes, but the question—is this still the master's house?—hovers over them. Indeed, it will continue to do so for the duration of their relationship. If Dana wonders whether Kevin is a racist (or at least an accomplice), then how can she keep from wondering whether she is a race traitor for choosing him as a partner? Of course, Kevin can no longer take anything for granted either. He must ask, "Do I look like someone you can come home to?" (51), and the relevance of this question never fades.

These high-stakes questions persist because the present and past are linked, as the *Roots* phenomenon demonstrated, and while *Kindred* highlights parallels between the 1800s and 1976, one of the most unsettling similarities involves writing and authorship, pillars in Dana's conception of achievement. In the nineteenth century, Dana writes mostly at Rufus's whim, and in the twentieth century, upon their arrival in their new home, Dana sorts books while Kevin is "either loafing or thinking" in his office. Thus, Butler suggests that, four years into their marriage, little has changed since they first met, when Dana had observed: "Kevin Franklin, his name was, and he'd not only gotten his book published, but he'd made a big paperback sale. He could live on the money while he wrote his next book. He could give up shitwork, hopefully forever" (54). As Wagers explains, "Kevin will live by his writing in broad daylight, while Dana continues to write at night and stumble through the minimum-wage jobs that support her" (31). In fact, Kevin had once said, "Yeah, don't you want to marry me? . . . I'd let you type all my manuscripts" (109). Dana resists this idea, refusing him enough to make him angry (ibid.). However, though Kevin seems to have accepted her refusal, she essentially fulfills a secretarial role when organizing their new house while he is "loafing or thinking" in his home office.

The parallel between Dana's writing at Rufus's whim and providing secretarial support for Kevin only intensifies the sense that she is falling short of her own definitions of success, which center on being free from traditional racial and gender constraints—in a word, free from history. At one point, Dana admits that because sharing Kevin's bed on the plantation is acceptable because nothing could be more normal than a slave sleeping with her master, "I almost felt as though I really was doing something shameful, happily playing whore for my supposed owner. I went away feeling uncomfortable, vaguely ashamed" (97). Dana says she *almost* felt like she was doing something degrading, but she cannot altogether escape these feelings, especially as racial transcendence seems less and less like a legitimate basis for her ideals. Clearly, Butler's text does not insist that modern interracial relationships are the same as those of the past, but that doesn't mean that the individuals in these relationships do not *wonder* if they are. The similarities cannot be easily ignored if there is to be any valid assessment of achievement.

Butler's *Kindred* suggests, in fact, that ignoring the similarities is pointless as long as, in Baldwin's words, "the great force of history comes from the fact that we carry it within, are unconsciously controlled by it." Note, for example, that Dana is disturbed by how easily she and Kevin fit into plantation life outside the bedroom. "Not that I wanted us to have trouble, but it seemed as though we should have had a harder time adjusting to this particular segment of history—adjusting to our places in the household of a slave holder. . . . For drop-ins from another century, I thought we had had a remarkably easy time" (ibid.). In conversation with Haley's *Roots*, Butler therefore suggests that slavery is not simply a "segment" of history; it cannot be cordoned off from 1976, the country's bicentennial, if for no other reason than the fact that slavery made the United States what it is.

Butler makes the parallels between the past and present more concrete than simply acknowledging that the country was built on a foundation of slavery, however. When Dana and Kevin reunite after he has been in the 1800s without her, their modern L.A. home reminds Dana of the Weylin house. She resists, "No. I shook my head, denying the impression. This house was nothing like the Weylin house" (193). Yet, as she watches Kevin get reacquainted with his surroundings, Butler has her note how he pauses in front of the shelf full of copies of "his most successful novel—the novel that had bought us this house" (ibid.). Dana thus highlights the dynamics that make their life possible. She lives in this suburban home not because her writing has taken off or because she can afford it with her minimum-wage jobs, but because her husband is white and therefore enjoys a level of (unopposed) success in American society that she and other black Americans do not. Again, although transcending race had been a key component of her definition of success and a confirmation of her homemaking achievement, she can no longer ignore the pillars of racism that prop up her house. Just as she is disturbed by the ease with which she and Kevin fit into slavery's expectations, there will always be uneasiness about the benefits she enjoys because the nation puts white men at an advantage. She had said of her time in slavery that Kevin was better protection than free papers (59). Like it or not, in the twentieth century, she cannot help wondering if there is still some truth to that.

As Dana and Kevin cling more intently to the relationship—trying to allay the insecurities created by that hovering question, *is this still the master's house?*—*Kindred*'s ending is particularly telling. In the Epilogue, Dana (as narrator) anxiously asserts the strength of the bond she and her white husband share because they have stayed together through their time-traveling ordeal. When they are safe from further interruptions from the nineteenth century, they visit the site of their encounter with slavery. The Maryland Historical Society has no records about the master's house that shaped their experience, so they have no material confirmation of the encounters that have fundamentally altered their relationship. They are disappointed but respond by assuring each other that their marriage (and the home they have made together in the suburbs) is stronger than ever. After all, only the two of them know that they are not crazy if they speak of the life-altering adventure of time travel as black woman and white man.

Butler does not treat Dana's choice of a white life partner as insignificant, and she underscores its many vexed implications with the text's most striking example of the power of embodied knowledge. Dana returns permanently from the nineteenth century when she kills Rufus, the man whose life she has been saving throughout the novel. Rufus is in utter despair because Alice has killed herself in response to his cruelty. He says he would rather be dead too, and Dana urges him to stay alive for his children; they are all he has left of Alice (256). Rufus insists that if Dana really cares about the children, then she should stay to replace their mother. This tense conversation continues. Rufus notes that, no matter what he has done, Dana has never hated him. He says Alice hated him "from the first time I forced her," but she had eventually stopped. Chillingly, Rufus says to Dana, "She had stopped hating me. I wonder how long it will take you" (259). Here, Rufus believes he has witnessed different responses to white violence; in fact, he has simply encountered black women pursuing different definitions of success. He pushes Dana onto the pallet, and she thinks about how much easier it would be to yield to him than to kill him.[12] Indeed, much of the action in this scene amounts to Butler's painstaking portrayal of Dana's ambivalence; Dana's thoughts become the details about her experience that she will never share with Kevin. However, she gathers herself enough to stab Rufus twice. His death releases her, and as she returns to 1976, she realizes that her arm is stuck in the wall of her new suburban house. She loses her arm from the elbow down, and Butler emphasizes that this is precisely where Rufus had been holding onto her. Seeing the wall of which her arm is now a part, she pulls hard and feels the pain, but she also hears Kevin's loving voice. Together, her rapist's grasp and the wall of her suburban home constitute her exit and entry point. There is no way to distinguish between peril and possibility.

Dana had not recognized Kevin when escaping the rapacious patroller earlier, so Butler marks a difference by allowing Dana to recognize Kevin's voice on this final return, but Dana's missing arm will always remind her of encounters with the past, the relevance of which refuse to fade. As readers encounter her in the community conversation of the 1970s and 1980s, it is clear that what is missing from Dana's body has been claimed by the wall of her suburban house no less than by slavery's rapacious grip. As long as her knowledge and her memories are inescapably embodied, she cannot avoid wondering if this is still the master's house.

Vulnerable Both Inside and Outside the Master's House

Beloved's protagonist Sethe defines achievement in terms of homemaking based on romantic coupling. In the tradition of *Incidents in the Life of a Slave Girl*, discussed in Chapter 1, choosing one's mate, not simply loving one's children, will be the surest sign she no longer occupies the master's house. Having fled slavery, Sethe lands at "124," the home of her husband's emancipated mother, Baby Suggs. Shortly after Sethe reaches

124 Bluestone Road, men arrive to re-enslave her. Determined to protect her children from bondage, she tries to kill them all but only succeeds with the baby, Beloved. The would-be slave catchers consider her insane and not worth taking back, so after a stint in jail, Sethe is left to make a life with her surviving children. Meanwhile, the violent intrusion upon the home she has made in freedom shakes Baby Suggs to the core. She stops preaching in the Clearing, where she had led community members in valuing themselves. No longer confident that an empowering space can be sustained, she retreats from life by staying in "the keeping room" and "pondering color" (Morrison 4). Soon thereafter, she dies, and Sethe is left to make a life in 124, which is full of the spirit of the dead baby, Beloved. Sethe's sons would not tolerate the spirit, so 124 is now occupied by Sethe, her daughter Denver, and her dead daughter Beloved, and practices of making-oneself-at-home drive the action. Sethe works to claim success—defined as creating a home distinct from the master's house— while also acknowledging the violence that answers black achievement. No longer hunted by slave catchers, Sethe seems to have a home of her own, yet the question of whether this is still the master's house hovers.

Homemaking can be achieved in many ways, of course, but Morrison depicts black women's pursuit of success in terms of making a home with a romantic partner. When Sethe becomes woman of the house after Baby Suggs's death, determining whether this is still the master's house revolves around romantic coupling. Paul D, who had been enslaved alongside Sethe and her (now missing) husband Halle, stumbles upon 124 and wants to become Sethe's life partner. *Beloved* lingers over the moments when Sethe and Paul D decide for (and against) drawing closer to each other. For him, the decision has to do with not feeling restless, not itching to leave.[13] Until finding her, he had never stayed anywhere for more than a few months at a time because "he had shut down a generous portion of his head, operating on the part that helped him walk, eat, sleep, sing" (49). To prioritize more than those necessities would have "required him to dwell" on his slave past at the Sweet Home plantation and the harsh realities of his life as a prisoner on a chain gang. In not always realizing he must find a way to live with his past, Paul D proves similar to Sappho in *Contending Forces*, yet, as *Kindred* shows—in concert with *Roots*—the past always demands a reckoning.

Even if he is not completely aware of the tangle with the past it will require, Morrison emphasizes Paul D's certainty about wanting to make a life with Sethe. Paul D is drawn to Sethe because she does not judge him for what he has endured. Because she creates a space for him to acknowledge his past without having his present limited by it, if he makes a home with her, it will not be the master's house. The nation's dehumanizing definitions will not reign in their home. With his pleased surprise at finding Halle's wife, "the closed portion of his head opened like a greased lock" (ibid.).[14] In other words, reuniting with Sethe makes him willing to have an interior life. Driven by his own desire, he makes this choice free from the power white people exercised over him on the plantation and on the chain gang. He revises his goals, and he soon encourages Sethe to do the same.[15]

Morrison highlights Sethe's difficulty giving herself permission to define success in ways that prioritize an interior life. After having sex with Paul D, Sethe lies in bed wondering, "would it be all right? Would it be all right to go ahead and feel? Go ahead and *count on something?*" (46). Despite their plans, Sethe's husband Halle has never joined her in the North, so "counting on something" feels dangerous. Unable to think clearly while lying with Paul D, she goes to the keeping room. For the first time, she sees her surroundings clearly and realizes why Baby Suggs had been so starved for color. Because of Paul D's presence, "emotions sped to the surface" and "things became what they were: drabness looked drab; heat was hot. Windows suddenly had view" (48). As Sethe and Paul D begin conceiving of achievement in terms that require an interior life, they begin "talking like a couple" after only one night. Indeed, "they had skipped love and promise and went directly to" Sethe saying it was "better than all right" for Paul D to find work in town and settle down there (51, 50).

However, as Sethe becomes more comfortable with the idea of "counting on something," Morrison uses her daughter, Denver, to make Sethe face the fact that she had not quite answered her own questions: *Would it be all right? Would it be all right to go ahead and feel?* Denver has been running "a mighty interference" and soon asks Paul D "how long he was going to hang around" (52). Paul D offers, "Maybe I should make tracks," and Sethe is surprised by how loud her spontaneous "no" is. She sends Denver out of the room, but soon finds herself issuing an ultimatum: "If I have to choose—well, it's not even a choice." To this, Paul D is unequivocal: "That's the point. The whole point. I'm not asking you to choose. Nobody would. I thought—well, I thought you could—there was some space for me" (54). Sethe points out that Denver is asking her to choose, but Paul D insists there's no need for an either/or scenario. He urges, "Tell her it's not about choosing somebody over her—it's making space for somebody along with her. You got to say it" (55). For Paul D, theirs can be different from the master's house, but that requires Sethe to give voice to what she wants.

Morrison makes clear that Paul D urges Sethe to help Denver accept his presence because he senses Sethe could be happier "on the inside" if she were open to letting a man catch her rather than doing everything on her own. He seems to believe she is being a matriarch, and he offers her relief from that role. By not having a life partner, Sethe has been refusing herself the option of "going inside." Paul D does not advise Sethe this way because he needs a place to live; he is a "walking man," after all. But "we can make a life, girl. A life" (ibid.). He asks Sethe to leave it to him and see how it goes. She says she will leave "some" of it to him, so he offers to take her and Denver to the carnival. This becomes Sethe's first outing in eighteen years (56).

Paul D does not understand why Sethe is worried about needing to choose between him and her children—a choice that would make their home too much like the master's house—but Morrison shows readers what he fails to recognize, that his arrival had indeed created an either/or situation. When he had begun kissing Sethe at the stove, Beloved had asked Sethe to choose, by shaking the house. Paul D had responded in kind. While fighting the spirit and the furniture it pitched, he had shouted, "Leave the place alone! Get the hell out" (22). The spirit thrust a table at him. He managed to grab it, and "he based it about, wrecking everything, screaming back at the screaming house, 'You want to fight, come on! God damn it'" (ibid.). More than this, he declared, "She got enough without you. She got enough!" (ibid.). Beloved would not have interpreted this declaration to mean Sethe has enough burdens without the burden of a haunted house. If Denver's insight means anything, then Beloved took this encounter as evidence that when asked to choose, Sethe would not choose her. As Denver says earlier, the ghost is not evil or even sad so much as rebuked and lonely (16).

Though Sethe conceives of success as a home based on romantic coupling, Morrison continues to foreground the question of whether Sethe must choose either motherly love or romantic love when Beloved appears in human form after being rejected in spirit form. Beloved's appearance is without explanation, but Sethe is not suspicious; she welcomes the stranger into her house, just as Baby Suggs had welcomed Sethe years before without asking questions. Meanwhile, Sethe continues to believe a home life with Paul D is possible and goes to the Clearing to make a final decision, which includes divorcing Halle in her heart (112). She takes Denver and Beloved with her. While standing on Baby Suggs's signature rock, which had served as her pulpit, Sethe feels fingers caressing her neck. When the caress becomes a stranglehold, Sethe is "more surprised than frightened," assuming it is Baby Suggs's spirit (113).[16] She does not allow herself to consider for long that it might be Beloved or even the spirit Paul D had cast out of her home. She immediately moves past the unsettling experience because the "ambition welling in her now" is so strong: "she wanted Paul D" (116). Morrison thereby emphasizes that Sethe's pursuit of success involves prioritizing romantic desire.

And yet, even as Sethe feels she can find happiness with Paul D, she believes doing so is wrong unless she can achieve the feat of balancing romantic and parental love. She is excited because "the glimpse of happiness she caught in the shadows swinging hands on the road to the carnival was a likelihood" (114). She is aware of barriers to this happiness, but she can refuse to erect them. A new life is "a likelihood—if she could just manage the news Paul D brought and the news he kept to himself. Just manage it" (ibid.). Convincing herself to grasp the success she glimpses, she coaches herself, "Just manage it. Not break, fall or cry each time a hateful picture drifted in front of her face. Not develop some permanent craziness like Baby Suggs' friend, a young woman in a bonnet whose food was full of tears. Like Aunt Phyllis, who slept with her eyes wide open. Like Jackson Till, who slept under the bed. All she wanted was to go on. As she had. Alone with her daughter in a haunted house she managed every damn thing. Why now, with Paul D instead of the ghost, was she breaking up? Getting scared? Needing Baby?" (ibid.). While uncertain she can manage an interior life and the vulnerability of intimacy—as Candice Jenkins argues, "intimacy simply cannot be made 'safe'" (20)—Sethe is determined to try. If she succeeds, this victory will be only the beginning. She must also balance romantic and parental love; only then can she believe she deserves a new life that includes the freedom to "go inside" (55).

She leaves the Clearing feeling confident that she can manage the balancing act, that she can live up to her definition of achievement, so she resolves to give the relationship a chance. Still heavy with what Paul D has shared about both Halle and himself, Sethe decides, "No matter what he told and knew, she wanted him in her life. . . . [T]hat is what she had come to the Clearing to figure out, and now it was figured" (Morrison

116). She is drawn to "the mind of him that knew her own. Her story was bearable because it was his as well—to tell, to refine and tell again. The things neither knew about the other—the things neither had word-shapes for—well, it would come in time: where they led him off to sucking iron; the perfect death of her crawling already baby" (ibid.). She feels sure she would "launch her newer, stronger life with a tender man" (117), but only because she is certain she has love enough for all (118).

With this, Sethe believes not only that 124 is not the master's house but also that it can become a home in which she shares with a romantic partner all she has experienced. In that sharing, her past could become usable as she creates the (home) life she wants. Through her home and reconfigured family, she will execute her vision for herself as a woman who has done the best she could under horrible conditions and claimed new and better circumstances. This achievement would be the ultimate in making-oneself-at-home, claiming accomplishment while knowing that doing so attracts the country's hostility.

Sethe believes that achievement depends on making a home less shaped by all that had characterized the master's house. Outside the text, the community conversation is aware of how often African Americans made a sense of home even in the master's house, but Sethe's goals are clear. As important, she makes her assessment in the context of others who had faced similar difficulties in their postslavery lives—that is, in their own homes—and had experienced varying degrees of success outside the master's house. Some make food that is full of tears, some sleep with their eyes wide open, some sleep under their beds. Like her, all have had their victories answered with white people's commitment to place "hateful pictures" in their minds. She will not ignore the violations responsible for creating her own "hateful pictures"; she acknowledges their significance. Nevertheless, she continues to pursue greater and greater freedom, the goal that had been her compass, even while at Sweet Home.

Though Sethe's definition of success requires the freedom to love her children and a man of her choice, she recognizes the opposition to black women's ability to do this, but remembering her journey to 124, she concludes it can be done in her case. Sethe pursues a life with Paul D because she is confident she "could do it. Just like the day she arrived at 124— sure enough, she had milk enough for all" (ibid.). Unfortunately, doubts arise again, but when they do, she worries less about her own limitations than about Paul D's. He comes to Sethe to confess about sleeping with Beloved, so he begins by admitting she will not like what he has to say.

Sethe braces herself by peremptorily accepting disappointment "because she didn't believe any of them—over the long haul—could measure up" (150). Paul D senses her lowered expectations and, instead of confessing, asks her to have a baby with him. This request scares Sethe, and she wonders: "What did he want her pregnant for? To hold on to her? Have a sign that he passed this way? He probably had children everywhere anyway" (155). She comes to a troubling conclusion: "No. He resented the children she had, that's what." She assumes he resents "sharing her with the girls. Maybe even the time spent on their needs and not his. They were a family somehow and he was not the head of it" (ibid.). Presuming Paul D resents not being head of household, Sethe increasingly suspects that, even when she succeeds in having enough love to give, only one kind of love can be sustained. If a child is not offended by the partner, then the partner is bothered by a child, it seems, so her capacity for love guarantees nothing.

The tension haunting Sethe, despite her confidence about having enough love for everyone, allows Morrison to remind readers of dynamics enforced during slavery to destroy black intimacy. In the process, the text draws a parallel between the master's house and Sethe's home in freedom because slaveholders sometimes tolerated black women's love for their children but never their love for a man of their choice. Harriet Jacobs highlighted these painful dynamics in the 1860s, and as readers encountered *Beloved* in the community conversation of the 1980s, they may have noted a modern version. Namely, the state increasingly functioned as a stand-in for slaveholders when it discouraged black nuclear families by denying resources to women who had partners.[17] *Caring for children? Sure! A partner of your choice? Not so fast!*

As Paul D unconsciously aligns with dominant discourses and practices, Morrison uses his limitations to highlight the many ways that American words and deeds constrain black women.

Given the consistency with which black women have been forced to choose between maternal and romantic love, it is significant that Sethe had seen in her own mother a glimpse of the possibility of expressing both. Though the dignity and tenderness are slight, they are emphasized and passed down through storytelling. Like most slave children, Sethe spent most of her time with an old woman assigned to care for youngsters while other women worked in the field. Sethe's caregiver, Nan, made a point of revealing that Sethe had been the only child her mother had not thrown away without a name. Soon after her mother was hanged,

Nan had drawn the distinction: "You she gave the name of the black man. She put her arms around him. The others she did not put her arms around. Never. Never. Telling you. I am telling you, small girl Sethe" (74). Nan speaks as a woman who had been "taken up many times by the crew," just as Sethe's mother had been. Perhaps they had supported each other by agreeing to refuse to put their arms around the men forced upon them.[18] Whatever the details, Nan is the best source Sethe has for information about her mother, whom she had seen only a few times. Nan attempts to give flesh to the sparse nurturing Sethe's mother was allowed to do on a plantation where women nursed their children for only two or three weeks before returning to work (72). Sethe's mother was gone all day and rarely spent the night. Sethe recalls, "By the time I woke up in the morning, she was in line. If the moon was bright they worked by its light. Sunday she slept like a stick" (ibid.).

As faint as it is, Sethe remembers her mother as a black woman who insisted upon attachment to both a man of her choice and a child. And, that was during slavery, in the master's house, so *Beloved*'s contribution to a *Roots*-inflected community conversation acknowledges practices of making-oneself-at-home . . . in the tradition of Jacobs, Keckley, Harper, and Hopkins. Sweet Home was never meant to be a home for the enslaved, especially not a sweet one, but that fact did not keep black women from working to create what was never intended.

Sethe never assumes black women will be allowed to balance parental and romantic love, but her glimpse of the possibility shapes her sense of what it means to make oneself at home in the midst of brutality. Her mother's remarkable feat has stayed with her, shaping her deepest desires. Paul D wants a life with her as much as she wants one with him, but as relentlessly as they march toward new definitions of success, they cannot simply erase their slave pasts. Forgetting the past would mean ignoring white violence but, as Butler shows through Dana, African Americans will go astray whenever trying to define and pursue success without accounting for the nation's commitment to racism. Thus, the entire time the novel tells of Paul D's and Sethe's love, it underscores their inability to escape the question: *Is this still the master's house?*

As *Beloved* engages whether the home of its emancipated characters might still be the master's house, Baby Suggs's homemaking efforts—and the shifting definitions of success that fuel them—prove as important as those of Paul D and Sethe. The new house is the first one in which Baby Suggs knows freedom, thanks to her son Halle's sacrifice. That freedom seems doomed to be marked by the absence of family, though, because even if this space is not the master's house, slavery has torn her family apart. Thus, *Beloved* joins the community conversation of the 1980s in exposing what is violently erased whenever black families are labeled pathological so that the nation's hostility toward them becomes a nonissue. The hope that Baby Suggs has for a reunited family rests in knowing her son had married and his wife is pregnant, though she has no idea where that wife might be. When Sethe arrives at 124, then, a fragment of Baby Suggs's family is reassembled; 124 had been a safe stopping place for Sethe because, when separated from her family, Baby Suggs had made it a homeplace for extended black community, but while the safety it provided had beckoned Sethe, it also set the stage for the betrayal of the very community Baby Suggs had served. Seeing how painful her bad hip makes simple movement, Halle has worked himself past exhaustion on his mother's behalf, so although the house represents freedom, it also represents alienation from family still in bondage. Seeing in Halle's face how much the accomplishment meant to him, she "never put to him the question she put to herself: What for? What does a sixty-odd-year-old woman who walks like a three-legged dog need freedom for?" (166). However, upon becoming free, she realizes he had understood its value in ways she had not.

When Baby Suggs relocates to Ohio to have a home of her own, Morrison highlights how naming practices create the greatest distance from the master's house. Garner, from whom her son is buying her freedom, helps her settle into her new life (ibid.). He had always called her "Jenny," and she finally asks why. Upon hearing his answer, she explains that, although "Jenny Whitlow" had been on her bill of sale, she always most identified with her husband Suggs, who had always called her "Baby." Garner advises, "If I was you I'd stick to Jenny Whitlow. Mrs. Baby Suggs ain't no name for a freed Negro" (167). Without contradicting him aloud, she rejects the advice because, like so many African Americans historically, she focuses on reassembling her family. She and her husband had always agreed to run away whenever they got a chance. He had done precisely that, and she assumes he had made it to freedom. Stepping into her new life in 124, she wonders, "Now how could he find or hear tell of her if she was calling herself some bill-of-sale name?" (168).

No longer occupying the master's house should mean Baby Suggs can reassemble her family, but ultimately, this is not the case. In two years of church networking, the information she gathers is "so pitiful she quit" (173). Cherishing the knowledge that her son Halle had gotten married and had a baby on the way, she has hope, but she remains alone, so she throws herself into "her own brand of preaching" (ibid.). Her heart seemed to start beating "the minute she crossed the Ohio River," so her ministry emerges when she makes up her mind about what to do with this newly beating heart (ibid.). While hoping to make her house a home when her family is reunited, she decides to enjoy what she can of freedom in the meantime: the two-story house at 124 Bluestone Road is hers to occupy "in return for laundry, some seamstress work, a little canning and so on (oh shoes, too)" (171). Baby Suggs had eagerly agreed to this arrangement because she is "excited about a house with steps—never mind she couldn't climb them" (ibid.). She will make do with the house until she can make it a home with her family.

In time, Baby Suggs decides that even if slavery prevents her new residence from becoming a family space, she can secure the victory of distinguishing it from the master's house by making it a community space. Relinquishing reunion hopes, but determined to live a full life, she creates a homeplace—"homes where all black people could strive to be subjects, not objects, where we could be affirmed in our minds and hearts despite poverty, hardship, and deprivation, where we could restore to ourselves the dignity denied us on the outside" (hooks 42). Therefore, when Sethe makes a miraculous escape from slavery, 124 is a safe place to land, a way station that is well-known because Baby Suggs had helped so many others. The day Sethe arrives at 124, having escaped slavery and made it there even after giving birth on the way, Baby Suggs begins celebrating with abandon.

Unfortunately, surviving and overcoming white violence, and making herself and her daughter-in-law at home, bring hostility. Community members view Baby Suggs's celebration as prideful; they do not approve. The novel consistently suggests that pride in women is a problem. Male beings, even roosters,[19] are expected to be proud, but it is somehow offensive in women. Accordingly, when what started as a gift of two buckets of berries from Stamp Paid, and the delight it brought to baby Denver, turned into "a feast for 90 people," the community partook but then resented Baby Suggs for it. Morrison's narrator reports, "Ninety people who ate so well, and laughed so much, it made them angry" (161). The next morning, remembering the revelry and the richness of the food, they "got angry" (ibid.). It was "too much, they thought. Where does she get it all, Baby Suggs, holy? Why is she and hers always the center of things? How come she always knows exactly what to do and when?

Giving advice; passing messages; healing the sick, hiding fugitives, loving, cooking, cooking, loving, preaching, singing, dancing and loving everybody like it was her job and hers alone" (ibid.). With Baby Suggs indicted, *Beloved* depicts a tendency Angela Davis had identified in the community conversation inflected by Black Power. Namely, the matriarch "is a cruel fabrication" and "a dastardly ideological weapon designed to impair our capacity . . . by foisting upon us the ideal of male supremacy" (Davis, "Role," 14).

In short, when Baby Suggs redefines success by no longer attending church with the hope of reassembling her family, she creates what bell hooks calls "homeplace." She uses her heart to give her community refuge, not only by preaching in the Clearing, but also by "giving advice; passing messages; healing the sick, hiding fugitives." However, it is exactly this service that makes her a target for community judgment.

Whether this dynamic is petty or not, the narrator exposes the white supremacist roots of the resentment: "Loaves and fishes were His powers—they did not belong to an ex-slave who had probably never carried one hundred pounds to the scale or picked okra with a baby on her back. Who had never been lashed by a ten-year-old whiteboy as God knows they had. Who had not even escaped slavery—had in fact, been *bought out* of it by a doting son" (Morrison 161–62, original emphasis). Interestingly, this account of Baby Suggs's life ignores details Morrison gives readers—namely, the years of labor that had broken down her body before she arrived at Sweet Home, where she performed less strenuous work because of her disabilities. Though this erasure is without justification, Morrison's text treats the neighbors' disapproval of what they consider "uncalled for pride" (162) as an understandable response, thereby obscuring the degree to which the judgment is gendered. The community's disapproval seems to align with the novel's moral universe, so it is easy to miss how skewed it is, but this kind of community judgment does not fall on men. Indeed, they are encouraged in this text to grasp whatever pride they can.

Pride is a problem only when supposedly detected in women, making their pursuit of success especially problematic, and this bias becomes clearest in relation to Sethe. When the sheriff escorts Sethe off the premises of 124 after she kills her baby, the "throng, now, of black faces stopped murmuring" because "a profile shocked them with its clarity. Was her head a bit too high? Her back a little too straight? Probably. Otherwise the singing would have begun at once, the moment she appeared in the doorway of the house on Bluestone Road. Some cape of sounds would have quickly been wrapped around her, like arms to hold and steady her on the way. As it was, they waited till the cart turned about, headed west to town. And then no words. Humming. No words at all" (179). Even black people who know the horrors of slavery judge Sethe because she does not seem ashamed or modest. Her crime, then, is claiming her definition of success and doing so unapologetically.

The gendered dynamics of the community's judgment must be understood within the context of the home (and homeplace) Baby Suggs succeeded in creating; after all, Baby Suggs's community-centered domesticity enables Sethe's bold actions. At one point, Stamp Paid meddles in Sethe's relationship with Paul D by sharing a newspaper clipping. Paul D comes to Sethe for assurance that Stamp Paid is confused if he thinks Sethe is the woman in the 18-year-old article. Sethe responds by telling her story as openly as Paul D had told his upon arriving at 124, even while knowing she "could never close in, pin it down for anybody who had to ask. If they didn't get it right off—she could never explain" (192). She recalls that, upon seeing the hat of schoolteacher, whose cruelty had shaped her life at Sweet Home, she knew he was there to take her and her children back. Hearing hummingbird wings beat in her ears, she flew into action. By the time she had looked schoolteacher in his eyes, "she had something in her arms that stopped him in his tracks. He took a backward step with each jump of the baby heart until finally there were none." She concludes, "I stopped him. . . . I took and put my babies where they'd be safe" (193). As she tells her story, she remembers a time "when the yard had a fence with a gate that somebody was always latching and unlatching . . . when 124 was a way station" (192). While she had been in jail, whiteboys "pulled it down, yanked up the posts and smashed the gate leaving 124 desolate and exposed" (193). Upon her return, "she was glad the fence was gone" partly because "that's where [the slave catchers] had hitched their horses" (192). Thus, when Sethe recalls that she had stopped schoolteacher, she marks her ability to do what the fence had not been able to achieve. That is, the safety that should accompany a home of one's own had been attacked. When denied that safety, she had scrambled to claim it nonetheless. Grabbing what society insists upon robbing her of, Sethe becomes vulnerable to judgment, including that of her own community and would-be life partner.

Morrison's narrator makes no such assertion, but what Paul D (and the community, as represented by the meddling Stamp Paid) find so objectionable about Sethe is that she acts on an agency that disregards the know-your-place aggression that empowers white people to play god with black people's lives. During slavery, most "masters" arrogated to themselves the power to breed "property," ignoring their kinship ties; Garner had acknowledged those ties and encouraged marriage, but he had no less played god.[20] From Paul D's perspective, "Garner called and announced them men—but only on Sweet Home, and by his leave" (260). Many assumed Garner's acknowledgment is what set "Sweet Home men" apart, but Paul D believes his brothers Halle and Sixo would have been men regardless. He is not sure he could say the same for himself (ibid.), and this doubt hovers over him as persistently as Beloved dwells in 124; his insecurity defines his experiences as much as Beloved's presence does. He is therefore repulsed by Sethe's definitions of safety and love, because they are valuables she has already claimed for herself and her children.

Sethe's self-determination disturbs Paul D because she had not needed him to secure what she believed she deserved; he sees her as a matriarch—a woman who emasculates men and therefore makes black households pathological. Sethe ends her story by declaring, "I took and put my babies where they'd be safe." Hearing "the pat she gave to the last word," Paul D concludes, "what she wanted for her children was exactly what was missing in 124: safety" (193). However, this conclusion only underscores Paul D's discomfort with seeing no role for himself. After all, "he thought he made [the house] safe, had gotten rid of the danger; beat the shit out of it; run it off the place" (ibid.). That is, by believing he had run the ghost out of 124, he thought his presence had transformed the space, had made it a domestic success. Until this moment, he had reasoned, "because she had not done it before he got there her own self, he thought it was because she could not do it. That she lived with 124 in helpless, apologetic resignation because she had no choice; that minus husband, sons, mother-in-law, she and her slow-witted daughter had to live there all alone making do" (ibid.). He convinces himself that while the Sethe he had known at Sweet Home was obedient, shy, and work-crazy "like Halle," "this here Sethe was new" (ibid.). Besides complicating the image of Halle as a real man, regardless of Garner or Sweet Home, this comparison grafts onto Sethe characteristics contradicted by her escape. The fact that she had claimed a home of her own should have been the first indication that she was not obedient, shy, and work-crazy "like Halle." Yet, Paul D holds on to his assessment, and Morrison records it: "This here Sethe talked about safety with a handsaw." Furthermore, "this here new Sethe didn't know where the world stopped and she began." In other words, he sees what Stamp Paid wanted him to see: "More important than what Sethe had done was what she claimed. It scared him" (ibid.).

What had Sethe claimed, exactly? I contend that she secured success and belonging, not at all cowered by the hostility of the world around her. She would keep marching toward achievement, and white men would not be the only ones who could decide what her or her children's future would be. Paul D insists her love is "too thick." She counters, "Love is or it ain't. Thin love ain't love at all." Paul D says her actions had not been effective, but she insists otherwise because her children are not at Sweet Home, and schoolteacher does not have them. Paul D suggests, "Maybe there's worse." Sethe then confirms what is unforgivable in her, her lack of regret for having exerted the kind of agency and meaning-making power that the nation insists whites should monopolize. She maintains her own conception of success, declaring: "It ain't my job to know what's worse. It's my job to know what is and to keep [my children] away from what I know is terrible. I did that" (194). A woman with that kind of clarity had made onlookers muse 18 years earlier: *Was her head a bit too high? Her back a little too straight?*

Again, Paul D's judgmental interpretations of Sethe's actions must be viewed in light of Baby Suggs's homemaking victories, which allow Morrison to illuminate painful American truths. Namely, black success inspires white aggression, and for women, it can also provoke the community's condemnation. When Sethe recalls the gate that "somebody was always latching and unlatching," the text highlights the consent that had characterized 124 as a way station, a homeplace. Baby Suggs's ability to offer her home as a space of safety and racial self-affirmation makes it the location at which Sethe can rest after the journey she should not have survived, especially without her husband (190). She could pause and try to create a life in a house that is not the master's house precisely because this is a homeplace. Of all that transpires, then, the most devastating is a simple fact: white people had come into Baby Suggs's yard. After this intrusion, Baby Suggs retreats into "pondering color" (4). She is determined to "fix on something harmless in this world" (211) because they had come into her yard, and she could not condone or condemn Sethe's response to that violation. Either way, Baby Suggs would be left with the fact that the black home is never safe. In the decades immediately after Emancipation—no less than in the 1980s, when *Beloved* is written—Americans claim that domesticity commands respect, but "the whitepeople came anyway. In her yard. She had done everything right and they came in her yard anyway" (247).[21]

The nation responds to black homemaking success with violence, and Baby Suggs finally submits to the country's demand that she accept "what I was put here to look for: the back door" (211). Knowing the odds against her, and even after Baby Suggs has died after surrendering to white violence by "pondering color," Sethe marches ahead, and her example is not lost on her daughter Denver, who continues the journey. As Denver represents another generation of black women who will pursue success, facing hostility yet undeterred by it, *Beloved* exemplifies the tendency among African Americans to engage in racial self-affirmation while acknowledging white violence. Denver wills herself forward via an exchange with her now deceased grandmother:

> But you said there was no defense.
> "There ain't."
> Then what do I do?
> "Know it, and go on out the yard. Go on." (288)

African American cultural production routinely notes that white Americans refuse to let black achievement simply yield respectability and safety. In *Beloved*, the black community's judgmental jealously is painful, but it cannot compare with the nation's much more viscous attacks. American culture works to obliterate black women's right to determine the quality of their lives, whether inside or outside the master's house.

*   *   *

As the community conversation of the 1970s and 1980s refined conceptions of achievement while engaging the brutality of the past and present, Octavia Butler's *Kindred* and Toni Morrison's *Beloved* considered precisely how slavery continued to shape American households. Unlike *Roots*, these were always presented as imaginative works of fiction. They therefore underscore the degree to which fiction does not inhabit a separate realm but is part of the dynamic, multivalent community conversation that includes objects, gestures, and embodied practices (such as cooking, dancing, debating, and kinkeeping) as well as artistic expressions of every genre and in every medium.

The community conversation of the 1970s and 1980s continued supporting black people in their preoccupation with accomplishment. African Americans did not respond to white violence so much as white violence emerged to erase evidence of black achievement. In exploring how *Roots* became a cultural phenomenon, Haley biographer Robert Norrell notes, "Moynihan said privately, 'Obviously one can no longer address oneself to the subject of the Negro family.' But, in fact, that was what Alex Haley had done—addressed himself to the black family—with a compelling account of family strength and survival" (Norrell 145). Of course, African American efforts at affirming themselves and each other with accounts of black victories—big and small, before slavery and in spite of it—was a long-standing tradition and an ongoing activity. Furthermore, embodied practices of belonging included debate and disagreement as community members worked to influence each other and develop collective goals.

While the idea circulated that black women have a history of identifying more with white families than with their own, Butler offered Dana, with her white husband and house in the suburbs. Thus, when Dana is pulled into the nineteenth century, readers might expect her to validate suspicions about slavery's lingering effects by betraying black people, especially black men. Instead, Dana becomes a mirror for such readers by looking down on the "female Uncle Tom." Ultimately, following Dana into the 1800s reveals how problematic such judgments are because her journey demonstrates the difference between reading about (or even witnessing) bondage and experiencing it. At the same time, however, the novel exposes Dana's folly in believing that life in 1976 is drastically different from life in the 1800s. Her assumptions about the past's irrelevance prove to be as faulty as assumptions that enslaved ancestors eagerly accepted subjugation.

The interracial marriage in *Kindred* creates urgency around the question of whether theirs is still the master's house, but Morrison's *Beloved* places equal weight on this question when focusing on a black couple and the difficulties they face when wanting to make a home that nurtures romantic, not just parental, love. Morrison explores the many negotiations required to create a space in which one's past can be acknowledged without becoming a limitation. Paul D enjoys that freedom because Sethe does not judge him for his experiences, but when given an opportunity to reciprocate, he says with disgust, "You got two feet, Sethe, not four" (194). Like Paul D, Sethe had been treated like an animal on the Sweet Home plantation, so when Paul D condemns Sethe by counting her feet, 124 feels like the master's house because her past is brought into the present as a bludgeon. The narrator describes Sethe and Paul D's resulting separation thusly: "Sweet, she thought. He must think I can't bear to hear him say it. That after all I have told him and after telling me how many feet I have, 'goodbye' would break me to pieces. Ain't that sweet" (195). As is true with Kevin and Dana in *Kindred*, black couples must be willing to face slavery's lasting impact; otherwise, without their being aware, it will shape their behavior and limit their ability to claim the success they deserve.

In a country built on slavery, homes of the present can bear an uncanny resemblance to those of the past. Butler and Morrison do not dispute this reality, but they insist the connections are complex and deserve careful examination that is prevented when black women are simply considered race traitors and matriarchs. As *Roots* and its masculinism steered the community conversation of the 1970s and 1980s, black women writers continued to work with the faith that real-life interlocutors can be awakened in ways that Paul D is not. For, if Paul D had understood he was speaking from slavery's premises, he might have refused to count Sethe's feet. Butler and Morrison therefore enter the community conversation on black success by encouraging readers to notice precisely how the nation's slave past continues to exert pressure. Only awareness of *how* Americans "carry [history] within" can give individuals any chance to resist being, in James Baldwin's words, "unconsciously controlled by it."

The Ultimate Home

Michelle Obama in the White House

Even while tracing generations of accomplishment, the community conversation of the 1970s and 1980s noted that African Americans often asked whether theirs was still the master's house. As Octavia Butler and Toni Morrison engaged this question, they undertook kinkeeping, offering narratives that linked readers to ancestors. While *Kindred* (1979) and *Beloved* (1987) circulated, African Americans also asked whether the White House would always belong to the "master" or if it could become their home, too. That is, would the country of their birth ever elect a black president?[1] The dynamic discussions prompted by these questions underscore the degree to which debate, like kinkeeping, is an embodied practice of belonging that produces homemade citizenship. Through the community conversation, African-descended people in the United States sustain themselves and each other in the march toward accomplishment. Community debates not only yield strategies for achievement but also identify its very contours and parameters—how to know if the individual or the group is successful.

Questions about the White House have had an enduring resonance in the community conversation, and poet Langston Hughes captures it in "Children's Rhymes." The poetic persona recalls the kinds of chants that punctuated their childhood and then notes what they now hear from neighborhood children: "*By what sends/the white kids/I ain't sent:/I know*

I can't be President" (390). The poem suggests that, for generations, the community conversation has wondered aloud whether African Americans would ever enjoy direct access to the nation's highest office and positions of honor in the White House. It is not surprising, then, that Barack Obama's presidency was passionately incorporated into the community conversation on success, and because the White House is the home "at the center of the nation's identity,"[2] many discussions focused on his wife as the first African American first lady. Like Harriet Jacobs's *Incidents in the Life of a Slave Girl*, which aimed to recruit white abolitionists, and Lorraine Hansberry's *A Raisin in the Sun*, which appeared on Broadway, Michelle Obama's public persona as first lady addressed mainstream audiences, but it also provided an access point to the community conversation on achievement. Perhaps her strongest contribution to that dynamic discussion was labeling herself *Mom-in-Chief.*[3] In claiming this label, she pursued success while acknowledging the violence inherent in how black women are typically understood, as welfare queens but also as servants in, not women of, the nation's house.

When read through the lens of achievement, the performance text of Mom-in-Chief reveals the labor required to remain undeterred in reaching goals on the national stage when unable to avoid the nation's aggression. Because conceptions of American citizenship are designed to include only straight white men with property, black women are pushed out of any sense of belonging within the category. Many weapons are marshaled to deny that they belong, including multivalent, meaning-making figures like the welfare queen and matriarch, as discussed in the Introduction and Chapters 4 and 5. However, mainstream culture consistently animates such figures because black women so often embody others, especially the strong black woman. As Melissa Harris-Perry puts it, the strong black woman has become "the citizenship imperative for African American women" (21). Yet, as I have argued, black people pursue accomplishment knowing that doing so will bring violence as often as praise. Therefore, to embrace the strong black woman while claiming success and asserting citizenship is to demonstrate awareness that know-your-place aggression routinely answers victories. Black women understand they cannot simply *be* in this country; they must be strong. Operating in harmony with these insights and practices, Michelle Obama embodied an intensified version of the strong black woman by performing Mom-in-Chief.

Mom-in-Chief gestures toward know-your-place aggression in two major ways. First, it draws attention to the fact that basing her public health program *Let's Move* on a presumed penchant for nurturing was more palatable than basing it on having been an administrator for the University of Chicago Medical Center. Second, it underscores the ridiculously high standard of femininity she had to maintain in order to avoid challenges not only to her capacity for representing American womanhood but also to her own status as a woman.[4] In other words, because it exposed know-your-place aggression (and prompted more of it), Michelle Obama's public persona is a text that reveals as much about the United States as about the individual black woman who succeeded against its steep odds.

As sketched in the Introduction, Barack and Michelle Obama's prominence created countless opportunities for observing how routinely American culture responds to black achievement with hostility. The first lady was far less powerful than the president, but know-your-place aggression circulated around Michelle Obama no less than her husband. In a nation that insists upon linking womanhood to whiteness, a black first lady was disturbing; for many Americans, it therefore became a patriotic imperative to negate her status as a homemaker. In the process, her heteronormative nuclear family somehow faded in importance in national conversations when it would have been cause for endless celebration if she (and it) had been white. Indeed, I contend that the runaway success of *The Help* constituted collective aggression toward the black female achievement Michelle Obama represented. *The Help* is a trite 2011 movie based on an utterly mediocre 2009 novel, but Americans of all backgrounds made it a blockbuster success. Whether white, black, Latinx, or Asian American and whether middle class or working class, everyone seemed to play some part in accepting this as a quintessentially American and therefore vaguely important work. What exactly made it so?? What about 2009 and 2011 created the conditions for countless Americans to become engrossed in a story featuring black women in the 1960s who work as maids???

As black feminist critic bell hooks observed, it is no coincidence *The Help* became a runaway hit in 2009, when a black woman held a place of unmistakable honor in the White House for the first time.[5] Mrs. Obama's visibility did not inspire a spate of popular culture representations of professional black women or of Mocha Moms, black stay-at-home mothers. Instead, it inspired an obsession with a presumably better time, when black women were domestics who needed white women's guidance. There was something askew, something vaguely *un*-American about a black first lady. The book and movie arrived to offer a reassuring message, that people who believe black women belong in a servant role are correct. It really does make more sense for black women to be housekeepers, not homemakers—and certainly not first ladies. *The Help*'s overwhelming popularity, becoming a franchise with everything from DVDs and T-shirts to packaged tea, cookbooks, and cookware, should be understood as an expression of the unconscious distress caused by seeing a black woman as *woman of the house*. The movie appeared at the right time with the right message and, drenched in everything the nation has taught us all, Americans of every background looked at this film's clichéd mediocrity and saw grand themes of American identity that would somehow make us better citizens if we would simply accept what it offered.

The Help's popularity amounted to know-your-place aggression toward the achievement Michelle Obama as FLOTUS represented, and the process was so overwhelming, yet so diffuse, that countless Americans participated in it. Even those who tried to ignore *The Help* could not, because their fellow Americans were so excited about it and invested in it. Avoiding conversations about *The Help* was nearly impossible (Wanzo). This fact underscores the most important function of know-your-place aggression: it impacts one's experience of achievements. Know-your-place aggression ensures that members of marginalized groups will not be treated according to their accomplishments. Being president does not mean a congressman won't shout insults during your speeches. Having been elected to lead the free world does not mean a lower-ranking politician will not shake her finger in your face as if you are a child.

Likewise, in rallying around a book and film that celebrate black housekeepers on the heels of Michelle Obama becoming the nation's most prominent homemaker, Americans sent and received powerful messages diminishing the significance of the nonwhite family occupying the White House. Americans' most common words and deeds are designed to exclude people of color from the nation's family portrait, and even an African American first family would not disrupt that tendency. In order to be considered an adult—a real American man or woman—a citizen must create a heteronormative nuclear family, and by that widely accepted measure, Mrs. Obama exemplified womanhood. However, because mainstream culture insists true women come in pale packages, her doing so inspired white hostility. Whenever Americans ignored or diminished the Obamas' domesticity, the nation continued its commitment to setting a bar for citizenship while aggressively refusing to recognize people of color even when they clear it. The nation has consistently claimed that individuals prove ready for full citizenship by first attaining domestic success, so the Obama power couple simply did what ordinary African Americans always have: meet or exceed requirements. As a group, African Americans have made a tradition of fulfilling mainstream standards, and in doing so, they have embodied their self-conceptions more than they have invested in the promise of civic inclusion. After all, they could never escape evidence of how worthless the nation's promises are.

Michelle Obama embodied Mom-in-Chief in much the same way less prominent women perform the strong black woman, and this parallel places her in the tradition of black club women of the 1890s and early 1900s. Club women literally taught others how to exemplify admirable womanhood with lessons about style, grooming, and comportment, and Michelle Obama's public persona continued that legacy. Through her performance of Mom-in-Chief, her creation of that multivalent figure (which involved decisions about her hair, clothes, and body), she exemplified all that U.S. society worked to prevent her from becoming: an impressive lady. Of course, the "lady" ideal reflects the fact that *all* women must prove their worthiness by following sexist rules, but an African American woman will likely meet the standard against the odds only to have the accomplishment purposely ignored and/or attacked. Indeed, white people's hostile reactions represented experiences that Mrs. Obama shared with 1890s black club women. Especially given these commonalities, the performance text of Mrs. Obama's public persona emerged from embodied practices of belonging, hailing black women even as other interlocutors could not be ignored.

Because American culture attaches pathology to black bodies, Michelle Obama's impeccable performance of Mom-in-Chief may seem to expose the workings of what black feminist critic Candace Jenkins calls the "salvific wish." Jenkins's concept refers to "a desire to rescue African Americans as a group from racist stigma" by embracing decorum and propriety (67–68). Despite evidence that "black moral rectitude" does not diminish racism,[6] African Americans throughout history have achieved it. However, as I have argued, black achievement emerges more from individual and collective self-conceptions than from a belief in the nation's promises. To read Mrs. Obama's public persona as an expression of the salvific wish would require attributing to her the desire to defend the race's reputation. Rather than focus on subjects and their presumably stable identities to uncover particular motivating desires, this project follows words, actions, gestures, and demeanors to discover how texts (both written and performed) engage in practices that produce homemade citizenship. That is, as a cultural project that African Americans engage in, the tendency to pursue success while acknowledging hostility proves to be an endeavor of articulation and performance that does not assume stable identity so much as discussion and debate as well as both harmony and discord in action.

One best understands the similarities between the first lady and 1890s black club women not by looking for evidence of stable identities with recognizable longings but by examining how words, actions, and demeanors are crafted to empower African Americans to move ahead while noticing the aggression designed to interrupt their success-oriented journeys. As demonstrated throughout this study, to pursue success while knowing violence will answer victories is to engage in practices of making-oneself-at-home. The community conversation sustains African Americans in those practices, enabling them to cultivate homemade citizenship. Far from a feature of black identity or subjectivity, homemade citizenship is constituted by practices, and it becomes legible when one examines the community conversation (which is never limited to words) while looking through the lens of success. Dominant discourses and practices are designed to deny black achievement and belonging, so the nation's most common responses to black victories (big and small) come in the form of aggression that reminds black people of their "proper" place as outsiders. Thus, as African Americans discuss their definitions of success, they are bound to address white violence—directly or indirectly—with their words and deeds, written texts and performance texts. Michelle Obama's performance on the national stage was no exception.

Mrs. Obama's Mom-in-Chief public persona—a performance text that contributed to the community conversation on black success—promoted traditional domesticity not because Mrs. Obama believed the nation's promise that homemaking yields respectability and safety; she did it while understanding that it likely would not. If, as all Americans are taught to believe, women gain society's respect and protection by creating domestic havens, then Michelle Obama should have been able to trust that she and her family would be revered and safe. Yet, as she embodied Mom-in-Chief, behaving in ways that presumably earned her that assurance, images of her husband in a noose provided the backdrop to her impeccable performances.

Homemade citizenship becomes legible whenever cultural producers refuse to ignore how consistently their community's successes inspire aggression, and this proved true for Mrs. Obama's public persona. Surely, the Michelle Obama who performed Mom-in-Chief was no less aware of the nation's racial politics than she had been before becoming First Lady. Please recall her February 2007 *60 Minutes* interview.[7] When asked if she fears for her husband's life because he is a black candidate, Mrs. Obama responded, "I don't lose sleep over it because the *realities* are that . . . *as a black man* . . . Barack can get shot going to the gas station" (emphasis added). Inevitably, Mrs. Obama's performance as Mom-in-Chief was inflected by her awareness that racist violence undergirds U.S. culture; even as Americans love announcing the arrival of a postracial society, know-your-place aggression routinely emerges. To recognize that her husband could be shot going to the gas station precisely because he is a black man was to note her family's vulnerability to racist violence (despite doing everything right, as Baby Suggs in *Beloved* had). Given the country's most common tendencies, she could not ignore the greater probability of her losing her husband and her children losing their father. Given the *realities* of the American past and present, Mrs. Obama evoked the racial profiling that leads to a disproportionate number of black and brown men dying at the hands of those sworn to protect and serve. However, even if one insists that, given her familiarity with gun violence in Chicago, Michelle Obama had been thinking of black men dying from other black men's gunfire, that would still gesture toward the country's systematic devaluation of black life. As cultural critic Ta-Nehisi Coates and others have explained, the structures that all but ensure African Americans' civic, social, and economic exclusion are the same as those that cause their deaths. "Spare us the invocations of 'black-on-black crime,'" Coates writes, "I will not respect the lie. . . . The most mendacious phrase in the American language is 'black-on-black crime,' which is uttered as though the same hands that drew red lines around the ghettos of Chicago are not the same hands that drew red lines around the life of Jordan Davis. . . . That which mandates the murder of our Hadiya Pendletons necessarily mandates the murder of Jordan Davis. I will not respect any difference. I will not respect the lie" ("On the Killing"). Michelle Obama also seemed to suggest that, whether ordinary citizens or political candidates, African Americans are targets because the nation so consistently attacks them and casts them as not only unworthy of inclusion but downright disposable.

African American success has always emerged in an environment that seeks to prevent it, to destroy it, and to obliterate evidence that it ever existed. As discussed in the Introduction and Chapter 2, it was never enough to lynch a man for competing with a white grocery store or for having received honors for military service; dominant discourse finished the job by insisting society was better without these victims because black men are natural rapists. Quite routinely, white Americans destroyed black families and households and swore they never existed. It is in this context that one must view black cultural production that spotlights successful black families and their households, and Mrs. Obama's public persona is one such cultural production.

Mom-in-Chief: The Creativity, Craft, and Labor of Impeccable Performances

Encouraging aspiration is arguably the job first ladies are most expected to do, and for Mrs. Obama, success in the role required herculean effort—no matter how elegant, glamorous, or fun she made it look. As historian MaryAnne Borrelli explains, a first lady's "gender role modeling becomes an aspect of the nation's identity. It is no longer an individual expression of self, but a country's statement about the nature of its female citizens" (147). Like all first ladies, Mrs. Obama had to work to gain the admiration of as many people as possible and to inspire as many women as possible to emulate her. However, a black woman is the last person Americans are taught to identify with, let alone actually admire, and this is especially true of a dark-skinned black woman. For Mrs. Obama, then, achieving the first lady's most important goal required relentless perseverance despite the attacks made inevitable by the nation's culturally ingrained messages. Even as first lady, Michelle Obama did what African Americans have always done—address each other, not just the mainstream—so, her public persona proves to be a cultural production that engaged the community conversation on success. Understanding this, one finds that her choices about hair, clothes, and bodily presentation revealed the complexity of her labor as a first lady as well as the power of embodied practices of belonging. Recognizing the efficacy of figures, which communicate through much more than words, she used semiotics to do her job well. That is, Michelle Obama constructed her persona recognizing the meanings produced through her hair, clothes, and body.

Michelle Obama's hair choices centered on encouraging women of all backgrounds to covet her style. Because she straightened her hair, countless women could walk into salons across the country with a picture of the First Lady. Women could ask their stylists to approximate the look because it was not particularly elaborate. For the vast majority of her time in the public eye, Obama wore a medium-length bob, attainable by most. If it had been longer, it would have been in fewer people's reach. If it had been shorter, fewer women would have wanted it, assuming it would not be flattering. While many may admire short hairstyles, most women find it hard to imagine having so little hair, given society's rigid conceptions of femininity. Also, if Mrs. Obama's hair had been kinky, braided, or locked, white women and Asian American women could not have easily aspired to and achieved it. One black woman—even if she was the First Lady—was not going to inspire a trend of white women requesting super-tight curly perms.[8] Given Western beauty standards, it was much more expedient for Mrs. Obama to wear her hair straight and therefore not have the majority of nonblack women hesitate to consider whether they can achieve the First Lady's look.[9]

Because she was the ultimate political wife, residing in the ultimate home, Michelle Obama could not disregard the meanings that the public might attach to her hair, even as she no doubt had her own beliefs about it. As cultural critic Nowile Rooks reminds us, black women's and girls' choices about their hair are not always about white people, but they often face situations in which that truth does not register. Their claiming freedom to adorn themselves will place them "in a trap of power relations, racial memories, and narrowly constructed identities. This is true because [the mainstream] can only imagine that ['ethnic'] styles are making a statement relative to white culture. They cease to mean in any other context" (290). Given this reality, what would have happened if First Lady Obama had not straightened her hair? Of course, Americans did not find out. Mainstream standards are too rigid to be tested this way by the woman who had to become Mom-in-Chief in order to lead *Let's Move* and represent U.S. womanhood. And, make no mistake, representing American womanhood meant adhering to standards that created a no-win situation. Some feminist critics insisted the focus on Mrs. Obama's beauty choices was trivial, but this was easy to say because she

Figure 4. During her husband's first campaign and for most of her time in the White House, Michelle Obama wore her hair in a modest bob. She appears here on January 18, 2009, at the Opening Inaugural Celebration at the Lincoln Memorial. (Photo Credit: Alex Brandon via AP Images)

made the "right" choices. If Michelle Obama had worn dread locks or even a modest afro, her hair would have suddenly ceased to be a trivial topic among these purportedly progressive critics.

However, white Americans were not the only people whose assessments had to be considered as the FLOTUS worked to encourage aspiration. Even as her on-the-job success required ensuring the widest path for nonblack women, she constructed her public persona to account for the messages (via semiotics) black women received. Though Mrs. Obama did not have dreadlocks or wear her hair in twists or braids, her hair may have been "natural" or free of chemical processing. Whether FLOTUS had a relaxer or not was a guarded secret; her hairdresser literally would not say.[10] Of course, the investment in leaving this detail up to the public's imagination and speculation pointed to the political weight black women's hair has always been made to carry. As discussed in Chapter 4, since the 1960s *Black Is Beautiful* movement, natural hair has been associated with self-love and self-esteem. Thus, for all else this guarded

Figure 5. Michelle Obama attended Nickelodeon's 25th Annual Kids' Choice Awards in Los Angeles on March 31, 2012. Her outfit was more attention-getting than elegantly understated, but she continued with a fairly plain hairstyle. (Photo Credit: Kevork Djansezian via Getty Images)

secret might have achieved, it affirmed the importance of black women as a constituency that not only could impact Mrs. Obama's approval ratings but also could be particularly helped or harmed by her decisions about how to represent American womanhood. Wearing one's hair natural is deemed to be self-loving, but it also comes with professional risks,[11] so a black woman's decision on this issue can be quite freighted. By straightening her hair but also leaving open the possibility that it was natural, Mrs. Obama affirmed both black women who wear their hair straight and those who do not, because she avoided tampering with the (now firmly established) idea that natural hair is the more loving choice.

As part of the performance text of her public persona, Mrs. Obama's hair choices suggested she knew she was not free to "go natural" conspicuously, but they also articulated an unwillingness to capitulate completely. Perhaps she refused to yield because she understood that acceptance of her as first lady was antithetical to the American way, just as civic inclusion for ordinary African Americans has always been. Maintaining

Figure 6. In the lead-up to the 2012 presidential election, Michelle Obama's hair remained consistent. She appears here with her husband at Hofstra University on October 16, 2012, after his second debate with Mitt Romney. (Photo Credit: Anthony Behar via AP Images)

privacy about some of her hair choices amounted to an assertion of agency because black women are expected to be open books, and the particular secret she kept created more flexibility for other black women, not less. To the extent that her decisions created space for other black women, they did valuable work because a prominent African American's choices are so easily used against their ordinary counterparts in everyday life.[12] By keeping space open for black women, Michelle Obama's public persona proved to be composed of embodied practices of belonging. It demonstrated that African Americans were among the "individuals whom she consider[ed] politically relevant and with whom she communicate[d]" as first lady (Borrelli 89). The contribution to the community conversation made by Michelle Obama's public image should be understood in terms of the people it supported. As historian Martha Jones argues, even after Michelle Obama left the White House, black women joined her in creating figures (multivalent images of themselves) that disregarded the limitations set by the nation. For instance, in Alabama's 2017 special senate election, "Democrat Doug Jones only narrowly bested Republican Roy Moore—thanks to 98 percent support from Alabama's black female voters. We can find their faces in photographs of rallies, prayer meetings and get-out-the-vote efforts. Such women are [Michelle] Obama's counterparts, discernible to us by their numbers and by the force of their political participation" (*Washington Post*). As I have shown, even seemingly conservative goals like political participation must be understood in terms of black people's belief in their right to resources. Especially when voter suppression is rampant (Berman), voting is a refusal to be deprived more than an expression of faith in the system. To return to Mrs. Obama, these particular hair choices suggested her understanding that, even if she had to become Mom-in-Chief to have a chance at being considered a real first lady, she could help the ordinary individuals forced to become strong black women to withstand the nation's daily assaults. Far more than they protest injustice, African Americans focus on keeping themselves and each other marching toward accomplishment.

Women of color could never be the only demographic with which Mrs. Obama communicated through the semiotics of the performance text that constituted her public persona, however. Because she always pursues success, despite knowing the odds against her, Michelle Obama (like countless other black women and girls) has been forced to learn important lessons about "how to be seen, by whom, and what the consequences are for not paying close attention when on the battlefield of self-representation" (Rooks 294). For better or worse, then, Michelle Obama could not go natural conspicuously; after all, the First Lady's hair choices were affected by her investment in succeeding in the role, which required convincing other women to emulate her, and mainstream culture interprets kinky hair as unattractive, if not hostile. As Rooks reminds us, "while hair may mean something particular within African American communities, once those understandings come into contact with the dominant culture, one may not be able to hold on to those original meanings" (292). There was simply no way for Michelle Obama, while pursuing success, to avoid the meanings dominant culture would attach to her every move.

Of course, Michelle Obama had no investment in popularity for popularity's sake; public approval had serious implications, which became clear months before the Obamas secured the White House. As soon as Michelle Obama became a target for remarks made in February 2008,

Figure 7. As first lady, Michelle Obama promoted healthy eating by emphasizing fruits and vegetables. Often photographed gardening, she also published a book about the White House garden. Here, she signs books at a Washington, D.C., Barnes & Noble store on June 12, 2012. (Photo Credit: Mark Wilson via Getty Images)

the Obama campaign took her out of the public eye. She had admitted, "for the first time in my adult lifetime, I am really proud of my country." White Americans generally responded with hostility,[13] essentially punishing her for feeling she had earned the right to speak her truth. Meanwhile, many African Americans thought she would become a public figure whose critiques aligned with their own, that she would acknowledge the vastly different experience this country offers to nonwhite people. Many people of color relished the possibility of hearing their typically suppressed truths uttered by a (potential) first lady. Given the punishing backlash,[14] however, it soon became clear that Mrs. Obama would make the most traditional choices imaginable in order to comfort those invested in downplaying the past and present injustices that had inspired her comment. Her comforting image hinged on her willingness to emphasize gardening and to insist upon performing Mom-in-Chief, despite her impressive professional background.[15] Another strategy she consistently used to succeed in the role of first lady, which should not have been surprising to anyone who knows this nation's tendencies toward black people, was to take what seemed to be every opportunity to teach white folk how to dance.[16]

As Mrs. Obama shifted from "militant" truth-teller to nonthreatening gardener and dancer, she used clothing to create continuity and decrease the likelihood that onlookers would notice how dramatically her demeanor had changed. According to social scientist Frederick Harris, a black political agenda conspicuously took a backseat during the Obama presidency,[17] and the first lady's public persona provided an important corollary for this assessment. Yet, despite a fairly dramatic shift, the foundation of Mrs. Obama's image remained intact: the accessibility of her look. Her introduction to the public as a J. Crew mom remained a crucial component of her public persona as she insisted upon labeling herself "Mom-in-Chief." Sharing that she shopped at J. Crew was important because the store's clothes are accessible to middle-class Americans, even if only those from the clearance rack. As First Lady, no less than when her husband was a candidate, and whether her public commentary acknowledged injustice or avoided it, Michelle Obama shaped perceptions by underscoring the accessibility of everything she made desirable while doing the job of inspiring admiration.

Keeping this accessible image convincing while occupying the White House required Mrs. Obama to craft the performance text of her public persona very deliberately, and she clearly took that work seriously. When her husband was reelected in November 2012, she wore a dress she had worn twice before. As *Daily Mail UK* put it, "Most women would seize the opportunity to buy a new outfit, but Michelle Obama chose to recycle [a patterned brocade Michael Kors dress]." Furthermore, as *People* had reported, it was an impromptu selection: "She said that she was so busy with the campaign and their kids that she had no time to think about an outfit and decided at the last minute."[18] Likewise, for the 2012 Democratic National Convention earlier that year, at which she delivered the speech asserting her Mom-in-Chief role and solidifying her popularity, she wore a dress by designer Tracy Reese. *CNN.com* reported, "Obama complemented Reese's art with a pair of

$245 rhubarb suede pumps from J. Crew, which she reportedly bought herself." This choice was important because "the outfit subtly reflected the Democratic Party's support of the middle class. Most dresses on Tracy Reese's website run between $250 and $450." The media noted, "That's a stark contrast to the Oscar de la Renta dress Ann Romney wore when addressing the Republican National convention, which reportedly cost $1,900."[19] Such decisions inevitably became part of Mrs. Obama's public persona, and she used them to place her husband's and the Democratic Party's ideals in a positive light. Indeed, her strategy aligned with one used by First Lady Rosalynn Carter. As Borrelli explains, "Rosalynn Smith Carter's decision to wear the gown she wore to her husband's gubernatorial inaugural ball to his presidential inaugural ball was at once sentimental and populist in its frugality" (1). Such wardrobe choices conveyed powerful messages; these women's clothes reinforced a political agenda centered on the middle class. For Democrats, this strategy was especially powerful because it showed that their willingness to advocate for purportedly "big" government in order to create a social safety net (that Republicans wanted to cut) did not amount to frivolous spending. Furthermore, such decisions demonstrated that their access to government resources would not translate into their spending as if there is no limit.

Even as she highlighted the constraints she willingly placed on her spending, Mrs. Obama did not sacrifice conveying the desirability of her style; indeed, she made it acceptable to aspire to her look. She wore clothes within a price range that middle-class Americans could imagine, she wore outfits more than once (like ordinary women), and she sent the message that one does not need professional help to achieve her look. As reported in the *New York Times* in 2008, "Michelle Obama apparently pulls off the feat of getting dressed on her own."[20] Though she had relationships with owners of boutiques in Chicago, she was not known to use a stylist. As *Vanity Fair*'s Amy Fine Collins[21] put it, "What's important here is that we're not starting from zero with Michelle Obama. I'm sure she's being advised. But there's nothing imposed on her that isn't generated by who she is. She has a very definite sense of herself."[22] So, the First Lady was like ordinary women in that she got advice from friends but did not pay a stylist. Making a similar observation, entertainment and lifestyle commentator Valerie Greenberg explained on Fox News: "Michelle brings such a unique, vibrant and youthful style, and the average woman can see herself wearing many of her outfits."[23]

The average woman can see herself wearing many of the First Lady's outfits. That may have been an understatement. In June 2012, in the run up to reelection, Mrs. Obama visited the talk show *The View* without her husband. She wore a leaf-print dress from the chain retailer White House/Black Market that she bought off the rack. It cost $148. And, what happened? That dress "sold out from all its locations within 48 hours of her TV appearance."[24] Yes, ordinary women could see themselves in Michelle Obama's clothes. Given that the first lady's most important job was to represent ideal American womanhood, this was evidence of her success in that position. And it is important to acknowledge that she accomplished this success *against the odds* because a black woman was never meant to be a citizen, let alone hold a place of honor in the White House. Americans should also recognize that Mrs. Obama's public success was an extension of the private achievement (as cherished wife and mother) that marked her journey long before she became first lady, and both were accomplishments that, for black women, inspire aggression as often as praise.

The performance text of her Mom-in-Chief public persona relied heavily on Michelle Obama's choices about hair and clothes, but the very deliberate presentation of her body proved equally important. As much as her clothing decisions helped determine perceptions of Michelle Obama's physique, her bodily presentation was a meaning-making endeavor unto itself. It helped create its own discourse—a discourse that very much fostered desire and underscored the appropriateness of the viewer's aspiration. First, in a culture in which most women know nothing about struggling to gain weight, Mrs. Obama's curvaceous figure made her body seem attainable. Simply by being a size no one would call skinny, she represented accessibility. To this, she added toned arms that others insisted upon making a topic of conversation.

As the first lady used semiotics in her favor, her arms proved significant not because other women found them envy-worthy but because she constantly highlighted exercise. Mrs. Obama's muscle tone likely had more to do with genetics than with working out, but she *played up* exercise to keep others aspiring. In fact, her emphasis on physical activity kept her arms from becoming a barrier as she worked for the popularity that would make her a successful first lady. Nothing is more annoying to American women than admiring another's arms, asking what she does to maintain them, and getting "nothing" as the answer. If that is one's truth, telling it is no way to win friends and influence people, and Michelle

Obama had to do precisely that. She therefore emphasized exercise and kept knowledge of her healthy habits *so much* in the public eye that no one really paused to consider that she might have had that muscle tone long before doing anything deliberate to keep it. The message was clear: you can have these arms if you are willing to *work for* them. This was genius. If you were not willing to work for them, you were not annoyed that she had them because she was willing to work in ways you were not. Of course, this did not stop the white supremacist violence of know-your-place aggression, but it contributed to her ability to make herself at home, to fuel ongoing achievement (for herself and others) in the midst of hostility.

Just as it was acceptable to want the first lady's clothes because they were not ridiculously expensive, her physique was also within reach, so wanting it was okay. In fact, wanting it was not mere vanity but more like a noble goal because aiming for it confirmed one's willingness to prioritize hard work and healthy choices. Indeed, wanting a body like Michelle Obama's seemed to be about discipline but not about starvation, which runway models are known to inspire.

Based on her approval ratings,[25] Michelle Obama was a successful first lady (which brought her aggression as often as praise), and her elaborate efforts at encouraging admiration played no small part. In a patriarchal society, no matter the sphere, a woman's appearance is treated as her most important contribution to it. Furthermore, her appearance is used as a basis for assessing her morality and merit. Attractive people are literally assumed to be more moral, reliable, and worthy of opportunity.[26]

Because women cannot avoid this dynamic, focusing attention on the aesthetics of one's home can be a way of putting some distance between gender expectations and one's body; Michelle Obama's use of the White House was therefore an especially important component of the performance text of her Mom-in-Chief persona. Almost by definition, the first lady is the nation's hostess, so the White House has always been a crucial site for her labor, but that function became more important during recent presidencies. As Borrelli notes, the role of national hostess can seem "marginal to the public-sphere responsibilities of political decision making, which are traditionally reserved to men," but "because symbols have such great meaning, and because the role of the nation's hostess empowers the first lady to frame and interpret such formidable political symbols as the White House, these duties have led to increased presidential interest in the work of the social office" (60). Modern presidents have understood that "the White House has given meaning and significance to presidential power" (89). "At its most effective, the first ladies' skillful use of the White House has elevated partisanship into leadership and transmuted power into authority" (ibid.). After all, the White House frames "both an enduring office and an effervescent administration" (59). Ideally, what the first lady accomplishes as national hostess will "encourage observers to draw constructive connections between a widely valued political symbol (the White House) and a sometimes controversial organization (the administration)" (ibid.).

As they have upheld, revised, or rejected White House traditions, first ladies have demonstrated an understanding of either their responsibility to maintain the status quo or their power to effect change. For example, Mamie Eisenhower made provisions for tours of the White House for African Americans, integrated the White House Easter egg hunt, and invited Mahalia Jackson to sing for her birthday party (Borrelli 68). "She also invited Lucille Ball and Desi Arnaz to the president's birthday celebration, seating them with her husband, even though Ball had been called before, and only grudgingly cleared by, the House Committee on Un-American Activities" (ibid.). Similarly, Jacqueline Kennedy made White House events more casual than those of the Eisenhower administration. For instance, the attire was black tie instead of white tie; for the first time, cocktails were served before dinner; and smoking was allowed (78). Mrs. Kennedy also preferred smaller gatherings than had been the tradition, so she looked for opportunities to make her social outreach at the White House more intimate (79). After the Kennedys left the White House, Lady Bird Johnson was even more attentive to the need for more inclusion of African Americans. As important, she and her husband used hospitality "to get action on legislation" and understood how to use "entertainment to further their pet projects."[27] Ultimately, she and her staff "had a gift for presenting the most appealing characteristics of the nation's identity" (ibid.). Taken together, the changes initiated during the Eisenhower, Kennedy, and Johnson administrations made the role of hostess "emphatically, unequivocally public" (83).

Through her use of the symbolic power of the White House, Michelle Obama continued the work of making 1600 Pennsylvania Avenue accessible to a broader segment of the citizenry—while contending with the ease with which the Obama administration could be accused of favoritism, yet another example of the know-your-place aggression used against people of color. A white leader's being surrounded by whites is not seen as having anything to do with race, but a nonwhite leader with even a handful of people of color around prompts accusations of racial bias. In this context, it matters that Michelle Obama helped choose pieces by African American artists to be displayed in the White House. Her having done so highlights her link to the first lady to whom she was most often compared: Jacqueline Kennedy. It was Kennedy who initiated the practice of using a combination of fundraising and collecting to decorate the White House (167). Michelle Obama continued this tradition in a way that acknowledged Americans' inevitable resistance to a first lady who is not white. In other words, her decorating choices evinced awareness of the challenges she faced as the first black woman to become woman of the nation's house. Her success would draw attacks, as demonstrated by her having to assert herself as not just a strong black woman but as Mom-in-Chief, but she could direct some of the inevitable assault away from her body and onto the White House.

As with the refusal to disclose whether or not her hair was chemically straightened, the presence of work by African American artists in the White House constituted an indirect affirmation of marginalized communities. The Obamas were hesitant about overt gestures that affirmed nonwhite people, and most art selections aligned with that tendency. The two most discussed African American artists in the Obama White House collection were Glenn Ligon and the late Alma Thomas. Ligon's piece was often described as "political" but only because many Americans deem "political" anything that acknowledges that whites are not the only people who exist and who contribute to American culture. Indirection was key, though. The work repeats a line from *Black Like Me*, the account of what happened to white journalist John Howard Griffin when he lived as a black man by darkening his skin in 1961. The words "All traces of the Griffin I had been were wiped from existence" are repeated, and with each iteration, the image becomes denser and the letters more difficult to decipher. The fact that these are the words of a white man helped create the indirection. There has always been a need for white people to acknowledge black experience in order for it to register as real and relevant, so the piece aligned with the Obamas' reality. Just as Ligon's art validates blacks' experience of racism by using a white man's words about his brief encounter with it, the Obamas needed white allies to gain entry to the White House. White voters helped tip the answer to the most enduring question of American belonging—do you have access to the presidency?—in their favor.

African Americans do not doubt their citizenship or their right to it, but the violence the country serves to them involves having their Americanness treated as a question, something to be proven. As art historian Maika Pollack poignantly noted, "I happened to visit Glenn Ligon's mid-career retrospective exhibition at the Whitney Museum, provocatively titled 'America,' the day Barack Obama released the long form of his birth certificate to the press. It was a fitting coincidence." After all, "The call for the President's birth certificate reminded us that there are still people for whom blackness and Americanness are incommensurate."[28] The fact that a painting that quotes a white man who briefly experienced the racism that African Americans encounter every day could be cast by most art critics as "political" is telling, but it also demonstrates how indirect the Obamas had to be about acknowledging that they had negative experiences they would not have encountered if they were white. Michelle Obama's art choices therefore reiterated the truth of the statement that forced her to withdraw from the public eye in 2008: African Americans' experiences in the United States rarely inspire pride because the country so seldom abides by its own standards of fair play. As James Baldwin put it, black people's "experience of the white world cannot possibly create . . . any respect for the standards by which the white world claims to live [because what they endure offers] overwhelming proof that white people do not live by these standards" (*Fire* 300).

It is worth considering whether Ligon's piece would have constantly been labeled "racial" and "political" if he had been a white artist, and similar questions should be asked about the work of the late Alma Thomas. Thomas's inclusion among the White House selections also generated much commentary, and one of her pieces was "quietly de-selected."[29] Thomas was the first African American woman artist to have a solo exhibition at the Whitney Museum, and her 1963 *Watusi (Hard Edge)* was destined for the first lady's office space, but it was never mounted. White House representatives insisted that the piece simply did not fit the space well, but it had started a firestorm, as right-wing media outlets insisted Thomas had essentially plagiarized Henri Matisse. Art critics immediately countered by educating the public on artistic traditions. As one put it, saying that Thomas was trying to pass her work off as a Matisse is like saying she was trying to get away with claiming the Mona Lisa as her original work.[30] The painting did not go into the first lady's office space as originally planned, but Thomas's 1973 painting *Sky Light* remained on the selection list and was mounted in the Obama's living quarters.[31]

Making the White House feel accessible to a wider swath of the citizenry seems to have been one measure of Michelle Obama's success (as it had been for Eisenhower, Kennedy, and Johnson), but including people of color is deemed generous for whites but suspicious for everyone else. Michelle Obama's art decisions were part of her public persona; she had to decorate her family's living space, the nation's most symbolic home. Michelle Obama's art choices integrated a more diverse citizenry into 1600 Pennsylvania Avenue—perhaps more than her husband's policies did—but often in ways that did not add to the visibility of nonwhite people. After all, the most discussed pieces by African Americans did not include images of African Americans; Thomas's two chosen works (including the one that was not displayed) were abstracts, and Ligon's was a text painting.[32] Ultimately, Michelle Obama's attempts at inviting certain populations into the White House (as Mamie Eisenhower had done with African Americans) could easily result in hostility for her as well as for such guests; apparently, nonwhite people's inclusion through their artwork was no less controversial.

It is useful to view the decisions that created Michelle Obama's public persona in relationship to Jacqueline Kennedy's, because many were skeptical of her ability to represent American womanhood too, although for very different reasons. The Kennedy family "thought that the American people's idea of a first lady was Bess Truman—a nice, matronly, dowdy, Midwestern American mother—and that someone like Jackie would just turn people off."[33] Over time, through her role as hostess, she proved an asset to the administration and an excellent representative for the nation's cultural potential. Maximizing her language skills, Mrs. Kennedy charmed and truly welcomed international guests, thereby putting the United States in a good light, as a place of hospitality and sophistication. Similarly, her interest in European art had been a liability, but because she made White House restoration a success, her role as hostess made the Kennedy administration appear admirable and productive (Borrelli 108–10). While these shifts represented public victories for Kennedy, they also allowed her to be true to her own interests.

If Jacqueline Kennedy won a battle, gaining some freedom to express herself, then Michelle Obama's victories might be gleaned in her moments of expressing—via her art choices—that she saw value in African

Americans as well as in other people of color.[34] To acknowledge this victory highlights the nation's dishonesty, given how frequently citizens claimed to be postracial during this particular administration. Mrs. Obama proactively affirmed and publicly valued African Americans by supporting their art, but the most discussed pieces avoided conspicuously representing nonwhite populations; her choices therefore expose the labor required to navigate the violent presumption that only white people truly belong. Facile color-blind declarations notwithstanding, the Obamas' time in the White House often revealed that Americans still conceive of civic inclusion—and certainly civic leadership—as a whites-only proposition.

*　*　*

Barack Obama's election was unquestionably historic. Few believed they would live to see a president who was not a white man. It proved even more momentous when he was reelected in 2012 despite voter suppression efforts that rivaled those of the 1890s (Berman), but the Obama presidency was also painfully revealing. Many claimed that Obama was "divisive" while others noted that the vitriol on display revealed truths about American citizens, not about Mr. Obama.

The latter characterization strikes me as more accurate because United States history has shown that black success beckons the mob, and responses to Michelle Obama should be seen in the same light. No matter who is in the position, public responses to the first lady reveal much more about the American people than about the president's spouse. Americans cannot know the first lady as a person. She simply seems to create "the relationships that bind the political system and the society together" (Borrelli 202). And, importantly, the first lady's influence is "examined and critiqued . . . by average citizens as well as by policy makers" (ibid.). If reactions to the first lady reflect the citizenry's character more than hers, then Michelle Obama was a particularly powerful mirror for the American public, even as many preferred ignoring their own reflections.

Above all, reactions to Michelle Obama highlighted the aggression woven into American culture that fuels the expediency of embodying the strong black woman. The need for a prominent woman of color to ratchet up her strong-black-woman performance to the level of Mom-in-Chief suggests that earning a place of honor in the ultimate home does not diminish the necessity of homemade citizenship, of making oneself at home while understanding you will be attacked for doing so. Michelle

Obama's success as a strong black woman with a "proper" home life landed her in the White House. Once there, it took deliberate effort to affirm herself, just as ordinary black women work to maintain their self-conceptions while being bombarded with the relentless discursive violence of stereotypes. As Melissa Harris-Perry might put it, she was simply "the most visible contemporary example of an African American woman working to stand straight in a crooked room" (271).

Laboring despite the odds against you takes a lot of effort, and Mrs. Obama spared none; she made careful decisions about everything, including hair, clothes, bodily presentation, and home décor. And her effort paid off in that she was indeed successful. However, for members of marginalized groups, success inspires aggression as often as praise, and the American public keeps renewing its commitment to this tendency. As the outsized celebration of *The Help* revealed, Americans still insist upon either ignoring black women's domesticity or viewing it only in terms of housekeeping.[35] Michelle Obama's place in the White House did not lessen the power of figures like the welfare queen, and it did not lead to more respect for black women as successful—downright admirable homemakers.

Coda

From Mom-in-Chief to Predator-in-Chief

Understanding know-your-place aggression takes the mystery out of why so many Americans were eager to see the country move from Mom-in-Chief to Predator-in-Chief. Because the nation's most common words and deeds aim to diminish people who are not straight, white, and male, those who are women and/or of color receive a very consistent message: *know your place!* Donald Trump's political ascendency highlighted what has always been most characteristic about the United States and its commitment to ensuring the unequal distribution of everything. That which American culture most consistently enacts (but denies) became visible in the demeanor adopted by Trump in relationship to Barack Obama and Hillary Clinton. Then, though Michelle Obama seldom engages the nation's ugliness directly (perhaps remembering the backlash to her 2008 "proud for the first time" comment), the First Lady publicly identified the aggression that shapes U.S. citizenship. American discourses and practices cast black women as irrelevant while making them some of the hardest hit targets, so Mrs. Obama continued the tradition of countless women before her, including those whose work has been examined throughout this book. In unusually explicit terms, she offered a cultural production comprised of especially keen observations and insightful critiques of the nation's tendencies.

As I argue in Chapter 6, know-your-place aggression guarantees that certain groups cannot simply enjoy the benefits that would otherwise accompany their success. Being elected to lead the free world, despite tireless voter suppression efforts (Berman), did not shield Barack Obama from unprecedented disrespect while occupying the office. Even more striking, it is now clear that denigrating the nation's first black president was literally the ticket to political ascendancy for a reality television star with no record of public service, no grace, and no knowledge of the Bible so many of his supporters claim to cherish. Besides winning support by standing against everything that would constitute Obama's legacy, Trump's rise perpetuated all the know-your-place aggression hurled at the Obama family throughout their time in the White House. As *The Guardian* put it, "Trump's political beginnings are rooted in an effort to deny the legitimacy of Obama's presidency" (Gambino). By taking Trump's demands for Obama's birth certificate seriously, American leaders and ordinary citizens did to the president what they do to all black people, thrust suspicion onto them, regardless of actual behavior. With so many respectable politicians tolerating Trump's efforts to delegitimize Obama, it is clear that Trump has never represented a fringe element of the population but the most agreed upon meanings of "the American way."

Having made himself a political contender by questioning Barack Obama's citizenship, Trump continued to expose the true nature of American culture when he officially launched his presidential campaign by calling Mexicans rapists. Trump was more explicit than most, but anti-Mexican sentiment is part of the very foundation of this country.[1] This rhetoric relied on long-standing hatred, so Trump gained momentum with it. Indeed, he benefited as he "conjured up images of 'bad hombres' [which] . . . resonated with the GOP's habit of labeling Latina mothers 'drop-and-leave' culprits and calling their children 'anchor babies'" (Chávez and Mitchell). Like the figure of the welfare queen, these stereotypes rely on images that provoke visceral reactions about who contributes to the nation and who takes away from it. As argued in the Introduction, figures are persuasive because they are multivalent and rely on the power of performance, the power of semiotics, and embodied practices. As Diana Taylor teaches, performance makes undeniable that "the affective is the effective" (*Performance* 92). These particular figures prove especially convincing because they are connected to the vilification of women: women have babies that they supposedly "drop and leave" or use as "anchors."

Of course, Trump's denigration of women has been as consistent as his racism, and this fact has never presented a problem because American institutions are designed to operate most smoothly when women of color are denigrated. Meanwhile, everyone is assured that these women cannot possibly be victims or experiencing anything significant because they are supposedly such a nonissue. National discourse ignores women of color even as it targets them; the ignoring is part of the discursive violence. Accordingly, when Trump publicly insulted a Latina in the mid-1990s, there was little outrage. Trump had "repeatedly called Venezuelan model Alicia Machado, the 1996 Miss Universe beauty pageant winner, 'Miss Piggy' and 'Miss Housekeeping'" (Chávez and Mitchell).[2] He was not a presidential hopeful at that point, but the degree to which he could have been, without such behavior hurting his chances, has now been thoroughly demonstrated. Ultimately, Trump's rise reveals what all American institutions have in common. The government is no different from a private corporation or a public university. They were all designed to ensure that white men can hoard power and status whether they deserve to (according to their own criteria) or not.[3]

Once he became the Republican nominee for president, Trump's demeanor toward Hillary Clinton exposed the nation's commitment to know-your-place aggression as clearly as his two terms of harassing Barack Obama. As was the case with disrespecting Obama, the cultural significance lies not simply in Trump's behavior but in the support he enjoys; it is clear that many share the beliefs that undergird his racist, sexist words and deeds. Even if one assumes most Americans do not support the ideas but simply tolerate them, it's important to understand *why* tolerance is such a common response.

In short, this country operates on the firmly held belief that white men are entitled to whatever they deem to be their right. In fact, there is nothing Americans believe in more than they believe in white male volition. Trump's coziness with Russia's Vladimir Putin underscores this fact. No matter how problematic a behavior is by their own standards, white men (who hold the power) will not curb white men's free will. White men will certainly presume to know what is best for women and deem themselves to be the best judges of whether or not people of color are worthy, but they will not intrude upon another white man's right to do as he pleases.[4]

Making citizenship a violent mechanism that carves white men's benefits out of everyone else's pain and deprivation is the American way, and this fact took center stage when Hillary Clinton became Trump's opponent. In other words, know-your-place aggression is simultaneously reactionary and productive. Relentless attacks on people who are not white *and* male even if—or especially because—they embody what the nation claims to respect, ensures that absolutely no standards are placed on white men. That is, white men are presumed deserving no matter what they do. As noted at the beginning of this study, citizenship is not respected based on behavior but based on demographic.

Witnessing the emergence of a woman presidential candidate inspired know-your-place aggression from ordinary citizens, not just Donald Trump, and this fact is telling. A person in a dominant demographic category need not be impressive by any measure in order for everything about American culture to encourage them to denigrate a far more impressive member of a marginalized group. As an American tradition, know-your-place aggression has meant that white mediocrity becomes merit, and white male villainy does, too. Near a Clinton rally held in Reno, Nevada, in August 2016, two men displayed a banner reading, "Trump that bitch" on their parked van, and "they waved and smiled, as people drove by" (Keith). Since March 2016, products with slogans like this have been common, and they were particularly well received at the Republican National Convention in Cleveland.[5] Speaking about many Trump rallies over time, Republican strategist Katie Packer noted that parents, who had their children with them, wore shirts and held signs describing Hillary Clinton in crudely sexual terms. Though staffers did not create the products, "there hasn't been a peep from the campaign about this stuff being offensive" (ibid.). "And, so, by not addressing it, they have encouraged it," Packer concluded. However, this trend revealed more than Packer noted, as made clear when considered in the context of John McCain's response to negative comments about Barack Obama in 2008. When a woman at his rally expressed misgivings based on her belief that Obama is not an American, McCain countered. McCain said, "He's a decent, family man, citizen, that I just happen to have disagreements with on fundamental issues. . . ." As a result, "McCain never became beloved by the base the same way his running mate, Sarah Palin, did" (ibid.). Given that the support of ordinary white Americans is a key indicator, denigrating certain populations is the most American thing a politician can do.

Trump supporters were not alone in their sexism toward Clinton, of course, and examples from the candidate himself further prove that his sexist beliefs are not at all uncommon; the investment in white male domination that dictated his every move is so widely shared that it sent him to the White House. In April 2016, Trump dismissed Clinton's impeccable credentials in the way that the credentials of any member of a marginalized group can be easily disregarded. He said she would not be a contender if she were not a woman (ibid.) and doubled down a couple weeks later. Clinton tried to turn this sexist idea on its head. In a campaign video released shortly afterward, she said, "If fighting for women's health care and paid family leave and equal pay is playing the woman card, then deal me in." However, the momentum of American culture cannot be outwitted. Because American citizenship has literally been constructed through know-your-place aggression, the nation ensures that being smarter or more righteous hardly matters. What matters most is being a white man or not being a white man.

To put it in the most neutral terms, "when men have monopolized the Oval Office and dominated the other branches of government for more than two centuries—and when women nationwide have had the right to vote for less than half that time, . . . the masculine template is a winning template" (Kurtzleben). For those reading through the lens of success, the neutrality of this phrasing serves as a reminder that the reality described is not at all neutral. Ninety-nine percent of the nation's presidents have been white men, and everyone is taught not only that this is fair but also that their white maleness had nothing to do with their achievements. No one is supposed to notice that their white maleness was (unjustly) interpreted as merit. Yet, if a woman gets close, her gender magically becomes evidence of an unfair advantage.

Still, what is most revealing about the know-your-place aggression of the Trump campaign and the steady support it enjoyed was how easily he cast his opponent as dangerous for the country. He nicknamed her *Crooked Hillary*, paving the way for enthusiastic chants of "Lock her up!" Without recounting the vitriol spewed throughout the campaign, its efficacy can be appreciated by considering the orientation of the 2016 Republican National Convention. As *The Wall Street Journal* put it, "if their convention speeches are any indication, most of the party's heavy hitters are less inclined to make a robust case for Mr. Trump than they are to make the case against Mrs. Clinton" (Hooks and Ballhaus). For instance, "Senate Majority Leader Mitch McConnell mentioned Mr. Trump just five times in his convention speech and Mrs. Clinton 24 times" (ibid.). Rick Tyler, a former aide to the Ted Cruz campaign summed it up this way: "The dominant message coming out of the convention is 'You may not like Donald Trump, but he is not Hillary Clinton.' If that's the dominant message, we've already lost" (ibid.). Clearly, Tyler did not understand know-your-place aggression. Everything about this country's culture is geared toward putting certain groups in their "proper" place, especially when these "others" are successful.

Given that Hillary Clinton had the kind of support that no other woman candidate had ever secured and the money to go along with it,[6] both leaders and ordinary citizens became (consciously and unconsciously) even more invested in countering those achievements. After all, it does not take much for voters, including women voters, to turn against women candidates.[7] As an insightful Trump supporter put it, "What the convention doesn't do to unify the GOP, Hillary Clinton will."

Another sign that know-your-place aggression determines American outcomes is the fact that Trump's family was his biggest asset at the convention. If Americans are honest with themselves, which they rarely are, there can be no better indication that demographics, not actual standards, determine how citizens view their leaders. The children who represented Trump on stage have different mothers, and he is on his third wife. This sort of family portrait simply would not have been an asset for anyone but a white man. Americans are taught to see value in white men, no matter what they do or don't do.

Trump himself said, "I could stand in the middle of 5th Avenue and shoot somebody and I wouldn't lose voters," and Americans delude themselves if they think this statement is hyperbole rather than an accurate reflection of their social and political reality. Know-your-place aggression is at the heart of U.S. citizenship. As I have argued in another context, all of American culture, including American jurisprudence, "has evolved to ensure that 'real' citizens (white men) keep their license to do harm because others must sometimes be reminded that they are not truly citizens."[8] So, when a white man kills someone, the nation's institutions mobilize to "manufacture innocence" for him, as cultural historian David Leonard has demonstrated so powerfully.[9] Serial killers in the United States are overwhelmingly white and male, and the response to them suggests that, no matter what, white men should continue to enjoy the rights and privileges of American citizenship. After all, that's the only reason American citizenship was created.

With white male license as its very reason for existing, the mechanisms of American citizenship flew into overdrive to oppose a female presidential candidate, so suggestions that Hillary Clinton was a problematic nominee only deflect from how thoroughly American culture was on display. Her success was used against her, as often happens for members of marginalized groups because American culture is geared toward reminding them of their "proper" place. Rebecca Traister summarizes the election cycle well:

> It is a piteous irony that in finding a way past the specific hurdles long set before women with presidential ambitions—fund-raising and the support of a major party—Hillary Clinton also offered up to her opponents, on the left and the right, the ammunition to undercut the historic nature of her candidacy. The very fact that she had close relationships with big donors and garnered the support of major political institutions made her part of the political elite, vulnerable to the anti-Establishment rhetoric of both Bernie Sanders and Donald Trump. It also kept her from being understood or celebrated as the historic outsider that, as a member of a gender historically denied access to executive power, she was. ("Shattered")

Understanding know-your-place aggression reveals that there is no irony here, only tradition.

Putting Clinton in her "proper" place—outside of the Oval Office—therefore has far-reaching implications and not just for those pursuing political positions. First, it affects the material realities of countless people who are not straight, white, and male because her loss translates into continued assaults on voting rights and reproductive health care and paves the way for Supreme Court appointees hostile to these populations. Of course, material violence and discursive violence go together, so the other consequences of Clinton's loss cannot truly be measured. As Traister predicted, Hillary Clinton proved to be a "screen upon which all of America's very long-standing, very complicated, fairly unattractive feelings about women [were] projected" ("Hot Mess"). It matters, then, that Clinton's supporters were also consistently "belittled for their cute investment in a non-male presidential power" (ibid.).

The reverberating violence of all these outcomes is especially clear when one recalls that the current mobilization of women in politics resulted partly from witnessing an accomplished woman experience a belittling ordeal on national television. EMILY's List, the nation's leading organization encouraging women to run for public office, was founded in 1985, but its originator says it gained widespread support in the wake of Anita Hill's testimony in the Senate confirmation hearings of Clarence Thomas, then a prospective Supreme Court judge. Thomas had sexually harassed Hill, and she shared her harrowing experience before the world only to see the all-male committee nevertheless confirm him. Women across the country watched along with her, and "by the following year, EMILY's List had grown to 23,000 members and raised more than $10 million" (Traister, "Shattered"). As important, "twenty new Democratic women were elected to Congress that year, and 1992 was dubbed 'the Year of the Woman.'" (ibid.). Most telling, "Pat Schroeder has recalled that afterward, when women's representation in the Senate was still just 7 percent and in the House was just over 10 percent, one of the Senate's 'old bulls' said to her, 'I really hope you're happy. This is beginning to look like a shopping mall'" (ibid.).

While many claim Clinton cannot be used to understand how Americans respond to women candidates because she has such a particular and troubled history with the American public, the only particularities about her case that really matter are her whiteness and her extraordinary level of accomplishment, which her whiteness facilitated. Because she is not only exceptionally credentialed but also white, rich, and well-connected, she makes clear what racial or economic disadvantages would otherwise obscure. That is, because her whiteness would normally make her achievements a cause for celebration, her experience exposes how thoroughly American citizenship operates specifically for the benefit of straight white men with property. In short, if a white man had Clinton's resumé, connections, and funding, he would have been a no-brainer for the American public. So, the effectiveness of the strategy used against Clinton reveals the nation's investment in keeping women, including the most privileged and powerful women, in their "proper" place. As cultural historian Ruby Tapia observes, "Both the 'Crooked Hillary' moniker and the 'Lock Her Up' chant became rhetorical pillars of the Hillary for Prison campaign, which was arguably, itself, as effective on behalf of Trump's presidential bid as the slogans 'Yes, we can' and 'Hope' were for Obama's campaign" ("Reading Race and Class"). Tapia rightly notes further, "The misogynistic criminalization of Hillary is based on an assumption—or perhaps acknowledgment—of her classed and racialized agency. She represents an able threat to the white masculinity of the state precisely because of her whiteness, her wealth, her power" (ibid.).

Know-your-place aggression springs into action whenever someone who is not a straight, white, propertied man knows they deserve to have their accomplishments recognized, respected, and rewarded. Thus, Trump's election "was an answer to women's success in securing legal recognition of their right to reproductive health services, including access to safe abortions. It was an answer to the success of DREAMers in persuading other Americans that they are not criminals, but human beings. It was an answer to black and brown people who recently began assuming that the White House and the government should work for their benefit, too" (Chávez and Mitchell). As Traister put it, seeing the Obamas with Hillary Clinton on the national stage on election night represented the degree to which "many groups of Americans who spent centuries disenfranchised . . . now felt they had the power to elect presidents" ("Shattered"). Clearly, nothing could inspire an aggressive *know your place!* response like that could.

Tapia argues that, in contrast to calls for Hillary Clinton's imprisonment because she posed a real threat to white male power, women of color are incarcerated at startling rates because "their *disempowerment* has been criminalized" ("Reading Race and Class"). However, know-your-place aggression prompts me to disagree. After all, accomplishments need not be extraordinary to inspire brutal reactions, as this book has shown when examining the incremental victories of enslaved people who nonetheless faced the full weight of the nation's hostility, with the Fugitive Slave Act as just one example. This is why it is crucial to recognize Trump's election as a response to the relatively modest advancements of all people of color, LGBTQ+ communities, and women.

To appreciate the know-your-place aggression of the 2016 election, one cannot stop with Barack Obama and Hillary Clinton; necessary insight emerges from a written text brought to life by a black woman, Michelle Obama.[10] On October 15, 2016, after the release of the recording of Trump saying he grabs women without their consent, Michelle Obama gave a speech in which she did what African American cultural production always has. She noted the achievements of marginalized groups, embodied clarity about their right to those achievements, and articulated the passion with which they must continue to aspire even as they identify the forces arrayed against them. Especially knowing Trump was elected a few weeks after this speech, Mrs. Obama's urging Americans to mobilize in support of Hillary Clinton can seem to have meant nothing, but it is worth looking not only more deeply but also through the lens of accomplishment.

When the speech clearly failed to win the election for Clinton, how does a reading practice oriented toward success shed light? It highlights the focus on achievement and the fact that this focus was never diminished by the blows Michelle Obama admits hit her personally. A general example first: Michelle Obama worked to convince her audience to support Hillary Clinton by appealing to Americans' respect for a good work ethic, even as that ideal has never actually driven U.S. practices. In reality, the nation has claimed to value a strong work ethic while never holding white men to such standards; purported ideals simply gave them license to judge others. When Michelle Obama brings these words to life, through a body that conjures up the history of people well aware of the nation's dishonesty, it is worth asking: *Does she really think Americans will step up and walk their talk about valuing hard work or does she suspect they won't?* I think the latter is likely, though we will never know.[11] Like ordinary African Americans, Michelle Obama has been unable to escape how ugly the real American way is. She knows the incredibly low standards to which white people hold themselves and each other, especially when the people harmed by their actions are not white men. Nevertheless, marching toward her own definition of achievement remains the goal. "When they go low, we go high" is one articulation of that march toward accomplishment, but so is leaving a record of the obstacles women face while they so often achieve anyway.

Thus, it is worth noting that she framed her remarks with the stark contrast American society offers women of accomplishment. She said she began her week with White House celebrations of the International Day of the Girl and her program Let Girls Learn. She spoke of absolutely relishing the events as important: "I thought it would be important to remind these young women how valuable and precious they are." This reassurance was necessary because she knows how routinely they receive a very different message: "See, because many of these girls have faced unthinkable obstacles just to attend school—jeopardizing their personal safety, their freedom, risking the rejection of their families, and communities." Such obstacles lend clarity: "I wanted them to understand the measure of any society is how it treats its women and girls." With this, Michelle Obama not only reiterated the intersectional analysis black women have offered for generations;[12] she identified the know-your-place aggression with which these girls are already familiar.

She then reminded the audience that they need not look at other societies for regressive responses to women and girls. She agonized, "And I can't believe I'm saying that—a candidate for President of the United States has bragged about sexually assaulting women. And I have to tell you that I can't stop thinking about this. It has shaken me to my core in a way that I couldn't have predicted." Because American culture not only sends a know-your-place message to certain populations but also insists that they are being too sensitive if they acknowledge receiving it, Michelle Obama paused to identify the impact. She was shaken by the import of all that had happened, more shaken than expected. She assured auditors that if they felt assaulted, that makes sense because the implications reverberate far beyond a single conversation.

Michelle Obama admitted she would prefer not addressing it, but "this was not just a lewd conversation, this was not just 'locker room banter.' This was a powerful individual speaking openly and freely about sexually predatory behavior and actually bragging about kissing and groping women." Trump's comments shed light on the fact that environments are shaped by powerful people; they set the tone for workplaces, organizations, countries. Mrs. Obama continued, "I've listened to this, and I feel it so personally. . . . The shameful comments about our bodies. *The disrespect of our ambitions and intellect*" (emphasis added). What is striking here is the clarity, as she notes that such behavior strives to put women's success in check. When they think their lives are about ambition and intellect, they will be reminded of their "proper" place. This is why it is so powerful that Mrs. Obama likened Trump's sexually aggressive speech to street harassment. She noted that it reminded her of when men address women in ways that make "you feel uncomfortable in your own skin." What better way to communicate that women are not at home? Even in their own skin, they should feel the force of the message that they are not at home, not true citizens.

Michelle Obama did not simply trace the violent impact of Trump's words and deeds, however; she made the case for all that Hillary Clinton brings to the table that could benefit the country. "The fact is, Hillary embodies so many of the values that we try so hard to teach our young people." As she had said in an earlier speech, "Hillary has never quit anything in her life," which should bring to mind Trump's bankruptcies as well as his divorces . . . but ultimately, the American people proved those facts did not matter. Americans have always cared more about demographics than actual standards. Obama continued, "And in this election, if we turn away from her, if we just stand by and allow her opponent to be elected, then what are we teaching our children about the values they should hold, about the kind of life they should lead? What are we saying?" Partly through indifference toward voter suppression, but also through the sincerity of 63 million people who cast their vote for Trump, the United States answered these questions in a way that aligns with its core values.

Mrs. Obama had been so accurate: "In our hearts, in our hearts, we all know that if we let Hillary's opponent win this election, that we are sending a clear message to our kids that everything they're seeing and hearing is perfectly okay." Sending this message was important because— no matter how often incremental progress for other groups might be tolerated—white men must always maintain the license to remind others that they are mere guests of the nation's true citizens. It therefore matters that 63 million Americans—including 53 percent of white women—voted for Trump. They articulated their beliefs regarding exactly what Michelle Obama said was at stake: "On November the 8th, we can show our children that this country is big enough to have a place for us all." *Room for all? Oh, no. That's not the American way!*

In so clearly identifying the stakes of the election, Michelle Obama highlighted not simply the violence of one powerful individual but the participation of countless ordinary citizens. There was no better way to tell women *"Know your place!"* than to elect a man known to be a predator of women. The pronouncements to all women include: *You can never truly be successful. Do not aim for achievement. Your achievements do not matter. You are not at home. You will always be in someone else's house.* The weight of such declarations is keenly felt by women of color, especially black women. As the saying goes, "When America catches a cold, black people get pneumonia." What hits women will hit black women especially hard.

Americans spoke loudly and acted out of their belief that citizenship might be for white men who damage communities and institutions, but it is certainly not for accomplished women. The United States has always sent this message, and black women have never let that stop them from marching toward their goals. Theirs is a history of moving from house slaves to housekeepers to homemakers, as Mrs. Obama highlighted when she spoke of her poised daughters coming of age in the White House, which was "built by slaves." She had also gestured toward the struggle of a black woman who inhabited the White House in a much less empowered way when she posed for her official portrait in 2008. By being photographed with Thomas Jefferson over her shoulder, as she wore a flattering, sleeveless dress while exuding confident self-possession, she honored Sally Hemings[13] and the countless other black women whose pain has been the very foundation of the nation's most important institutions. As Mrs. Obama continues to craft her public persona outside of the White House, she will continue to contribute to a community conversation on success that understands the nation's ongoing investment in insisting that African Americans are not citizens and will never be at home. As they always have, African Americans use that dynamic, multivalent discussion to cultivate homemade citizenship, to make themselves at home nonetheless.

Notes

Introduction

1. U.S. citizenship is also built on settler colonialism and the denial of Indigenous sovereignty. See Dunbar-Ortiz, *An Indigenous Peoples' History*, and Brandzel, *Against Citizenship*. While subduing Native populations, the United States also excluded African Americans, despite the lack of a color designation in initial ideas of citizenship. See Hyde, *Civic Longing*, as well as Mills, *Racial Contract*.

2. Know-your-place aggression emerges in response to the accomplishments—big and small—of all marginalized groups, so I refuse to speak only of African Americans here, even though the book focuses on them. For the most comprehensive account of the concept, see Mitchell, "Identifying White Mediocrity and Know-your-place Aggression," which addresses not only racism but also (hetero)sexism, trans antagonism, ableism, and Islamophobia.

3. I begin with the Civil War, but see Kendi's *Stamped* for earlier examples, such as the 1699 legislation demonstrating that planters perceived imported Africans to be hopelessly incapable, except when the issue was instructing them on "the complexities of proslavery theory, racist ideas, tobacco production, skilled trades, domestic work, and plantation management" (65).

4. The same can be said for Native Americans and immigrants.

5. In addition to the examples in this study's first chapter, the *Narrative of Henry Box Brown* shows keen awareness of opposition to every victory. See Mitchell, "Beyond Protest," *Race in American Literature and Culture*, edited by John Ernest, Cambridge UP.

6. "By *embodied practice*, I mean any bodily act that conveys meaning. The term is deliberately broad, building on Performance Studies, which emphasizes the centrality of performance in how human beings make culture and live their lives. Embodied practices can include speaking or singing, grimacing or gesturing, hugging or hitting, reading a script dramatically or performing in full costume" (Mitchell, *Living with Lynching*, 5, emphasis in original).

7. Like much important scholarship, Christina Sharpe's *In the Wake* gestures toward possibilities not completely overtaken by white supremacy, but it is primarily committed to a thorough accounting of "the wake": the unrelenting antiblackness upon which Western "democracy" is built. I appreciate her gestures, but my study's goals are different in that I want to be clear that *black success is the reason antiblackness became "the weather."*

8. Cultural criticism typically approaches black art as a response. Examples are too plentiful to list, but the orientation is so ubiquitous that it has shaped otherwise immeasurably valuable work. For instance, Hazel Carby traced "the ways in which black women, as writers, addressed, used, *transformed*, and on occasion *subverted* the dominant ideological codes" (20–21, emphasis added). Similarly, Claudia Tate insisted that black domestic romance "provided both a ready formula for liberal black self-construction and *relief* for black readers from direct encounters with racism. . . . Hence, in amazing opposition to the violent resurgence of racial oppression that marked this period, these novels focus by and large on happy domestic settings without directly addressing interracial turmoil" (14, emphasis added). According to Tate, "racial *protest* displaces racial affirmation" in the early 1900s (17, emphasis in original). Tate also stated that African Americans defied the low expectations of dominant discourses that cast African Americans as immoral and unprepared for full citizenship. In my reading, such depictions arose to counter already existent black success.

9. Given its cultural studies framework, this study uses "discourses and practices" to gesture toward the many ways that dominant ideologies, such as racism and sexism, are articulated and advanced not only through individual words and deeds but also through the nation's laws, political rhetoric, public policies, and popular culture.

10. I use "citizens of color" deliberately here. I do not believe immigrants are less worthy of belonging than those born inside the nation's current borders, but American discourse claims as much. In accord with the community conversation, I am underscoring the violence of excluding even those who fit stated criteria.

11. See Rodgers and Robinson, "How the News Media Distorts Black Families," and Chávez and Mitchell, "Step Up!"

12. Donald Trump's use of "bad hombre" tapped into a longstanding strategy among conservatives. See Chávez and Mitchell.

13. Just as being considered white or Native American determined who got land and resources in the early days of the republic, demographics still dictate the distribution of everything from job opportunity to safety, as well as freedom from contaminated air and water. Scholarly investigations of inequity abound, including Lipsitz, *Possessive Investment*, and Alexander, *The New Jim Crow*.

14. Diana Taylor's *The Archive and the Repertoire* shapes my understanding of the interaction between a culture's written documents and its embodied practices. I see the nation's most common discourses and practices, most common words and deeds, as always deeply related. Given this partnership, words and deeds that align with racism, sexism, heterosexism, and classism (for example) are persuasive and efficacious.

15. Examples of "broken home" rhetoric in supposedly neutral news coverage about victims of color include the Fox News report by the Associated Press, "Teenager Killed by Chicago Police Officer Came from Troubled Past, Broken Family," *Fox News*, November 26, 2015, www.foxnews.com/us/2015/11/26/ teenager-killed-by-chicago-police-officer-came-from-troubled-past-broken -family.html, and the many stories that led to Nick Wing, "When the Media Treats White Suspects and Killers Better than Black Victims," *Huffington Post*, August 14, 2014, www.huffingtonpost.com/2014/08/14/media-black-victims _n_5673291.html. A piece that is more transparent about its conclusions coming from its author's perspective is Mary Mitchell, "More than Bullets Killed Laquan McDonald," *Chicago Sun-Times*, November 21, 2015, chicago.suntimes.com/2015/11/22/18445007/mitchell-more-than-police -bullets-killed-laquan-mcdonald.

16. Harris-Perry finds that, when Americans do not feel empowered to change outcomes, they blame victims rather than admit situations are unfair. For more detail and a discussion of the implications for nonwhite people, see *Sister Citizen* 188–91.

17. Traditional domesticity's limits have been demonstrated, for example, with Spillers's "Mama's Baby, Papa's Maybe," in *Black, White* and Collins's emphasis on the value of other-mothering (180–92). Also see George, "Recycling"; Reddy, "Home, Houses, Nonidentity"; and Ferguson, *Aberrations*.

18. The nation's history of creating systems and policies that block nonwhite people from the American dream is consistent and well documented. See, for example, Coates's "The Case for Reparations," which cites longer studies.

19. This practice has been well documented, but a particularly striking example of not only its violence but also black women's determination to

march toward success, no matter how much they must change their definition of it, emerges in Dierdre Owens's *Medical Bondage*, via the testimony of Mrs. Everett (57–58).

20. Representations of black women who love black men of their own choice abound. Examples in slavery-era texts include the narratives of Frederick Douglass, William Wells Brown, and Henry "Box" Brown, as well as William (and Ellen) Craft's *Running a Thousand Miles for Freedom* and Harriet Jacobs's *Incidents in the Life of a Slave Girl*.

21. See H. Williams, *Help Me*. Also, the post-slavery existence of "paramour rights," laws to make a black woman's sexual will irrelevant, suggests that negating black people's humanity and agency required deliberate action and the cooperation of state power. See the documentaries *The Other Side of Silence* and *The Curtain of Secrecy: The Story of Ruby McCollum*, as well as C. Arthur Ellis Jr.'s book, *Zora Hurston and The Strange Case of Ruby McCollum*, Ringgold, Ga.: Gadfly Publishing, 2009.

22. Violence against LGBTQ+ individuals is legible to scholars; we are used to grappling with aggression toward those who do not conform—"punks, bulldaggers, and welfare queens," as Cathy Cohen puts it. Indeed, Jack Halberstam conceives of the refusal to meet society's standards in terms of the "queer art of failure," which celebrates the practices of a figure who "quietly loses, and in losing . . . imagines other goals for life, for love, for art, for being" (88). Because "queer failure" entails seeking and creating alternatives, African American artists often use figures that are so *un*interested in failure that they do not seek alternative ways of being. The cultural productions I study highlight the fact that violence comes even to those who have done everything "right." The structural injustice of American citizenship is foregrounded when violence pursues even those who epitomize the most conservative, mainstream values. Nevertheless, to my mind, Halberstam's queer art of failure actually gestures toward achievement. Those individuals and communities have succeeded in knowing they are human and deserve rights even when they don't conform to dominant discourses and practices that insist that only certain kinds of people deserve anything other than violence.

23. Spires's *Practice* and Hyde's *Civic Longing* demonstrate that citizenship was not initially tied to whiteness, so legislation and court rulings made the link more and more explicit throughout the 1800s. That process has continued, even as Americans go through periods of claiming to value abstract ideals and corresponding behaviors rather than demographics.

24. This is the case even though Mrs. Obama made a joke of calling her husband her baby daddy in 2004 (see http://transcripts.cnn.com/TRANSCRIPTS/0411/02/se.06.html). Fox commentators were not eager to corroborate the ironic humor of her remark or the rapport such humor might facilitate within the community conversation.

25. See, for example, Julie Hirschfeld Davis, "Obama's Twitter Debut, @POTUS, Attracts Hate-Filled Posts," *New York Times,* May 21, 2015. https://www.nytimes.com/2015/05/22/us/politics/obamas-twitter-debut-potus -attracts-hate-filled-posts.html and https://funnyjunk.com/Change+hope +hang+rope/funny-pictures/5380752/.

26. See Erik Ortiz, "Is this an anti-Obama lynching? Texas man hangs chair from tree inspired by Clint Eastwood speech." *New York Daily News,* September 21, 2012. https://www.nydailynews.com/news/politics/anti-obama -lynching-texas-man-hangs-chair-tree-inspired-clint-eastwood-speech-article -1.1164520.

27. Of course, this is similar to Michel Foucault's "discourse," and I am certainly indebted to his theorizing, but I distinguish my object of study with emphasis on "imagined community" and the other issues raised throughout this Introduction.

28. For infanticide and suicide in the antebellum era, see A. Davis, *Women, Race, and Class,* and Owens, *Medical Bondage,* among others.

29. The American Colonization Society is just one example of how thoroughly white Americans believed black people could remain in the United States only if enslaved; if they insisted upon freedom, black people should go elsewhere. However, African Americans also made impassioned arguments for leaving the United States. Black advocates for emigration include Mary Ann Shadd Cary, Henry Highland Garnett, and Martin Delany in the 1850s, Henry McNeal Turner in the 1890s, Marcus Garvey in the 1920s, and the many throughout the twentieth century and today devoted to cultural heritage tourism in and migration to Ghana; Bahia, Brazil; and various sites of slavery in the U.S. South, such as the Carolina Sea Islands. (The latter tradition is discussed in Commander, *Afro-Atlantic Flight.*)

30. It is difficult to define the parameters of Afro-pessimism, but Jared Sexton's "The Social Life of Social Death" is a useful overview, and it casts the work of people like Frank Wilderson as representative. What I identify as Afro-pessimism (that is in opposition to my goals) has to do with giving white supremacy too much credit, suggesting it shapes everything about black people's experiences. Moten's work represents "black optimism" in Sexton's overview, but this Introduction has already suggested how I part ways with it. Some of Hartman's work figures similarly in this Introduction. The sophisticated theorizing in Calvin Warren's *Ontological Terror* is one particularly emblematic example of Afro-pessimism, insisting black being itself has been put under erasure. Sharpe's *In the Wake* also somewhat represents the approach.

31. See, for example, Hartman's "Venus," *Scenes of Subjection,* and *Wayward Lives;* Daphne Brooks's *Bodies in Dissent;* Sarah Haley's *No Mercy Here;* and Deirdre Owens's *Medical Bondage.*

32. The concept of *the politics of respectability* was developed by Evelyn Brooks Higginbotham and has shaped much black feminist criticism, including my own. Brittney Cooper's *Beyond Respectability* illustrates how the concept has led many to overlook what is clearly represented in black women's intellectual thought. My project uses the lens of success to come to conclusions similar to Cooper's, understanding that neither my insights nor Cooper's would be possible without the foundation Higginbotham provided.

33. The cult of true womanhood held sway in the nineteenth century. Barbara Welter's account of this ideology and its impact remains the most definitive.

34. Even if it addresses a gap by engaging literature and art, this book is certainly not alone in building on the foundation laid in the 1980s and 1990s. It joins, for example, Roderick Ferguson's *Aberrations in Black*, Candice Jenkins's *Private Lives, Proper Relations*, and Salamishah Tillet's *Sites of Slavery*.

35. See Hyde, *Civic Longing*, and Spires, *Practice*, on the deliberate steps taken to attach citizenship to propertied white manhood.

36. Aside from the aforementioned Fox News "baby mama" label, see Peter Slevin's biography for discussion of racist, sexist responses to Mrs. Obama, especially 291–92.

37. She initially applied the term to herself in a 2008 interview, but the more deliberate use began with this speech. Interestingly, in her memoir, she mentions only the 2008 interview and says, "I'd said it casually, but the phrase caught hold and was amplified across the press" (Obama 329).

38. For a critical review of such arguments, see Brittney Cooper, "Lay Off Michelle Obama: Why White Feminists Need to Lean Back," *Salon*, November 29, 2013, www.salon.com/2013/11/29/lay_off_michelle_obama_why _white_feminists_need_to_lean_back/. For a somewhat neutral overview, see Lonnae O'Neal Parker, "Four Years Later, Feminists Split by Michelle Obama's 'Work' as First Lady," *Washington Post*, January 18, 2013, www .washingtonpost.com/lifestyle/style/feminists-split-by-michelle-obamas-work -as-first-lady/2013/01/18/be3d636e-5e5e-11e2–9940–6fc488f3fecd_story .html. A standard example is Kay Hymowitz, "Let's Face It: Michelle Obama Is a Feminist Cop-Out," *Time*, November 25, 2013, ideas.time .com/2013/11/25/lets-face-it-michelle-obama-is-a-feminist-cop-out/. Also see Slevin, especially 286–89.

39. See Kessler, *In the President's Secret Service*.

40. Kun Kyung Kim, "NRA Ad Brings Obama Kids into Gun Debate; White House Fights Back," *Today*, June 16, 2013, www.today.com/news/ nra-ad-brings-obama-kids-gun-debate-white-house-fights-1B7995875.

41. hooks has made this point while speaking more than once. I believe I first heard it when she was in public dialogue with Valerie Lee on October 13, 2011, during one of hooks's residencies at Ohio State University.

42. Hollywood is as political as any other sector of American life, so Academy of Motion Pictures voters made a statement (through these nominations and awards) about the debate that had been raging about black actors being relegated to servile or criminal roles and whether such limitations are a problem.

Chapter 1. A Home of One's Own

1. See, for example, Mills, *Racial Contract*, and Roberts, *Killing*.

2. In *Birthright Citizens*, Martha Jones distinguishes between colonization and emigration, arguing the former represented white interests and the latter was embraced as self-determination.

3. As historian Daina Berry finds, enslaved people had a sense of their value that was not dependent on the amount of money for which they could be sold. She calls it "soul value," and "enslaved people often expressed their soul values by running away" (*Price* 62).

4. The Constitution was full of proslavery compromises, and the North consistently upheld them. See M. Berry, *Black Resistance*.

5. In *Birthright Citizens*, legal historian Martha Jones demonstrates that the aggressive decision rendered by Roger Taney was not as far-reaching as often presumed. Still, by highlighting the degree to which Taney was responding to the challenges Baltimore's black citizens represented to white supremacy, her analysis confirms the validity of my viewing American jurisprudence as a violent response to black success. Also see Hyde's *Civic Longing* on Taney's aggressive revision of how citizenship was defined (36–40).

6. For more on freedom suits, see Wong. Particularly striking in her discussion of this case: "The Dred Scott opinion stands in infamy for its . . . failure to deliver justice to an elderly slave who embraced law and legal process in an eleven-year struggle to contest his enslavement and secure his freedom. [However, this case was] profoundly shaped by gender and kinship. Harriet and Dred Scott *together* dedicated over a decade of their lives to the struggle for a legal freedom that would extend to their two daughters" (130, original italics).

7. Parallels in the lived world were plentiful, and Jones views legal activity in these terms throughout *Birthright Citizens*. For instance, even being in debt is a way of acting like a "rights bearing citizen."

8. Both texts' reception histories underscore the value of this study's focus on success and community conversation. *Incidents* targeted white readers in hopes of fueling abolitionism, but it was published while slave states were seceding, so as Frances Smith Foster has argued, interest in slave narratives decreased (*Written* 117). Jacobs's work still earned positive reviews in American periodicals and commanded enough attention to warrant a British printing (Foster, *Written*, 117–18; Foster and Yarborough vii). When encountered in

the twentieth century, scholars assumed it to be a fictional narrative written by the editor, Lydia Maria Child (Yellin xxv). It therefore took movements for Black Studies and Women's Studies in the 1970s and 1980s to inspire recuperative efforts, and Jean Fagan Yellin's archival findings authenticated Jacobs's authorship in 1981 (Yellin xxv). Yellin's recovery included acknowledging its contribution to the community conversation: "Jacobs's book may well have influenced Frances Ellen Watkins Harper's pioneering novel *Iola Leroy; Or, Shadows Uplifted* (1892), which in turn helped shape the writings of Zora Neale Hurston and other foremothers of black women writing today" (ibid. xxix). The publication of *Behind the Scenes* created a sensation, but it also sparked know-your-place aggression, damaging Keckley's reputation. Furthermore, Keckley "received no royalties and she lost most of her wealth. . . . After the book, she could depend only upon the twelve dollars a month pension she received as a widow whose only son was killed in [Civil War] combat" (Foster, *Written*, 129). Corroborating the present study's focus on success, Janet Neary argues, "Correctly perceiving *Behind the Scenes* as an attack on the racial status quo, contemporary reviewers painted [its author] as a servant 'who had forgotten her place'" (58). When *Behind the Scenes* was rereleased in 1931, a prominent notice said Keckley had never existed and the narrative was fictional and written by a white journalist. Like *Incidents*, then, it had to be recuperated by scholars invested in black women's voices and victories.

9. Wong traces how American jurisprudence also simultaneously denied and relied on black humanity and personhood. (See especially her Introduction and Chapter 3.) Manne's "Humanizing Hatred" chapter in *Down Girl* corroborates the violence of this pattern.

10. Given the hierarchy of homebuilding, Linda's discussion of black men who "give their masters free access to their wives and daughters" (38) is strikingly contradictory. If denying captives the right to choose (or stay faithful to) partners of their selection supports slavery, this is as true for enslaved men as for enslaved women.

11. As argued in the Introduction, the assumption that one must have trouble seeing another's humanity in order to be cruel to them is faulty. Also see Kate Manne's "Humanizing Hatred" chapter in *Down Girl*.

12. F. Foster reaches the same conclusion. See *Written*, 122–26.

13. Importantly, Keckley demonstrates her love and acceptance of the child she had because of rape by naming him after the black man who lovingly treated her as his daughter. See Lewis, "Elizabeth Keckley," 9.

14. Given that Hyde's "political subjunctive" is accessible through "extralegal discourses of citizenship" (16, 17), Jacobs's blending of biography and sentimental romance proves particularly significant for asserting black belonging.

15. See Kelley, *Right to Ride*, and Mitchell, Introduction to *Iola Leroy*.

16. Some clearly believed dying in victory meant setting the terms of one's own death. Jacobs often speaks of praying for death (49, 53, 65, 66, 67, 71) and Keckley includes the story of an uncle who hangs himself (30). Also see D. Berry, *Price*, especially the story of Isaac and his insurrectionist comrades (146).

Chapter 2. No, Really

1. The reception history of these works corroborates this study's focus. According to Hazel Carby, and given William Still's original 1892 introduction, *Iola Leroy* was immediately considered suitable for black Sunday School classes. Though I argue elsewhere that Harper likely published *Iola Leroy* as a bound book in order to reach readers who were not African American (Introduction), examining it for its contribution to the community conversation remains relevant. (In the same spirit, I do not disregard contributions to the community conversation because Jacobs hoped to convert white readers into abolitionists, Hansberry reached Broadway, or Obama was first lady.) Like *Iola Leroy*, *Contending Forces* was Hopkins's sole "fiction published in book form [as opposed to serially] during her lifetime" (Yarborough, Introduction, xxx). Even if bound book formats suggest a hope for wider circulation, Hopkins used the Colored Co-operative Publishing Company, an independent black press whose size led to the novel being "released with little fanfare and apparently no comment from the white mainstream literary community" (ibid. xliv). It is appropriate to interpret these works with an eye toward the impact on community.

2. These post-Reconstruction narratives continue the tradition traced by Tess Chakkalakal in earlier works: "As a marital relation that had little to do with either property or power, the slave-marriage came to embody principles of an ideal marriage, a union of souls that transcended the earthly concerns upon which legal marriage was based" (6).

3. See Bederman, *Manliness*, 11–25.

4. As Hartman argues, "the nonevent of emancipation" revealed the nation's investment in "the resubordination of the emancipated" (*Scenes* 116); freedpeople bore "the onerous responsibilities of freedom with the enjoyment of few of its entitlements" (*Scenes* 121).

5. See note 1 above.

6. Following the lead of literary historians Carla Peterson, Meredith McGill, and Andreá Williams, I sometimes use "Watkins Harper" to remind readers that she was a public figure even before she was married and even without benefiting from the social acceptance that later came with being a widow.

7. Iola expresses similar sentiments and motivations (117–18).

8. In highlighting the violence black women suffered at the hands of white women, the novel speaks to lived experience, corroborating the findings of historian Thavolia Glymph.

9. Traditional literacy is not the only valuable skill depicted. Tom had gathered information about the Civil War by listening to white people's conversations (15–16). This required expertly performing ignorance and a lack of interest. Even when denied literacy, enslaved people demonstrate intelligence, and the characters inside the text as well as the text itself preserve evidence of it.

10. Robert knew John Salters as John Andrews during the war (174).

11. With this emphasis on choosing a mate with whom one can do "racial uplift" work, the novel also contributes to the tradition of creating "black homes," traced by Robert Reid-Pharr in *Conjugal Union*.

12. These passages remind readers that the insights offered by Michelle Alexander's *The New Jim Crow* and by Douglas Blackmon's *Slavery by Another Name* were understood long ago.

13. Violence against children was also woven into mainstream literary and performance culture. As Robin Bernstein demonstrates, even alphabet books enacted violence against African American children and connected their "learning and by extension their social advancement to violence" (75).

14. John Langley threatens to expose her to her fiancé Will, whom Langley insists will not be understanding or compassionate (317).

15. Monsieur Louis tells Sappho he knows she does not love him, but he would relish being able to provide for her and her child as long as he lives and beyond the grave via his will (357–58).

16. To say "otherwise abused" suggests rape, especially because the wife and daughter died the next day. Their deaths underscore their virtue at a time when true women were believed incapable of living after sexual violation. This is why Sappho's survival is infused with so much shame, and it gestures toward the shame that black women, as a group, were expected (and often made) to feel.

17. Beaubean's threat of legal action suggests naive faith in American courts and may be a commentary on how people of color seem to maintain faith when others have dispensed with it. As historian Estelle Freedman demonstrates in *Redefining Rape*, courts seldom contradicted the "popular belief that a man was justified when, in a fit of passion, he killed the scoundrel who had debauched his wife or his daughter" (40). Beaubean would have acted more in accordance with American expectations by killing his brother. His hesitation may have been caused by the fact that he was not considered white, but his brother was, which surely also helped his brother become a state senator.

Chapter 3. New Negroes, New Homes

1. The majority opinion in *Plessy v. Ferguson* includes this logic: "We consider the underlying fallacy of the plaintiff's argument to consist in the assumption that the enforced separation of the two races stamps the colored race with a badge of inferiority. If this be so, it is not by reason of anything found in the act, but solely because the colored race chooses to put that construction upon it" (see *Iola Leroy*, Appendix A, 264).

2. Race riots demonstrated an investment in telling African Americans, "know your place!" They erupted all over the country, with the most prominent being those in Wilmington, Delaware, in 1898; New Orleans, Louisiana, in 1900; Atlanta, Georgia, in 1906; Springfield, Illinois, in 1908; and East St. Louis, Illinois, in 1917. An even more intense wave of violence came in 1919 as soldiers returned to the United States after serving in WWI. The latter part of 1919 proved yet again that black success beckons the mob. Black soldiers had been honored for their bravery overseas and were greeted by crowds cheering as they marched down American streets. However, know-your-place aggression is the flexible, dynamic array of forces that answer the achievements of marginalized groups such that their success brings aggression as often as praise. Especially because lynching soldiers in their uniforms became as meaningful as the scripts played out in black people's homes during night-riding raids, white mobs conveyed that African Americans' contributions to the Allied Forces' victory would not translate into victory at home. By the end of 1919, beginning in what came to be known as "Red Summer," race riots had erupted in Longview, Texas; Washington, D.C.; Chicago, Illinois; Omaha, Nebraska; and Elaine, Arkansas.

3. Referring to Wilkerson, *The Warmth of Other Suns*.

4. Regarding mobility and modernity, especially as related to how racism shaped American culture while it became technologically advanced, see Hale, *Making Whiteness*.

5. See Feimster, *Southern Horrors*, and "Ida B. Wells and the Lynching of Black Women," *New York Times*, April 28, 2018. https://www.nytimes.com/2018/04/28/opinion/sunday/ida-b-wells-lynching-black-women.html.

6. See Feimster, *Southern Horrors*; Rosen, *Terror*; and Freedman, *Redefining Rape*.

7. The reception history for both *Quicksand* (1928) and *Their Eyes Were Watching God* (1937) suggests the value of reading for how the protagonists define success without simply bowing to white violence or the community's investment in race motherhood. Upon release, *Quicksand* received attention in mainstream publications and applause from W. E. B. Du Bois in *The Crisis* (T. Davis 277–84). Because Du Bois praised its contrast to Claude McKay's *Home to Harlem*, which focused on characters deemed far from respectable,

black male authors suggested the novel was not necessarily good but show-cased the characters that gatekeepers like Du Bois wanted represented in black art (Hutchinson 277–92). *Quicksand* went out of print not long after publication, and while the tendency among black men to support each other more than black women artists surely contributed, it's also true that "by the time *Quicksand* left the presses in 1928, most of the fire and verve of the Re-naissance were over, and much of its attendant significance, the opportunities for publishing, had actually decreased even while the number of new writers had increased" (T. Davis 281). Similarly, *Their Eyes* was published well after the Renaissance's heyday but at a time when The New Deal offered relief, including for art. The novel received attention in mainstream outlets, includ-ing critiques from the likes of Richard Wright that put it in its "proper" place as unimportant to black people's struggles—as if black women's challenges were irrelevant politically and otherwise. The recovery efforts of the 1960s and 1970s privileged black men and white women, so it took decidedly black feminist efforts to bring these texts back into circulation. The recuperation has been impressive, making these works canonical and resulting in circu-lations unheard of during the authors' lifetimes. Indeed, both women died with little money, but Larsen's novels *Quicksand* and *Passing* "sold more than 160,000 copies" in 2012, making her work Rutgers University Press's "best seller," and HarperPerennial profits from "close to 500, 000 copies of [Hurston's] books still sold annually, fifty years after her death." See https://news.rutgers.edu/feature-focus/new-location-puts-rutgers-university-press-center-campus-life/20130218#.XS37JJNKii5 and https://www.harpercollins.com/corporate/press-releases/more-than-70-years-after-publication-of-zora-neale-hurstons-classic-novel-their-eyes-were-watching-god-harper-perennial-and-the-zora-neale-hurston-trust-extend-their-publishing-relationship-into-the/. I cannot help but think that, even with the well-deserved status these texts now enjoy, allowing me to see the focus on success despite the violence it invites, know-your-place aggression achieved its goal in that these indi-vidual black women artists are *not* the ones who benefit from their labor and achievements.

8. This is a fictional place suggestive of Tuskegee Institute in Alabama. See Thadious Davis's notes in the Penguin Classics edition of Larsen's *Quicksand*.

9. Helga believes, the narrator reports: "In Naxos between teacher and student, between condescending authority and smoldering resentment, the gulf was too great, and too few had tried to cross it. It couldn't be spanned by one sympathetic teacher. It was useless to offer her atom of friendship, which under the existing conditions was neither wanted nor understood" (9).

10. Marlon Ross sees a similar dynamic temporarily at play: "Helga thinks that she wants a strong man to motivate her submission, one so worthy that

his mastery can justify the subordination of her own will through a sexual desire that is so bound to racial service that it rises to purity" (372).

11. Helga experiences the erotics of religion in a way that seems very similar to her sexual pleasure (110–15). For more on this, see Lindsay Reckson, *Realist Ecstasy: Religion, Race, and Performance in American Literature*, New York: New York UP, 2020.

12. Helga repeatedly wonders why people of color have children (76–77, 104, 130–31).

13. The idea that African Americans descend from kings and queens on the African continent is often associated with the Black Power Movement, but Deborah Gray White's "aristocracy of the soul" suggests the gesture toward royalty is much older. Indeed, it may underscore the importance of nineteenth-century "Ethiopianism," examined by Scott Trafton and Eric Sundquist.

14. Phoeby had been much more blunt when speaking to her husband: "[the funeral director] got uh lovely place tuh take her to. . . . Better'n her house Joe left her" (106).

15. Janie also argues that even if Tea Cake has a fondness for property, that fact would not make him any less desirable than others, especially those courting her. After all, there are three other widows in town, but men are not lining up for those without an inheritance (107).

16. As Ann duCille argues, sensuality and intimacy were never absent. Authors attuned to black Victorian values simply used marriage as the mechanism for their portrayal (*Coupling* 32–36).

Chapter 4. Home as Human Right and Black Power

1. One example: the 1943 Detroit massacre of African Americans that "erupted on June 20 at the segregated city beaches and an amusement park" (Harris and Teborg-Penn 17).

2. Black attorneys faced countless indignities as well as physical violence while trying to gain the education to become lawyers and after achieving that goal. See Mitchell, *Living with Lynching*, 115–46.

3. The United States routinely used black progress to assert its superiority over the Soviet Union. See Cheryl Higashida, Erik McDuffie, William Maxwell, and Richard Iton.

4. A reference to Cathy Cohen's crucial essay.

5. Mildred demonstrates understanding that white people are not superior but hold themselves and each other to incredibly low standards. Examples from *Like One of the Family* include Mildred's dressing down of the employer who asks for her health card (43), her offer to vouch for her employer so that another housekeeper will work for her (72), her assessment of rich people

who create problems because they don't have real ones (90), her telling an employer that she is ruining her child and revealing her own inadequacy (133–36), and her confrontation with white employers who see themselves as decent but do nothing about the injustice she and her community face (171–73).

6. See Lipsitz, *Possessive Investment*; Katznelson, *Affirmative Action*; and Coates, "Reparations."

7. The script calls it a "riot," but this is better understood as an urban rebellion or uprising because black people are rebelling against unfair contracts and poor living conditions. It differs from the riots that begin this chapter in which white people attack black people to remind them of their "proper" place.

8. My "community conversation" approach is worth reiterating in relationship to the plays' production histories. *Raisin* broke ground on Broadway, and *Wine* initially aired as a teleplay on Boston Public Television. Because black newspapers took *Wine* seriously, the interest the black press generated helped support stage productions soon after it aired. A flyer for a New York production preserved in ProQuest's *Black Drama* database proclaims the show is "Back by Black Demand," so it may be easier to understand that this work targeted, and was eagerly received by, African Americans. Even works that cannot ignore mainstream audiences engage the community conversation, though. In fact, considering *Raisin* in the same way this study approaches *Incidents in the Life of a Slave Girl* (1861) or Michelle Obama's first lady persona is instructive. One result is grappling with the possibility that some of Hansberry's comments in interviews had to do with the intense white gaze on her work and the constant assumption that her work proved her investment in "assimilationist politics" (Perry 113). I think white misunderstandings led to moments when she defended Mama Lena as fiercely as Lena defends Walter Lee to Beneatha (see Smith, *Visions*, 322). I say this because Imani Perry explains, "[Hansberry] had written a masterpiece but its meaning had been excruciatingly submerged by the admiration of so many," so "she resisted ever running the risk of writing in a way that her politics might be misunderstood again" (112). In other words, Hansberry's support of Mama Lena in interviews may have more to do with avoiding giving white people reason to denigrate Mama Lena without understanding the pressures under which she is operating, but that does not obliterate the need to recognize the more complex address to black audiences.

For more production history as well as interpretations that may be even more performance-based than mine here, see Colbert, "A Pedagogical Approach" and *Theatrical Body*, and C. Davis, *Prefiguring*, as well as standard texts like Hatch and Shines's *Black Theatre U.S.A.*

9. I reiterate my acknowledgment that, in tracing black people's investment in belonging, I am tracing African American participation in settler

colonialism, capitalism, and imperialism (especially given my emphasis on conservative goals like serving in integrated military units).

10. Baraka offered this as a reassessment in 1987, admitting he had been unable to appreciate many aspects of the play during its initial run because activists like him felt it was "middle class."

11. See Anastasia Curwood on how marriage offered high moral ground for African Americans in a society that thrives on devaluing them (15–30). For more on the positive assumptions attached to marriage in American culture, see Nancy Cott.

12. For those who believe Lena is a matriarch, she might be said to exemplify legal scholar Anita Hill's assertion that "to the extent that it existed, matriarchy was what black women got handed, not what they planned" (69).

13. For more on the Hansberry desegregation case, see Kamp, "History."

14. This argument is very much influenced by Brandon Manning, who took my Spring 2012 Black Feminist Criticism seminar. His final paper argued that Lena operates as a patriarch and that scholars have labeled her "matriarch" uncritically, as a simple counterpart to "patriarch." His argument was so convincing I could never read the play or the scholarship the same way again. I have come to a slightly different interpretation, that she operates as a proxy, but these ideas grew from Manning's insight.

15. As Lena directs her son's performance of her husband's persona, the play demonstrates a key function of conservative domesticity: "The domestic is an arena in which complex ideological negotiations are conducted to make the transition from past social practices in the process of meeting the pressures of the present" (George 11).

16. This antiwoman logic aligns with the government's assault on black women, as detailed by Dorothy Roberts, and American culture's overall refusal to provide a public safety net. As Nancy Cott shows, marriage and nuclear families became important not because Americans were concerned about emotional support and nurturing but were committed to keeping children off of government support (32, 48–49, 169–72, 221–22).

17. The tendency to silence voices that do not align with the experience of heterosexual black men has been extensively theorized. See, for example, duCille's "Monster, She Wrote," Crenshaw's "Mapping," and Simien's Introduction.

18. That Hansberry sometimes defended Lena's approach seems evident in Judith Smith, *Visions*, 322. Also see note 8 above.

19. Perry is far from alone in this. See, for example, Tricia Rose, "Hansberry's *A Raisin in the Sun* and the 'Illegible' Politics of (Inter)personal Justice," *Kalfou* 1.1 (Spring 2014): 27–60.

20. Powerfully, when Mama Lena beats Walter Lee, stage directions indicate, "Beneatha *goes to them and stops it*" (129).

21. Morrison often notes in interviews that segregation was more conducive to there being successful black doctors, lawyers, and entrepreneurs than communities have enjoyed since integration.

22. Even if Bill's parents lived in a suburb with black neighbors, his association of their goals with conformity remains key, suggesting his values formed in opposition to those presumably cherished by people like the Youngers in *Raisin.*

23. In this way, Bill's character aligns with Elda Román's findings about novels tracing upward mobility among nonwhite Americans: "Status seekers thus act as the initial investors in a hierarchical and ownership-oriented value system, and latter generations can either accept or refuse this ideological inheritance and reinterpret the end goal of mobility. The artist figures in these novels reject materialist pursuits for more creative paths" (24).

24. Childress's columns in black newspapers became *Like One of the Family.* See *Like One of the Family* as well as Higashida, *Black Internationalist Feminism,* 202.

25. See all references by Margo Crawford; Keisha Blain, *Set the World*; Ashley Farmer, *Remaking Black Power*; and Robyn Spencer, *Revolution.*

26. Also see Tanisha Ford on black women's agency via fashion choices.

27. Tommy's domestic yearning resonates powerfully with the history Robyn Spencer traces, whereby black women's romantic desires were constantly sacrificed for the Black Panther Party, making the organization unsustainable. For instance, men dated outside the party because they were believed capable of converting women, but party women were assumed susceptible to being pulled out of the organization if dating outsiders.

28. Though most understand Black Power only in masculine terms, Margo Crawford argues it is impossible (and indeed irresponsible) to separate Black Power philosophies from black feminist critiques of masculinism. After all, "black women were responding to the masculinism, with force and frustration, *as* it unfolded" ("Family Affair" 199). Also see Farmer.

29. Notably, Walter Lee and his wife Ruth in *Raisin* avoid anything that seems African. When Beneatha reveals her natural hair, Ruth says, "You expect this boy to go out with you with your head all nappy like that?" (Hansberry 80). Before the rise of "Black Is Beautiful," respectability was linked to straightened hair.

30. See C. Davis, *Prefiguring,* and Colbert, "A Pedagogical Approach," for more on class stratification.

Chapter 5. Still the Master's House?

1. This book's investment in foregrounding racial self-affirmation aligns with Kevin Quashie's elegant theorizing in *The Sovereignty of Quiet,* which begins by engaging this moment at the Olympics.

2. The Kerner Commission Report argued that the government should initiate aggressive solutions because it had created the conditions that led to riots in cities such as Detroit, Michigan; Newark, New Jersey; and Washington, D.C. See http://web.stanford.edu/dept/csre/pdfs/Kerner_Executive_Summary .pdf.

3. Tellingly, this figure even obscured Linda Taylor, the woman who inspired the myth but whose actual crimes victimized African Americans, not white taxpayers. See Josh Levin, *The Queen: The Forgotten Life behind an American Myth*, New York: Little, Brown and Company, 2019.

4. Neither book was the cultural phenomenon that *Roots* was, but Morrison's *Beloved* always sold well, being her fourth novel and yet another demonstration of her formidable presence. *Kindred* was never a failure as a novel, but its canonical status has formed in the years following Butler's Nebula and Hugo Awards in 1985 and MacArthur Fellowship in 1995. In both cases, sales figures are less important than maintaining a focus on these works' contribution to the community conversation.

5. Before it appeared in *Women, Race, and Class*, "The Black Woman's Role in the Community of Slaves" was published in the December 1971 issue of *The Black Scholar*.

6. For historical parallels, see Hunter's *Bound in Wedlock*.

7. For real-life corollaries to such practices, see Penningroth.

8. In harmony with my insistence that black intimacies need not be read as acceptance of dominant conceptions of success and belonging, Hortense Spillers warns, "We might choose to call this connectedness 'family,' or 'support structure,' but that is a rather different case from the moves of a dominant symbolic order, pledged to maintain the supremacy of race. It is that order that forces 'family' to modify itself when it does not mean family of the master, or dominant enclave" (219).

9. Spoken by the central nun character in Faulkner's short story "Requiem for a Nun."

10. See James Baldwin, "The White Man's Guilt," *Ebony*, August 1965. Expanded and reprinted as "Unnameable Objects, Unspeakable Crimes," in *The White Problem in America*, Chicago: Johnson Publishing, 1966.

11. Also, she does not assume that being "accused" of antislavery activity is the same as having actually been involved in such activity.

12. This seems a key moment when readers understand how unwilling Dana is to judge enslaved women who might have found a way to make peace with their immeasurable sexual vulnerability. If even Dana (with all her advantages in the 1800s) thinks it would be easier to submit, then the condemnation of the militant 1960s, which Dana had not immediately rejected, is misguided.

13. Paul D's lack of restlessness results from vague awareness that Sethe could be what Sixo had called "a friend of your mind" (321).

14. Before reuniting with Sethe, Paul D would have sung songs around the house as he does in 124, but the lyrics would have been about putting his shoes and hat back on rather than about keeping them off (48–49).

15. Interior life aligns with Kevin Quashie's theorization of *quiet*. While Americans routinely assume "black subjectivity exists for its social and political meaningfulness rather than as a marker of the human individuality of the person who is black," Quashie's conception of quiet "is a metaphor for the full range of one's inner life—one's desires, ambitions, hungers, vulnerabilities, fears" (4, 6).

16. Perhaps it is easier to believe it is Baby Suggs's spirit because Sethe visits the Clearing essentially to divorce her son Halle.

17. One study that discusses the denial of benefits to women with partners is "Aid to Dependent Children: The Legal History" by Linda Gordon and Felice Batlan. It notes, "One of the first AFDC cases to reach the U.S. Supreme Court, *King v. Smith* (1968), challenged an Alabama regulation allowing for AFDC termination if a recipient 'cohabitated' with a man." https://socialwelfare.library.vcu.edu/public-welfare/aid-to-dependent-children-the-legal-history/.

18. It is not clear whether "the crew" represents "breeders" acting on orders from a "master" or men who raped of their own accord.

19. When Paul D speaks of Mister, a rooster at Sweet Home, he assumes the validity of the rooster's pride in ways never extended to female beings (85–86, 124–25).

20. Underscoring Garner's similarity to other enslavers, Baby Suggs recalls how Garner continued to extract labor and life from her son while allowing him to "free" her into the "care" of his liberal friends, who also demanded her labor (165–69).

21. Racism's arbitrary power and black people's cognizance of it appear throughout history. For instance, as Ta-Nehisi Coates shares from a conversation he had with the mother of a slain classmate, he reports: "She alluded to *Twelve Years a Slave* [1853]. 'There he was,' she said, speaking of Solomon Northup. 'He had means. He had a family. He was living like a human being. And one racist act took him back. And the same is true of me. I spent years developing a career, acquiring assets, engaging responsibilities. And one racist act. It's all it takes'" (*Between the World and Me* 145).

Chapter 6. The Ultimate Home

1. To name one discussion prompt, Jesse Jackson's 1984 national campaign to seek the presidency was successful enough to make his 1988 run quite credible.

2. C-Span quoted in Hill, *Reimagining Equality*, xxiv.

3. Mrs. Obama first used this term in an interview with Harriette Cole in 2008 (see Cole). She more intensely embraced the moniker in her 2012 Democratic National Convention speech, as her husband battled for reelection.

4. Denying womanhood to black women is an American tradition. Besides the foundational examples from slavery, one might note the ease with which *New York Times* columnist Maureen Dowd suggested Michelle Obama could "wind up and punch out Rush Limbaugh, Bernie Madoff and all the corporate creeps who ripped off America." As Harris-Perry argued, "Dowd is tapping her own racial imagination when she perceives the First Lady as capable of engaging in a street brawl with grown men. This fantasy of the super-strong, masculine black woman who could easily best a man in a physical altercation is a crooked image" (279).

5. First lady is not the only honorable role, however. In the *Washington Post*, Martha S. Jones reminds us of Mary McLeod Bethune's presence as a member of Franklin D. Roosevelt's "Black Cabinet."

6. Jenkins, *Private Lives*, 68.

7. *60 Minutes*, February 11, 2007. Archived at http://www.cbsnews.com/videos/michelle-obama-on-security/.

8. Super-tight curly perm trends are not unheard of, though. When I visited Japan in 1998, I learned some people used this strategy to achieve dreadlocks.

9. Women's looks have always been crucial to group identity. Often, men are affirmed in their identities because of how "their women" look. This is as true for wealthy white men whose wives must be blonde and slim as it is for Afrocentric men whose wives must wear their hair natural. For other considerations of the power of women's appearance, see Chapman, *Prove It on Me*; Gill, *Beauty Shop Politics*; and Ford, *Liberated Threads*.

10. Mrs. Obama has remained with stylist Johnny Wright for the majority of her time in the spotlight, beginning around 2008. There were literally years during which he would not answer whether or not her hair was chemically processed. This was especially the case as I did research in 2011, 2012, and 2013. The tune seems to have changed in 2014. For instance, on *HuffPost Live* in August 2014, he declared, "I love how her hair has grown so long, and it's all 100 percent natural." http://www.dailymail.co.uk/femail/article-2724388/The-secret-Michelle-Obamas-perfect-waves-First-Ladys-stylist-reveals-100-natural-just-uses-conditioner-hair-tie.html. In May 2015, *The Root* Associate Editor Danielle Belton reported Wright told her "Michelle Obama has been completely natural for years now (he straightens her hair with a flat iron)." This story even suggests she may wear an afro at some point. See http://www.theroot.com/articles/culture/2015/05/from_relaxed_to_all_natural_johnny_wright_the_man_behind_first_lady_michelle.html.

11. In addition to the analysis offered by Nowile Rooks about schools reprimanding black girls, see, for example, *Clutch* magazine's September 2015 online feature, "Because Our Hair Is Always Political: 6 Black Women Fired for Their Hairstyles." http://www.clutchmagonline.com/2015/09/women-fired-for-their-hairstyles/.

12. I am referring to the common practice of using prominent black people to judge other African Americans. Oprah Winfrey and the Obamas are commonly used this way.

13. Biographer Peter Slevin reminds us that some white people understood Mrs. Obama's comment perfectly well (rather than willfully misunderstanding it as unpatriotic), but the campaign deliberately treated it as a gaffe (224–29).

14. Of course, not all backlash to Mrs. Obama's comment about being proud for the first time came from white people.

15. Mom-in-Chief is especially remarkable because so many Americans applauded Jill Biden for not abandoning her career.

16. The tendency to expect black people to put whites at ease by singing and dancing has a long history, and it has been critiqued in African American literature. For instance, Ralph Ellison's novel *Invisible Man* devotes a scene to a debate about whether it was insulting that another guest asked the protagonist to sing when he attends a party hosted by the Brotherhood, a progressive organization.

17. Frederick Harris, "The Price of a Black President," *New York Times*, October 27, 2012. http://www.nytimes.com/2012/10/28/opinion/sunday/the-price-of-a-black-president.html. Also see his book, *The Price of the Ticket: Barack Obama and the Rise and Decline of Black Politics*. New York: Oxford UP, 2014.

18. http://www.dailymail.co.uk/femail/article-2229247/Michelle-Obama-recycles-Michael-Kors-dress-Ann-Romney-embraces-Republican-red-Election-night.html.

19. Arielle Hawkins, *CNN*, "Michelle Obama Convention Speech Dress Dazzles, Scores." http://politicalticker.blogs.cnn.com/2012/09/05/michelle-obama-convention-speech-dress-dazzles-scores/comment-page-5/.

20. Guy Trebay, "Michelle Obama's Style: She Dresses to Win," *New York Times*, June 8, 2008. http://www.nytimes.com/2008/06/08/fashion/08michelle.html?_r=0.

21. Collins oversees the International Best Dressed List.

22. Another quotation from Trebay, note 20.

23. Quotation from "Election Night Style-off!" https://www.dailymail.co.uk/femail/article-2229247/Michelle-Obama-recycles-Michael-Kors-dress-Ann-Romney-embraces-Republican-red-Election-night.html.

24. Another quotation from Hawkins, note 19.

25. The first lady's poll numbers have been repeatedly tracked and have often been quite strong. See Slevin. Also see Jeffrey Jones, "Michelle Obama Remains Popular in U.S.," *Gallop.com*, May 30, 2012. http://www.gallup.com/poll/154952/michelle-obama-remains-popular.aspx. Also, after leaving the White House, polls revealed her to be the nation's "most admired" woman. See Veronica Stracqualursi, "Michelle Obama Bests Hillary Clinton To Be Voted Most Admired Woman by Americans, Poll Shows," *CNN*, December 27, 2018. https://www.cnn.com/2018/12/27/politics/michelle-obama-hillary-clinton-gallup-poll/index.html.

26. See research-based articles, such as Abigail Tucker, "How Much Is Being Attractive Worth?" *Smithsonian Magazine*, November 2012. http://www.smithsonianmag.com/science-nature/how-much-is-being-attractive-worth-80414787/?no-ist, and Melissa Stanger, "Attractive People Are Simply More Successful," *Business Insider*, October 9, 2012. http://www.businessinsider.com/attractive-people-are-more-successful-2012–9.

27. Journalist Nancy Dickson, who covered the Johnson administration, quoted in Borrelli 99.

28. Maika Pollack, "American Like Me: Glenn Ligon at the Whitney," *Observer*, May 10, 2011. http://observer.com/2011/05/american-like-me-glenn-ligon-at-the-whitney/.

29. See, for example, Randy Kennedy, "Off the Wall: White House Drops Painting," *New York Times*, November 4, 2009. http://artsbeat.blogs.nytimes.com/2009/11/04/off-the-wall-white-house-changes-mind-about-painting/?_r=0.

30. Mona Lisa comparison from Blake Gopnik, "Alma Thomas's 'Watusi (Hard Edge)' Won't Hang in White House," *The Washington Post*, November 5, 2009. http://www.washingtonpost.com/wp-dyn/content/article/2009/11/04/AR2009110405053.html. Similar points were made in many pieces, including Christopher Knight, "More Art Fabrications from the Right Wing," *Los Angeles Times*, October 13, 2009. http://latimesblogs.latimes.com/culturemonster/2009/10/more-art-fabrications-from-the-right-wing.html.

31. Charlotte Higgins, "What Barack and Michelle Obama's Taste in Art Says about Them," *The Guardian*, October 7, 2009. http://www.theguardian.com/culture/charlottehigginsblog/2009/oct/07/art-barack-obama.

32. Interestingly, the artist with the largest number of selections, the late William H. Johnson, features African Americans in his realistic work, but these pieces were not discussed nearly as much as Ligon's and Thomas's, so I am not treating them as significant to Mrs. Obama's public persona. Johnson was trained in Scandinavia in the 1930s, and four of his pieces were chosen for display.

33. Bradford qtd. in Borrelli 109. Sarah Bradford, *America's Queen: The Life of Jacqueline Kennedy Onassis*. Thorndike: Thorndike Press, 2001.

34. The work of Native American artists, inventors of color, and other under-represented groups received a nod via Michelle Obama's selections. See Blake Gopnik, "1600 Penn and Ink: Obamas' Choice of Works on Loan to White House Reflects a Discerning Eye," *The Washington Post*, October 7, 2009. http://www.washingtonpost.com/wp-dyn/content/story/2009/10/06/ST2009100603682.html?tid=a_inl.

35. While with her two small children in New York City's Central Park, a friend of mine was asked by more than one white person if she was a nanny (because they could use some help). In 2017, no less than in 1917 or 1817, certain people just never look the part of homemaker. See R. Gates.

Coda

1. The country's foundational anti-Indigenous ethos is also worth noting. See Brandzel.

2. Also see "Shamed and Angry: Alicia Machado, a Miss Universe Mocked by Donald Trump," in *The New York Times*. https://www.nytimes.com/2016/09/28/us/politics/alicia-machado-donald-trump.html.

3. As I often say, given that white men created the standards shaping American institutions, they are the ones most poised to meet them, but they often don't. Criteria are then changed for them, but those changes are never considered a "lowering" of standards. The bar is "lowered" only if someone benefits who is not straight, white, and male. This has always been how American institutions work, but more people seem willing to notice because Trump provides such an extreme and ubiquitous example.

4. An example of this was when NFL owners began to support kneeling at football games after Trump said teams should fire players who kneel. It was clearly not about supporting Colin Kaepernick and his cause but about banding together to insist that the rich white men who own NFL teams will not be told what to do. Sources for this insight include Rod Morrow of *The Black Guy Who Tips* podcast and journalists Bomani Jones and Jemelle Hill.

5. See "Anger in Cleveland" video. https://www.theatlantic.com/video/index/492473/anger-in-cleveland/.

6. Her campaign was far better financed than Trump's at every stage. See "Tracking the 2016 Presidential Money Race," *Bloomberg*, December 9, 2016. https://www.bloomberg.com/politics/graphics/2016-presidential-campaign-fundraising/.

7. The primary obstacle often becomes whether the woman candidate is considered "likeable," a wildly vague and subjective criterion conducive to discrimination. Evidence is overwhelming. See, for example, Kathleen Dolan,

"Gender Stereotypes, Candidate Evaluations, and Voting for Women Candidates: What Really Matters?" *Political Research Quarterly* 67.1 (2014): 96–107.

8. "In America, White Women Can Get Away with Almost Anything," *The Huffington Post*, March 16, 2018. https://www.huffingtonpost.com/entry/opinion-mitchell-brianna-brochu-roommate_us_5aabfb61e4b0337adf83827f.

9. See David Leonard, "The Unbearable Invisibility of White Masculinity: Innocence in the Age of White Male Mass Shootings," *Gawker*, January 12, 2013.

10. Michelle Obama has a speech writer, but it matters that she delivered the words, giving them life with her gestures and embodied presence. For full text, see https://medium.com/hillary-for-america/michelle-obama-just-gave-one-of-the-most-powerful-speeches-of-this-campaign-dc61fd8a86a0.

11. We will never know Michelle Obama's innermost thoughts and feelings. Her memoir's publication did not change this. She will always be more of a mirror for Americans than a personality or identity accessible to the public. And that is as it should be.

12. Kimberlé Crenshaw coined *intersectionality* in 1989, but the idea has appeared throughout the intellectual work of black women. See studies such as Cooper's *Beyond Respectability* and Foreman's *Activist Sentiments*.

13. For more, see Chapter 7 of Harris-Perry's *Sister Citizen*.

Works Cited

Abdur-Rahman, Aliyyah. *Against the Closet: Black Political Longing and the Erotics of Race.* Durham, N.C.: Duke UP, 2012.

Alexander, Michelle. *The New Jim Crow: Mass Incarceration in the Age of Colorblindness.* New York: The New P, 2010.

Anderson, Benedict. *Imagined Communities. Reflections on the Origin and Spread of Nationalism.* Rev. ed. New York: Verso, 2006.

Anderson, Carol. *White Rage: The Unspoken Truth of Our Racial Divide.* New York: Bloomsbury USA, 2016.

Andrews, William. "Slave Narratives, 1865–1900." *The Oxford Handbook of the African American Slave Narrative.* Ed. John Ernest. New York: Oxford UP, 2014. 219–33.

Avilez, GerShun. "Housing the Black Body: Value, Domestic Space, and Segregation Narratives." *African American Review* 42.1 (2008): 135–47.

Baldwin, James. *The Fire Next Time.* 1963. *James Baldwin: Collected Essays.* Ed. Toni Morrison. New York: Library of America, 1998. 291–347.

———. *Nobody Knows My Name.* 1961. *James Baldwin: Collected Essays.* Ed. Toni Morrison. New York: Library of America, 1998. 135–285.

Bambara, Toni Cade. *The Black Woman: An Anthology.* New York: New American Library, 1970.

Baraka, Amiri. "A Wiser Play than Some of Us Knew." *Los Angeles Times,* March 22, 1987.

Bay, Mia, et al., Eds. *Toward an Intellectual History of Black Women.* Chapel Hill: U of North Carolina P, 2015.

Bederman, Gail. *Manliness & Civilization: A Cultural History of Gender and Race in the United States, 1880–1917*. Chicago: U of Chicago P, 1995.

Berman, Ari. *Give Us the Ballot: The Modern Struggle for Voting Rights in America*. New York: Farrar, Straus, and Giroux, 2015.

Bernstein, Robin. *Racial Innocence: Performing American Childhood from Slavery to Civil Rights*. New York: New York UP, 2011.

Berry, Daina. *The Price for Their Pound of Flesh: The Value of the Enslaved from Womb to Grave in the Building of a Nation*. Boston: Beacon P, 2017.

Berry, Mary Frances. *Black Resistance/White Law: A History of Constitutional Racism in America*. New York: Penguin, 1995.

Blackmon, Douglas. *Slavery by Another Name: The Re-enslavement of Black People in America from the Civil War to World War II*. New York: Doubleday, 2008.

Blain, Keisha. *Set the World on Fire: Black Nationalist Women and the Global Struggle for Freedom*. Philadelphia: U of Pennsylvania P, 2018.

Blassingame, John. *The Slave Community: Plantation Life in the Antebellum South*. New York: Oxford UP, 1972.

Bonner, Marita. "On Being Young—a Woman—and Colored." 1925. *The Norton Anthology of African American Literature, Third Edition, Volume 1*. Eds. Henry Louis Gates Jr. and Valerie Smith. New York: Norton, 2014. 1266–69.

Borrelli, MaryAnne. *The Politics of the President's Wife*. College Station: Texas A&M UP, 2011.

Brandzel, Amy. *Against Citizenship: The Violence of the Normative*. Urbana: U of Illinois P, 2016.

Brown, Henry "Box." *Narrative of the Life of Henry Box Brown, Written by Himself*. 1851. Ed. John Ernest. Chapel Hill: U of North Carolina P, 2008.

Brown, William Wells. *Narrative of the Life and Escape of William Wells Brown. Clotel; or The President's Daughter: A Bedford Critical Edition*. Ed. Robert S. Levine. Boston: Bedford/St. Martins, 2011. 49–80.

Butler, Judith. *Bodies That Matter: On the Discursive Limits of "Sex."* New York: Routledge, 1993.

Butler, Octavia. *Kindred*. 1979. Boston: Beacon P, 2004.

Camp, Stephanie. *Closer to Freedom: Enslaved Women and Everyday Resistance in the Plantation South*. Chapel Hill: U of North Carolina P, 2004.

Carby, Hazel. *Reconstructing Womanhood: The Emergence of the Afro-American Woman Novelist*. New York: Oxford UP, 1987.

Chakkalakal, Tess. *Novel Bondage: Slavery, Marriage, and Freedom in Nineteenth-Century America*. Urbana: U of Illinois P, 2011.

Chapman, Erin. *Prove It on Me: New Negroes, Sex, and Popular Culture in the 1920s*. New York: Oxford UP, 2012.

Childress, Alice. *Like One of the Family*. 1956. Ed. Trudier Harris. Boston: Beacon P, 1986.

———. *Wine in the Wilderness*. 1969. Ed. James Hatch and Ted Shine. *Black Theatre U.S.A.: Plays by African Americans, The Recent Period, 1935–Today*. Revised and Expanded. New York: The Free Press, 1996. 345–62.

Coates, Ta-Nehisi. *Between the World and Me*. New York: Spiegel & Grau, 2015.

———. "The Case for Reparations." *The Atlantic*, June 2014.

———. "On the Killing of Jordan Davis by Michael Dunn." *The Atlantic*, February 15, 2014.

Cohen, Cathy. "Punks, Bulldaggers, and Welfare Queens: The Radical Potential of Queer Politics?" *Black Queer Studies: A Critical Anthology*. Eds. E. Patrick Johnson and Mae Henderson. Durham, N.C.: Duke UP, 2005. 21–51.

Colbert, Soyica Diggs. *The African American Theatrical Body: Reception, Performance, and the Stage*. Cambridge: Cambridge UP, 2011.

———. "A Pedagogical Approach to Understanding Rioting as Revolutionary Action in Alice Childress's *Wine in the Wilderness*." *Theatre Topics* 19 (March 2009): 77–85.

Cole, Harriette. "The Real Michelle Obama." *Ebony*, September 2008. 72–84.

Collins, Patricia Hill. *Black Feminist Thought: Knowledge, Consciousness, and the Politics of Empowerment*. 2nd ed. New York: Routledge, 2000.

Colored Conventions. coloredconventions.org.

Commander, Michelle. *Afro-Atlantic Flight: Speculative Returns and the Black Fantastic*. Durham, N.C.: Duke UP, 2017.

Coontz, Stephanie. *Marriage, A History: From Obedience to Intimacy, or How Love Conquered Marriage*. New York: Viking, Penguin Books, 2005.

Cooper, Anna Julia. *A Voice from the South*. 1892. Ed. Mary Helen Washington. New York: Oxford UP, 1988.

———. [Continued Discussion of the Intellectual Progress of Colored Women since Emancipation]. May Wright Sewall, Ed. *The World's Congress of Representative Women*. Chicago: Rand, McNally & Company, 1894. 712–15.

Cooper, Brittney. *Beyond Respectability: The Intellectual Thought of Race Women*. Urbana: U of Illinois P, 2017.

Cott, Nancy. *Public Vows: A History of Marriage and the Nation*. Cambridge, Mass.: Harvard UP, 2000.

Craft, William. *Running a Thousand Miles for Freedom; Or, the Escape of William and Ellen Craft from Slavery*. London: William Tweedie, 1860. Docsouth.org.

Crawford, Margo. *Black Post-Blackness: The Black Arts Movement and Twenty-First-Century Aesthetics*. Urbana: U of Illinois P, 2017.

———. "Must Revolution Be a Family Affair? Revisiting *The Black Woman*." *Want to Start a Revolution? Radical Women in the Black Freedom Struggle*.

Eds. Dayo F. Gore, Jeanne Theoharis, and Komozi Woodard. New York: New York UP, 2009.

———. "Natural Black Beauty and Black Drag." Ed. Lisa Gail Collins and Margo Natalie Crawford. *New Thoughts on the Black Arts Movement.* New Brunswick, N.J.: Rutgers UP, 2006. 154–72.

Crenshaw, Kimberlé. "Demarginalizing the Intersection of Race and Sex: A Black Feminist Critique of Antidiscrimination Doctrine, Feminist Theory and Antiracist Politics." *University of Chicago Legal Forum* (1989).

———. "Mapping the Margins: Intersectionality, Identity Politics, and Violence against Women of Color." *Stanford Law Review* 43.6 (1991): 1241–99.

Curwood, Anastasia. *Stormy Weather: Middle-class African American Marriages between the Two World Wars.* Chapel Hill: U of North Carolina P, 2010.

Davis, Angela Y. "Reflections on the Black Woman's Role in the Community of Slaves." *The Black Scholar* 3.4 (December 1971): 2–15.

———. *Women, Race, and Class.* New York: Vintage, 1983.

Davis, Carol. *Prefiguring Postblackness: Cultural Memory, Drama, and the African American Freedom Struggle of the 1960s.* Jackson: UP of Mississippi, 2015.

Davis, Thadious. *Nella Larsen: Novelist of the Harlem Renaissance.* Baton Rouge: Louisiana State UP, 1994.

Douglass, Frederick. *Narrative of the Life of Frederick Douglass, an American Slave, Written by Himself.* 1845. Eds. William L. Andrews and William S. McFeely. New York: W. W. Norton, 1997.

duCille, Ann. *Coupling Convention: Sex, Text, and Tradition in Black Women's Fiction.* New York: Oxford UP, 1993.

———. "Monster, She Wrote." *Skin Trade.* Cambridge, Mass.: Harvard UP, 1996. 60–80.

Dunbar, Erica Armstrong. *Never Caught: The Washingtons' Relentless Pursuit of Their Runaway Slave, Ona Judge.* New York: Atria, 2017.

Dunbar-Ortiz, Roxanne. *An Indigenous Peoples' History of the United States.* Boston: Beacon P, 2014.

Fanon, Frantz. 1952. *Black Skin, White Masks.* Trans. Charles Markmann. New York: Grove Press, 1967.

Farmer, Ashley. *Remaking Black Power: How Black Women Transformed an Era.* Chapel Hill: U of North Carolina P, 2017.

Feimster, Crystal. *Southern Horrors: Women and the Politics of Rape and Lynching.* Cambridge, Mass.: Harvard UP, 2009.

Ferguson, Roderick. *Aberrations in Black: Toward a Queer of Color Critique.* Minneapolis: U of Minnesota P, 2004.

Ford, Tanisha. *Liberated Threads: Black Women, Style, and the Global Politics of Soul.* Chapel Hill: U of North Carolina P, 2015.

Foreman, P. Gabrielle. *Activist Sentiments: Reading Black Women in the Nineteenth Century.* Urbana: U of Illinois P, 2009.

Foster, Frances Smith. *Written by Herself: Literary Production by African American Women, 1746–1892.* Bloomington: Indiana UP, 1993.

Foster, Frances Smith, and Richard Yarborough. "Introduction/Contexts/Criticism." *Incidents in the Life of a Slave Girl.* 1861. Eds. Frances Smith Foster and Richard Yarborough. New York: W. W. Norton, 2019.

Foster, Guy. "'Do I Look Like Someone You Can Come Home to from Where You May Be Going?': Re-Mapping Interracial Anxiety in Octavia Butler's *Kindred.*" *African American Review* 41.1 (Spring 2007): 143–64.

Foucault, Michel. "The Subject and Power." *Critical Inquiry* 8.4 (1982): 777–95.

Franklin, John Hope, and Alfred Moss Jr. *From Slavery to Freedom: A History of African Americans.* 8th Ed. New York: Knopf, 2015.

Freedman, Estelle. *Redefining Rape: Sexual Violence in the Era of Suffrage and Segregation.* Cambridge, Mass.: Harvard UP, 2013.

Gaines, Kevin. *Uplifting the Race: Black Leadership, Politics, and Culture in the Twentieth Century.* Chapel Hill: U of North Carolina P, 1996.

Gambino, Lauren. "First Ladies Club: How Michelle Obama Became Hillary Clinton's Unlikely Ally." *The Guardian,* October 28, 2016. https://www.theguardian.com/us-news/2016/oct/28/michelle-obama-hillary—clinton-campaign-first-lady-election.

Gates, Henry Louis, Jr. *The Signifying Monkey: A Theory of African-American Literary Criticism.* New York: Oxford UP, 1988.

Gates, Raquel. "What Snooki and Joseline Taught Me about Race, Motherhood, and Reality TV." *Los Angeles Review of Books,* October 21, 2017. https://lareviewofbooks.org/article/what-snooki-and-joseline-taught-me-about-race-motherhood-and-reality-tv/#!.

George, Rosemary. "Recycling: Long Routes to and from Domestic Fixes." Ed. Rosemary George. *Burning Down the House: Recycling Domesticity.* Boulder, Colo.: Westview Press, 1998. 1–20.

Gill, Tiffany. *Beauty Shop Politics: African American Women's Activism in the Beauty Industry.* Urbana: U of Illinois P, 2010.

Glymph, Thavolia. *Out of the House of Bondage: The Transformation of the Plantation Household.* Cambridge: Cambridge UP, 2008.

Green, Joyce. "Black Romanticism." *The Black Woman: An Anthology.* Ed. Toni Cade Bambara. New York: New American Library, 1970. 137–42.

Halberstam, Jack (Judith). *The Queer Art of Failure.* Durham, N.C.: Duke UP, 2011.

Hale, Grace. *Making Whiteness: The Culture of Segregation in the South, 1890–1940*. New York: Vintage, 1999.

Hansberry, Lorraine. *A Raisin in the Sun*. 1959. Introduction by Robert Nemiroff. New York: Vintage, 1994.

Harper, Frances Ellen Watkins. *Iola Leroy; Or, Shadows Uplifted*. 1892. Edited and Introduction by Koritha Mitchell. Ontario: Broadview P, 2018.

Harris, Robert, and Rosalyn Terborg-Penn. *The Columbia Guide to African American History since 1939*. New York: Columbia UP, 2006.

Harris, Trudier. *Saints, Sinners, Saviors: Strong Black Women in African American Literature*. New York: Palgrave, 2001.

Harris-Perry, Melissa. *Sister Citizen: Shame, Stereotypes, and Black Women in America*. New Haven, Conn.: Yale UP, 2011.

Hartman, Saidiya V. *Scenes of Subjection: Terror, Slavery, and Self-Making in Nineteenth-Century America*. New York: Oxford UP, 1997.

———. "Venus in Two Acts." *Small Axe* 26 (June 2008): 1–14.

———. *Wayward Lives, Beautiful Experiments: Intimate Histories of Social Upheaval*. New York: W. W. Norton, 2019.

Hatch, James, and Ted Shine, Eds. *Black Theatre U.S.A.: Plays by African Americans, The Recent Period, 1935–Today*. Revised and Expanded. New York: The Free Press, 1996.

Higashida, Cheryl. *Black Internationalist Feminism: Women Writers of the Black Left, 1945–1995*. Urbana: U of Illinois P, 2011.

Higginbotham, Evelyn Brooks. *Righteous Discontent: The Women's Movement in the Black Baptist Church, 1880–1920*. Cambridge, Mass.: Harvard UP, 1993.

Hill, Anita. *Reimagining Equality: Stories of Gender, Race, and Finding Home*. Boston: Beacon P, 2012.

Hine, Darlene Clark. "Rape and the Inner Lives of Black Women in the Middle West: Preliminary Thoughts on the Culture of Dissemblance." *Signs* 14.4 (1989): 912–20.

Holland, Sharon. *The Erotic Life of Racism*. Durham, N.C.: Duke UP, 2012.

hooks, bell. *Yearning: Race, Gender, and Cultural Politics*. New York: South End P, 1999.

Hooks, Janet, and Rebecca Ballhaus. "Donald Trump Accepts GOP Nomination, Promises to Fix America." *Wall Street Journal*, July 22, 2016. https://www.wsj.com/articles/donald-trumps-convention-speech-to-attack-establishment-promise-to-fix-america-1469144391.

Hopkins, Pauline. *Contending Forces: A Romance Illustrative of Negro Life North and South*. 1900. Edited and Introduction by Richard Yarbrough. New York: Oxford UP, 1988.

Hughes, Langston. *The Collected Poems of Langston Hughes*. Ed. Arnold Rampersad. New York: Vintage Books, 1995.

Hunter, Tera. *Bound in Wedlock: Slave and Free Black Marriage in the Nineteenth Century*. Cambridge, Mass.: Harvard UP, 2017.

———. *To 'Joy My Freedom: Southern Black Women's Lives and Labors after the Civil War*. Cambridge, Mass.: Harvard UP, 1997.

Hurston, Zora Neale. *Their Eyes Were Watching God*. 1937. Foreword, Mary Helen Washington. New York: Harper & Row Perennial Library, 1990.

Hutchinson, George. *In Search of Nella Larsen: A Biography of the Color Line*. Cambridge, Mass.: The Belknap Press of Harvard UP, 2006.

Hyde, Carrie. *Civic Longing: The Speculative Origins of U.S. Citizenship*. Cambridge, Mass.: Harvard UP, 2018.

Iton, Richard. *In Search of the Black Fantastic: Politics and Popular Culture in the Post–Civil Rights Era*. New York: Oxford UP, 2008.

Jacobs, Harriet. *Incidents in the Life of a Slave Girl*. 1861. Eds. Frances Smith Foster and Richard Yarborough. New York: W. W. Norton, 2019.

Jenkins, Candice. *Private Lives, Proper Relations: Regulating Black Intimacy*. Minneapolis: U of Minnesota P, 2007.

Johnson, E. Patrick. *Appropriating Blackness: Performance and the Politics of Authenticity*. Durham, N.C.: Duke UP, 2003.

Jones, Martha S. *Birthright Citizens: A History of Race and Rights in Antebellum America*. Cambridge: Cambridge UP, 2018.

———. "Michelle Obama and the Black Women of the White House." *Washington Post*, February 18, 2018.

Kamp, Allen R. "The History behind Hansberry v. Lee." *U.C. Davis Law Review* 20.3 (1986): 481–99.

Katznelson, Ira. *When Affirmative Action Was White: An Untold History of Racial Inequality in Twentieth-Century America*. New York: W. W. Norton, 2005.

Keckley, Elizabeth. *Behind the Scenes, or, Thirty Years a Slave and Four Years in the White House*. 1868. Ed. James Olney. New York: Oxford UP, 1988.

Keith, Tamara. "Sexism Is Out in the Open in the 2016 Campaign. That May Have Been Inevitable." *Morning Edition. National Public Radio*, October 23, 2016. https://www.npr.org/2016/10/23/498878356/sexism-is-out-in-the-open-in-the-2016-campaign-that-may-have-been-inevitable.

Kelley, Blair Murphy. *Right to Ride: Streetcar Boycotts and African American Citizenship in the Era of Plessy v. Ferguson*. Chapel Hill: U of North Carolina P, 2010.

Kelley, Robin D. G. *Freedom Dreams: The Black Radical Imagination*. Boston: Beacon P, 2002.

Kendi, Ibram X. *Stamped from the Beginning: The Definitive History of Racist Ideas in America*. New York: Nation Books, 2016.

Kessler, Ronald. *In the President's Secret Service: Behind the Scenes with Agents in the Line of Fire and the Presidents They Protect*. Updated reprint edition. New York: Broadway, 2010.

Kihss, Peter. "'Benign Neglect' on Race Is Proposed by Moynihan." *New York Times*, March 1, 1970.

King, Tiffany Lethabo. *The Black Shoals: Offshore Formations of Black and Native Studies*. Durham, N.C.: Duke UP, 2019.

Kurtzleben, Danielle. "Trump and The Testosterone Takeover of 2016." *National Public Radio*, October 1, 2016. https://www.npr.org/2016/10/01/494249104/trump-and-the-testosterone-takeover-of-2016.

Larsen, Nella. *Quicksand*. Edited and Introduction by Thadious Davis. New York: Penguin, 2002.

Lewis, Janaka. "Elizabeth Keckley and Freedom's Labor." *African American Review* 49.1 (2016): 5–17.

Lipsitz, George. *The Possessive Investment in Whiteness: How White People Profit from Identity Politics*. 1998. Rev. and Expanded. Philadelphia: Temple UP, 2006.

Litwack, Leon. *Trouble in Mind: Black Southerners in the Age of Jim Crow*. New York: Knopf, 1998.

Manne, Kate. *Down Girl: The Logic of Misogyny*. New York: Oxford UP, 2018.

Matthews, Kristin. "The Politics of 'Home' in Lorraine Hansberry's *A Raisin in the Sun*." *Modern Drama* 51.4 (2008): 556–78.

Maxwell, William. *F.B. Eyes: How J. Edgar Hoover's Ghostreaders Framed African American Literature*. Princeton, N.J.: Princeton UP, 2015.

McDowell, Deborah. *The Changing Same: Black Women's Literature, Criticism, and Theory*. Bloomington: Indiana UP, 1995.

———. "Witnessing Slavery after Freedom—Dessa Rose." *Slavery and the Literary Imagination*. Ed. Deborah McDowell and Arnold Rampersad. Baltimore: Johns Hopkins UP, 1989.

McDuffie, Erik. *Sojourning for Freedom: Black Women, American Communism, and the Making of Black Left Feminism*. Durham, N.C.: Duke UP, 2011.

McKittrick, Katherine. *Demonic Grounds: Black Women and the Cartographies of Struggle*. Minneapolis: U of Minnesota P, 2006.

McMurry, Linda O. *To Keep the Waters Troubled: The Life of Ida B. Wells*. New York: Oxford UP, 1998.

Mills, Charles. *The Racial Contract*. Ithaca: Cornell UP, 1997.

Mitchell, Koritha. "Identifying White Mediocrity and Know-Your-Place Aggression: A Form of Self-Care." *African American Review* 51.4 (2018): 253–62.

———. Introduction. *Iola Leroy*. Ontario: Broadview P, 2018.

———. *Living with Lynching: African American Lynching Plays, Performance, and Citizenship, 1890–1930*. Urbana: U of Illinois P, 2011.

———. "Love in Action: Noting Similarities between Lynching Then and Anti-LGBT Violence Now." *Callaloo* 36.3 (2013): 689–717.

Mitchell, Koritha, and Alex Chávez. "An Open Letter to White People from Two Professors of Color: Step Up!" *The Huffington Post*, March 21, 2017. https://www.huffingtonpost.com/entry/professors-of-color-to -white-people-step-up_us_58d17651e4b0e0d348b34885.

Morrison, Toni. "A Bench by the Road," *World: Journal of the Unitarian Universalist Association* 3:1 (January/February 1989): 4–5, 37–41. https:// www.uuworld.org/articles/a-bench-by-road.

———. *Beloved*. 1987. New York: Vintage, 2004.

———. "Home." *The House That Race Built*. New York: Vintage, 1998. 3–12.

———. *Playing in the Dark: Whiteness and the Literary Imagination*. New York: Vintage, 1992.

Moten, Fred. "Blackness and Nothingness (Mysticism in the Flesh)." *South Atlantic Quarterly* 112.4 (2013): 737–80.

———. "The Case of Blackness." *Criticism* 50.2 (2008): 177–218.

[Moynihan, Daniel P.] United States Department of Labor Office of Policy Planning and Research. *The Negro Family: The Case for National Action*. Washington, D.C.: Department of Labor, 1965.

Neal, Larry. "The Black Arts Movement." *The Norton Anthology of African American Literature, Third Edition, Volume 2*. Eds. Henry Louis Gates Jr. and Valerie Smith. New York: Norton, 2014. 784–87.

Neary, Janet. *Fugitive Testimony: On the Visual Logic of Slave Narratives*. New York: Fordham UP, 2016.

Nelson, Alondra. *The Social Life of DNA: Race, Reparations, and Reconciliation after the Genome*. Boston: Beacon P, 2016.

Ngai, Sianne. *Ugly Feelings*. Cambridge, Mass.: Harvard UP, 2005.

Norrell, Robert. *Alex Haley and the Books That Changed a Nation*. New York: St. Martin's P, 2015.

Obama, Michelle. *Becoming*. New York: Crown, 2018.

Omi, Michael, and Howard Winant. *Racial Formation in the United States: From the 1960s to the 1990s*. 2nd ed. New York: Routledge, 1994.

Owens, Deirdre Cooper. *Medical Bondage: Race, Gender, and the Origins of American Gynecology*. Athens: U of Georgia P, 2017.

Painter, Nell Irvin. *The History of White People*. New York: W. W. Norton, 2010.

Paulin, Diana. "De-Essentializing Interracial Representations: Black and White Border Crossings in Spike Lee's *Jungle Fever* and Octavia Butler's *Kindred*." *Cultural Critique* 36 (1997): 165–93.

Penningroth, Dylan. *Claims of Kinfolk: African American Property and Community in the Nineteenth-Century South.* Chapel Hill: U of North Carolina P, 2003.

Perry, Imani. *Looking for Lorraine: The Radiant and Radical Life of Lorraine Hansberry.* Boston: Beacon P, 2018.

Quashie, Kevin. *The Sovereignty of Quiet: Beyond Resistance in Black Culture.* New Brunswick, N.J.: Rutgers UP, 2012.

Rankine, Claudia. *Citizen: An American Lyric.* Minneapolis: Graywolf Press, 2014.

Reddy, Chandan. "Home, Houses, Nonidentity: Paris Is Burning." Ed. Rosemary George. *Burning Down the House: Recycling Domesticity.* Boulder, Colo.: Westview Press, 1998. 355–79.

Reid-Pharr, Robert. *Conjugal Union: The Body, the House, and the Black American.* New York: Oxford UP, 1999.

Roberts, Dorothy. *Killing the Black Body: Race, Reproduction, and the Meaning of Liberty.* New York: Vintage, 1997.

Robinson, Cedric. *Black Marxism.* 1983. Updated Ed. Chapel Hill: U of North Carolina P, 2000.

Rodgers, Nicole, and Rashad Robinson. "How the News Media Distorts Black Families." *Washington Post,* December 29, 2017.

Roediger, David. *The Wages of Whiteness: Race and the Making of the American Working Class.* New York: Verso, 1991.

Román, Elda. *Race and Upward Mobility: Seeking, Gatekeeping, and Other Class Strategies in Postwar America.* Stanford, Calif.: Stanford UP, 2018.

Romero, Lora. *Home Fronts: Domesticity and Its Critics in the Antebellum United States.* Durham, N.C.: Duke UP, 1997.

Rooks, Nowile. "Wearing Your Race Wrong: Hair, Drama, and a Politics of Representation for African American Women at Play on a Battlefield." Eds. Michael Bennett and Vanessa Dickerson. *Recovering the Black Female Body: Self-Representations by African American Women.* New Brunswick, N.J.: Rutgers UP, 2001. 279–95.

Rosen, Hannah. *Terror in the Heart of Freedom: Citizenship, Sexual Violence, and the Meaning of Race in the Postemancipation South.* Chapel Hill: U of North Carolina P, 2009.

Ross, Marlon. *Manning the Race: Reforming Black Men in the Jim Crow Era.* New York: New York UP, 2004.

Rowell, Charles H. "Interview with Octavia Butler." *Callaloo* 20.1 (1997): 47–66.

Sexton, Jared. "The Social Life of Social Death: On Afro-Pessimism and Black Optimism." *Tensions* 5 (Fall/Winter 2011): 1–47. http://www.yorku.ca/intent/issue5/articles/jaredsexton.php.

Sharpe, Christina. *In the Wake: On Blackness and Being*. Durham, N.C.: Duke UP, 2016.

Shaw, Stephanie. *What a Woman Ought to Be and to Do: Black Professional Women Workers during the Jim Crow Era*. Chicago: U of Chicago P, 1996.

Shockley, Evie. Remarks on *Black Art Matters: African American Scholar/Artists Creating Home within the Academy and the Arts*. Roundtable at the American Studies Association Annual Conference. Denver, Colorado. November 2016.

Simien, Evelyn. Introduction. *Gender and Lynching: The Politics of Memory*. New York: Palgrave Macmillan, 2011. 1–13.

Slevin, Peter. *Michelle Obama: A Life*. New York: Knopf, 2015.

Smith, Judith. *Visions of Belonging: Family Stories, Popular Culture, and Postwar Democracy, 1940–1960*. New York: Columbia UP, 2004.

Spencer, Robyn. *The Revolution Has Come: Black Power, Gender, and the Black Panther Party in Oakland*. Durham, N.C.: Duke UP, 2016.

Spillers, Hortense. *Black, White, and In Color: Essays on American Literature and Culture*. Chicago: U of Chicago P, 2003.

Spires, Derrick R. *The Practice of Citizenship: Black Politics and Print Culture in the Early United States*. Philadelphia: U of Pennsylvania P, 2019.

Sundquist, Eric. *To Wake the Nations: Race in the Making of American Literature*. Cambridge, Mass.: The Belknap Press of Harvard UP, 1993.

Tapia, Ruby. "Reading Race and Class in the Feminist Criticism of 'Lock Her Up.'" Remarks on *Embattled Rhetorics: Claiming Otherness, Recasting Privilege*. Roundtable at the Modern Language Association Annual Convention. Philadelphia, Pennsylvania. January 2017.

Tate, Claudia. *Domestic Allegories of Political Desire: The Black Heroine's Text at the Turn of the Century*. New York: Oxford UP, 1992.

Taylor, Diana. *The Archive and the Repertoire: Performing Cultural Memory in the Americas*. Durham, N.C.: Duke UP, 2003.

———. *Performance*. Durham, N.C.: Duke UP, 2016.

Thompson, Lisa B. *Beyond the Black Lady: Sexuality and the New African American Middle Class*. Urbana: U of Illinois P, 2009.

Tillet, Salamishah. *Sites of Slavery: Citizenship and Racial Democracy in the Post–Civil Rights Imagination*. Durham, N.C.: Duke UP, 2012.

Trafton, Scott. *Egypt Land: Race and Nineteenth-century American Egyptomania*. Durham, N.C.: Duke UP, 2004.

Traister, Rebecca. *All the Single Ladies: Unmarried Women and the Rise of an Independent Nation*. New York: Simon & Schuster, 2016.

———. "I'm a Hot Mess for Hillary." *Elle*, October 1, 2015. https://www.elle.com/culture/career-politics/a30203/hillary-clinton-hot-mess/.

———. "Shattered." *The Cut*, November 12, 2016. https://www.thecut
.com/2016/11/hillary-clinton-didnt-shatter-the-glass-ceiling.html.

Wagers, Kelley. "Seeing 'from the Far Side of the Hill': Narrative, History,
and Understanding in *Kindred* and *The Chaneysville Incident*." *MELUS*
34.1 (2009): 23–45.

Wallace-Sanders, Kimberly. "Dishing Up Dixie: Recycling the Old South in
the Early-Twentieth-Century Domestic Ideal." *Burning Down the House:
Recycling Domesticity*. Ed. Rosemary George. Boulder, Colo.: Westview
Press, 1998. 215–31.

Wanzo, Rebecca. "Love 'The Help,' But Please Stop Asking Me to Do the
Same." *The Huffington Post*, August 12, 2011. http://www.huffington
post.com/rebecca-wanzo/the-help-movie_b_925550.html.

Warren, Calvin. *Ontological Terror: Blackness, Nihilism, and Emancipation*.
Durham, N.C.: Duke UP, 2018.

Wells, Ida B. *A Red Record*. 1895. *Southern Horrors and Other Writings:
The Anti-Lynching Campaign of Ida B. Wells, 1892–1900*. Ed. Jacqueline
Jones Royster. New York: Bedford/St. Martin's, 1997. 73–157.

———. "Our Women." 1887. *The Portable Nineteenth-Century African
American Women Writers*. Eds. Hollis Robbins and Henry Louis Gates
Jr. New York: Penguin, 2017. 564–65.

———. *Southern Horrors: Lynch Law in All Its Phases*. 1892. *Southern Horrors and Other Writings: The Anti-Lynching Campaign of Ida B. Wells,
1892–1900*. Ed. Jacqueline Jones Royster. New York: Bedford/St. Martin's,
1997. 49–72.

Welter, Barbara. "The *Cult of True Womanhood*: 1820–1860." *American
Quarterly* 18. 2 (1966): 151–74.

White, Deborah Gray. *Too Heavy a Load: Black Women in Defense of
Themselves, 1894–1994*. New York: Norton, 1999.

Wilkerson, Isabel. *The Warmth of Other Suns: The Epic Story of America's
Great Migration*. New York: Vintage, 2011.

Williams, Andreá. *Dividing Lines: Class Anxiety and Postbellum Black Fiction*. Ann Arbor: U of Michigan P, 2013.

Williams, Fannie Barrier. "The Intellectual Progress of the Colored Women
of the United States since the Emancipation Proclamation." May Wright
Sewall, Ed. *The World's Congress of Representative Women*. Chicago:
Rand, McNally & Company, 1894. 696–711.

Williams, Heather Andrea. *Help Me to Find My People: The African American Search for Family Lost in Slavery*. Chapel Hill: U of North Carolina
P, 2012.

Wong, Edlie. *Neither Fugitive Nor Free: Atlantic Slavery, Freedom Suits, and
the Legal Culture of Travel*. New York: New York UP, 2009.

Yarbrough, Richard. Introduction. *Contending Forces: A Romance Illustrative of Negro Life North and South.* New York: Oxford UP, 1988. xxvii–xlviii.

Yellin, Jean Fagan. Introduction. *Incidents in the Life of a Slave Girl: Written by Herself.* Cambridge, Mass.: Harvard UP, 1987. xiii–xxxiv.

Young, Elizabeth. *Disarming the Nation: Women's Writing and the American Civil War.* Chicago: U of Chicago P, 1999.

Young, Harvey. *Embodying Black Experience: Stillness, Critical Memory, and the Black Body.* Ann Arbor: U of Michigan P, 2010.

Index

KORITHA MITCHELL is an associate professor of English at The Ohio State University and the author of *Living with Lynching: African American Lynching Plays, Performance, and Citizenship, 1890–1930*.

The University of Illinois Press
is a founding member of the
Association of University Presses.

———————————————————

University of Illinois Press
1325 South Oak Street
Champaign, IL 61820-6903
www.press.uillinois.edu